“Why is personhood such a pivotal issue? A[illegible]
whenever the principles of human dignity a[illegible] of life are questioned, the
rule of law is automatically thrown into very real jeopardy. No one, then, is absolutely secure, because absoluteness is removed from our legal vocabulary. When the right to life is abrogated for at least some citizens, all the liberties of all the citizens are at risk. Suddenly, arbitrariness, relativism, and randomness have entered into the legal equation. This, then, is the pivotal issue of our age.”

George Grant, Ph.D., Author of
Grand Illusions: The Legacy of Planned Parenthood

“This book will encourage you, and at the same time, challenge you to reconsider and readjust the priorities of your life. Though his personal testimony and also by thoroughly and logically stating the facts and nature of our struggle, Daniel Becker encourages us to be like the men and women of courage who, throughout history, acted on a personal conviction of conscience without looking back to see who was following. Gideon's army was only 300 men, but they were following a higher vision for a better world—a vision that moved them to action. Likewise, we must act. Life, the greatest and primary gift to humankind, is under threat at its very core. To inspire us to engage in this battle, each author in this book "blows the shofar" and gives us a clear call to action: To uphold the sanctity of human life and therefore, remove the curse from our land.”

Tony Sperandeo, International Jewish speaker and author; Chairman of Be'ad Chaim, the Israeli movement for the protection of the unborn child and its mother

"*Personhood: The Tree of Life* seeks to influence public opinion and public policy toward these [pro-life] ends. By broadening our vision to include the many scriptural facets of the sanctity of life and human dignity, the authors have, by their faith-based example, demonstrated a model of pro-life victory in the 21st century. I commend them for their faithfulness."

Bishop David Kagan, DD, PA, JCL,
Bishop of the Diocese of North Dakota

“Pro-lifers know the infanticide holocaust is the moral crisis of the age. Finally, a book has come forward to show the movement how to end it once and for all.”

Steve Deace, Conservative Review

"Life is a gift from God that must be treasured and defended. Whether you agree with everything in this book or not, it will make you think and challenge you to defend human life."

Rick Santorum, former Republican Presidential Candidate, served in US Senate and US House of Representatives

"Ever wonder why there can be no compromise or exception possible for the right to life for preborn children? This new book edited by Daniel Becker comprehensively and persuasively answers that question and many more. Full protection for the life of children in the womb is the only legitimate goal of the pro-life movement and Personhood lays out a path steering clear of unethical concessions to the culture of death."

John-Henry Westin,
Co-Founder and Editor-in-Chief, ***LifeSiteNews.com***

"There are two compelling reasons to rethink our pro-life strategy. The one reason is that the pro-life movement has to become more successful. The other reason is that society and technology are changing fast and posing new challenges to human life and dignity. I agree with Mr. Becker that we have to base our activities on this firm foundation: man created in the image of God."

Alex van Vuuren, Executive Committee member of One of Us, European Federation for Life and Human Dignity

"Personhood is the alarming end-time wake-up call to stop the evil destruction of God's creation through the corruption of science. In this book, Personhood Alliance exposes this danger by urging the pro-life movement and society to step up to face far-reaching issues that have already brought dramatic consequences."

Bert P. Dorenbos, President
Schreeuw om Leven (Cry for Life) Holland

"This book has many of the missing pieces to a lot of pro-life literature. I'm excited to see this compilation of work come from my friend Dan Becker and pray that this will help all of us to remember that the central issue in abortion is the image of God He places on a *person* in the womb."

James K. Lansberry, Executive V.P. Samaritan Ministries, President, Alliance of Health Care Sharing Ministries, Founder and National Director of The Morning Center

PERSONHOOD THE TREE OF LIFE

The Biblical Path to Pro-Life Victory in the 21st Century

Edited by Daniel C. Becker
President and Founder, Personhood Alliance

May 20, 2017

TKS Publications
Alpharetta, Georgia

TKS Publications
777 Rivendell Lane, Alpharetta, GA 30004
World Wide Web: www.tkspublications.com
Email: email@tkspublications.com

First Edition

Cover Design: Carolyn McKinney
Cover Image: Olive Tree licensed from Alexandr Bakanov
Illustrations and photos on pages 18 and 28 by Daniel Becker

ISBN-10: 0983190372
ISBN-13: 9780983190370

Printed in the United States of America

Library of Congress Control Number: 2017905609

REL012110	RELIGION / Christian Life / Social Issues
REL084000	RELIGION / Religion, Politics & State
POL043000	POLITICAL SCIENCE /Political Process / Political Advocacy
SOC046000	SOCIAL SCIENCE / Abortion & Birth Control

In the United Kingdom

HRAM2	Religion and politics
HRAM1	Religious ethics
JFMA	Ethical issues: abortion and birth control

---

24 23 22 21 20 19 18 17 16 15 14 13 12 11 10 9 8 7 6 5 4 3 2 2

This book is dedicated to today's Gideon army of selfless servants who have faithfully committed all to see the sanctity of life and human dignity defended biblically in their time in history.

Table of Contents

SECTION III PERSONHOOD AND MEDICAL ETHICS

SECTION IV PERSONHOOD AND THE LAW

SECTION V PERSONHOOD AND POLITICS

SECTION VI TESTIMONIES OF LIFE

Acknowledgements

I wish to express my grateful thanks to the following persons for aiding the production of this work, for without their dedication and help, it would not have been possible. Thank you, Karen LaBarr, Rick and Judy McClure, Sarah Quale, and Greg and Jan Winchester for your support of the sanctity of life in our time.

The chapters in this book serve as a critical contribution to the conversation from individuals and organizations who, as diverse as they may be, are unified on the biblical principles of the sanctity of life and human dignity for all those created in the image of God, without exception and without compromise. To each of the authors who contributed to this work, thank you.

Contributors

Daniel C. Becker, President and Founder of Personhood Alliance; Former President, Georgia Right to Life; Former board member, National Right to Life

Nancy Elliott, Chairman, Euthanasia Prevention Coalition USA

Kitti Hataway, Development Director, Personhood Florida

Rev. Walter B. Hoye II, President and Founder of the Issues4life Foundation, the California Civil Rights Foundation, and the Frederick Douglass Foundation of California; core member of the National Black Pro-Life Coalition

Dr. J. Patrick Johnston, D.O., Director, Association of Pro-Life Physicians; President, Personhood Ohio

Gualberto Garcia Jones, National Policy Director, Personhood Alliance; Executive Director, International Human Rights Group

Bill Kee, Executive Director, Defend Life Nebraska

Rebecca Kiessling, Esq., President and Founder, Save the 1; Co-founder, Hope After Rape Conception

Christopher Kurka, Executive Director, Alaska Right to Life

Dr. Patricia McEwen, President, Life Coalition International; Vice President, Personhood Florida

Tim Overlin, Executive Director, Personhood Iowa

Darlene Pawlik, New Hampshire Right to Life PAC; Vice President, Save the 1

Sarah Quale, President and Founder, Educe

Les Riley, President, Personhood Mississippi; Executive Director, Morning Center (Memphis)

Jay Rogers, President, Personhood Florida Education

Matt Sande, Legislative Director, Pro-Life Wisconsin

Brad and Jesi Smith, Personhood Michigan; Founders, Keeping Our Faith; Speakers, Save the 1

The Biblical Path to Pro-Life Victory

"And God said 'Let us make man in our image and after our likeness...'" Genesis 1:26

"Open your mouth for the mute,
for the rights of all who are destitute.
Open your mouth, judge righteously,
defend the rights of the poor and needy."
Proverbs 31:8-9

"Rescue those who are being taken away to death;
hold back those who are stumbling to the slaughter. If you say, 'Behold, we did not know this,' does not he who weighs the heart perceive it? Does not he who keeps watch over your soul know it, and will he not repay man according to his work?"
Proverbs 24:11-12

"...Children must not be put to death for crimes committed by their parents." Deuteronomy 24:16 (CEV)

"Can wicked rulers be allied with you, those who frame injustice by statute? [speaks to endorsement standards]
Psalms 94:20

"They band together against the life of the righteous and condemn the innocent to death. [speaks to legislative action]
Psalms 94:21

"Like a muddied spring or a polluted fountain is a righteous man who gives way before the wicked."
Proverbs 25:26

"Yet this you have: You hate the works of the Nicolaitans, which I also hate. He who has an ear, let him hear what the Spirit says to the churches. To the one who conquers I will grant to eat of the tree of life, which is in the paradise of God.'"

Revelation 2:6

FOREWORD

By Bishop David Kagan, DD, PA, JCL, Bishop of the Diocese of North Dakota, Bismarck

"Then God said,[1] 'Let us make man in our image, after our likeness.' So God created man in his own image, in the image of God he created him; male and female he created them."[2]

"Then the Lord God formed the man of dust from the ground and breathed into his nostrils the breath of life, and the man became a living creature."[3]

In both citations from the Book of Genesis, it is crystal clear that God is the Creator and man is the creature. Man does not and cannot create himself. Thus, it is man who has his origin in and from God.

God Creates Us in His Image

It is equally clear that man is unique among all creation. He is created in the "image and likeness" of God.[4] Mankind—male and female—receives this likeness to God from that which comes from God Himself,

---

[1] Genesis 3:22; Genesis 11:7; Isaiah 6:8
[2] Genesis 1:26-27
[3] Genesis 2:7
[4] Genesis 1:26

His "breath of life."[5] Thus, mankind—male and female—is not only created by God as all of creation is created by Him, but unlike the rest of creation, mankind is created in His image and likeness, possessing God's breath of life and therefore, is a "living being."[6]

God Creates Us Persons

Two essential truths can be deduced from these scriptures. The first is that the human person is essentially distinct from all of the rest of creation because this person is created in the image and likeness of God and has been given God's breath of life so as to become a living being. Human "exceptionalism" is God's plan. Thus, not only the person, but also the person's dignity, is God-given and not something the person can self-generate or do with and dispose of arbitrarily.

The second truth, following upon the first truth, is that the human person has an eternal destiny or end because of Jesus Christ, the eternal Word through Whom and for Whom all has been created.

Mankind Has Rejected This Truth

Not all acknowledge these foundational truths. Error surrounds those who reject this Divine revelation. The root of the erroneous definitions of the person is found in the philosophy of rationalism. *Rationalism* became widespread in the early 18th century, and it asserts that human reason is the sole and final authority for establishing what is the truth. By extension, rationalism claims that faith and the practice of religion must then be limited only to what human reason establishes as the truth.

---

[5] Genesis 2:7
[6] Genesis 2:7

Rationalism gave rise to modernism in the mid- to late-19th century and to the pervasive philosophy of the 20th and 21st centuries known as secularism. What rationalism does is exclude God, the supernatural, and the spiritual, and it exalts the person as self-made, self-sufficient, and the ultimate authority unto himself or herself. The pro-life movement is not immune to these deadly influences.

The Consequences of Error

Each error regarding the human person and human dignity has a specific and slightly different method, yet all have a shared basic premise. The premise is: The person and the person's dignity are relative to what is able to be observed and measured externally. That is, the person is not a subject in his or her own right, having an objective origin (God) other than oneself. Instead, the person is really the object of other finite realities in the sense that the person's identity and dignity are not inherent, but assigned. These errors consider the person an object to be used, not a subject to be respected and defended.

Here is the absolute truth about the person and the person's intrinsic human dignity. The first conclusion is clear and self-evident. Each person, from the first moment of conception to the last moment of life by natural death, possesses one, absolute, and inviolable human right—the right to life. The second conclusion, following upon the first and binding all persons, as well as all groups, is a strict matter of human justice. No person or group has any individual or inherent right to destroy or to mutilate innocent human life but has the binding duty to protect and defend innocent human life in all of its stages of development.

The third conclusion to be drawn is that the binding teaching on the person and the person's intrinsic human dignity is a matter to be recognized by all persons and groups as objectively true. No individual person, no group of persons or any political and social agency or government, can change or re-define the person, the person's human dignity, and the person's singular status within creation as defined by God.

Personhood: The Tree of Life seeks to influence public opinion and public policy toward these ends. By broadening our vision to include the many scriptural facets of the sanctity of life and human dignity, the authors have, by their faith-based example, demonstrated a model of pro-life victory in the 21st century. I commend them for their faithfulness.

Bishop David Kagan, DD, PA, JCL,
Bishop of the Diocese of North Dakota

PREFACE

Personhood The Tree of Life

"Personhood is the right to have rights."

Personhood[7] is a mighty tree of life. Just as a tree has many branches that all share the same trunk, the Personhood movement[8] grows from one sturdy premise: The life and dignity of every innocent human being from earliest biological beginning until natural death should be protected by law. This premise is firmly rooted in the biblical concept of *Imago Dei,*[9] that is, every human being is made with great dignity in the image and likeness of God Himself.

---

[7] *Personhood* is the legal right to have rights. A functional definition is the governmental recognition of the God-given sanctity of life and human dignity that is to be acknowledged from our earliest biological beginning until natural death in all areas of culture, public policy, and law.

[8] Any Christian ministry that supports a Personhood Amendment being amended to its nation's constitution

[9] *Imago Dei* is the biblical doctrine of human exceptionalism that arises from our being God's designated representatives in this world. Humans are the only created being declared by God to be created in His image and after His likeness (Genesis 1:26-27).

Each branch of the Personhood tree is a response to threats against human dignity and innocent persons. As the leaves on the branches, distinct Christian ministries gather the Son's light and transform its rays into life-giving energy, producing fruit for the whole Kingdom of God.[10] The tree grows in strength and fruitfulness as its branches stay steadfastly attached to trunk and root, impacting our culture through education, legislation, political action, and vision.

In the 20th century, it was enough for pro-life groups to oppose abortion, euthanasia, physician assisted suicide, destructive embryonic stem cell research, and infanticide.[11] In the 21st century, we face an increasing array of issues that directly violate human life *and* human dignity.[12] Personhood offers a single moral and legal construct from which we can launch all life-protecting initiatives. Personhood, with its biblical expression of the doctrine of *Imago Dei,* can be applied to all human rights advocacy, public policy, and political strategy in order to establish legal protections for the most vulnerable in our midst.

Our culture's worldview has changed from post-Christian to increasingly anti-Christian and is fraught with the challenges of the emerging biotechnologies of our day. To remain relevant and effective,

---

[10] "Its leaves were beautiful and its fruit abundant, and in it was food for all," describing Nebuchadnezzar's kingdom in Daniel 4:12. How much more should the Kingdom of God manifest these traits?

[11] National Right to Life Committee Mission Statement, "Our areas of concern include abortion, infanticide, euthanasia, assisted suicide, and the killing of preborn children for their stem cells." Retrieved from http://www.nrlc.org/about/mission/

[12] Cameron, N. (2005). National Right to Life Convention speech. "In the 20th century it was enough that we were pro-life, but in the 21st century, we must also be pro-human." Nigel Cameron is the former dean of the Wilberforce Forum.

the pro-life community must re-tool. We must increase our scope of policy, strategy, and actions beyond what has become an outdated paradigm.

Personhood's Deep Roots and Broad Branches

The extreme forces generated by storms are enough to rip a mighty tree from the ground unless it is anchored by an extensive network of roots that are deeply interlaced into the soil and rock. Personhood's root structure is faith-based. For over 2,000 years, a uniquely Christian worldview has confronted the cultures of death and emerged victorious. The Gospel of Jesus Christ has transformed many Pagan cultures, which now embrace human dignity and the biblical sanctity of human life. As such, the Personhood movement does not ally itself with groups like Atheists for Life, Lesbians for Life, and other organizations that oppose the basic historical tenets of our faith. This foundation of faith separates Personhood from many other pro-life efforts and creates tension when Personhood advocates encounter unbiblical policy and strategy in the halls of government and in national leadership.

As aforementioned, the branches of the Personhood tree are responses to threats against human dignity and innocent persons. In addition to abortion and assisted suicide, other threats arise from within biotechnology, cybertechnology, bioethics, and animal rights efforts; still others include human trafficking, population control, and variant family structures. In future years, there will be assaults from unforeseen sources. The good news is that Personhood answers all such threats. It is foundational to who we are as human beings, and it derives its strength from God's revealed Word and ways.

The chapters in this book address the roots and trunk of the Personhood tree, as well as the branches on which the 21st century pro-life movement must focus, including abortion, euthanasia, biotechnology, marriage and family, human dignity, and human exceptionalism.

Biotechnology Branch

Today's biotechnology branch must include strong restraints on deadly human experimentation, not only at an embryonic level, but also across the human lifespan to combat the erosion of medical standards. We must challenge the policies of hospital ethics boards by affirming human life and dignity, especially regarding neonatal abnormalities and end-of-life decisions.

The biotechnology industry is awash in emerging areas of concern. Many technologies cause death in the research phase. Many others assault the basic idea of human dignity. Such "advances" include creation of human-animal hybrids, human germline modification, cryopreservation, artificial wombs, and human cloning.

Assisted reproductive technology has moved quickly and not always with respect for life or dignity. Three-parent children created with DNA from a mother, father, and female donor have already been born. Egg donation, gestational surrogacy, abuses in *in vitro* fertilization methods, pre-implantation genetic diagnosis, and selective reductions all have grave ethical dimensions for which a Personhood perspective provides discernment.

Personhood principles require that strong, biblically based pro-life ethics and law challenge and guide these advancements. In providing this leadership, we lay the foundation for generations of fruitful harvest.

Marriage and Family Branches

Defending biblical marriage is an important branch of the Personhood tree. The doctrine of *Imago Dei* is found in the same passage of Scripture that also refers to marriage between one man and one woman.[13] There is an unbreakable link between life issues and marriage. Abortion and single parenting have a direct relationship.[14] Divorce and dysfunctional families are prominent factors in teen pregnancy and abortion.[15] In addition, some homosexual couples use reproductive technologies that jeopardize life and are an affront to human dignity.

Human Dignity Branches

Additional branches must be added to confront denial of Personhood in the realm of human dignity. Human slavery is one such branch. The very word in Latin for person is *persona*, a term that was used exclusively to describe legal protections and rights of the citizens of ancient Rome. The term was never accorded to slaves. This ancient branch of human dignity has multiple modern offshoots that need the healing touch of the Gospel of Jesus Christ, including forced human labor (i.e., the boat boys of Indonesia), child labor, child sex trade,[16] and all other forms of human

---

[13] Genesis 1:26-27

[14] Miller, T., PhD. (2012). The welfare state, abortion, and the growth in single-parent families, 12-14. Retrieved from http://visionandvalues.org/docs/familymatters/Miller_Tracy.pdf?cbb716

[15] McClanahan, S., & Bumpass, L. (1988, July). Intergenerational consequences of family disruption. *American Journal of Sociology, 4*: 130-52. Retrieved from http://www.journals.uchicago.edu/doi/10.1086/228954

[16] The average age for commercial child sexual bondage is 13 years old. See: Daly, J. (2015). *The dignity and sanctity of every human life*, p. 153. Retrieved

trafficking. A proper understanding of personhood leads to a compassionate biblical response to help rescue and heal the diseased foliage, in this example, young children who face significant hurdles in overcoming their victimization.[17]

Human Exceptionalism Branch

Another branch that requires our gardener's touch is that of biblical human exceptionalism, which lies at the core of personhood. Are humans unique in God's order of creation? Are they therefore the only God-given recipient of the legal protections of personhood? Or will animals, computers with artificial intelligence, robots that pass the Turing test,[18] and alleged space aliens also have a claim? A legal debate on "Personhood—Beyond the Human"[19] is currently taking place, yet the Christian voice is largely silent. Can we afford to allow "truth to stumble in the public square"[20] in our absence?

---

from https://www.flipsnack.com/Focus/the-dignity-and-sanctity-of-every-human-life-resource-guide.html

[17] As pregnancy resource centers in the 1980s were God's way of meeting the victimization of woman through abortion, God is now raising up ministries of compassion to help these young children.

[18] The Turing Test assesses a machine's ability to exhibit intelligent behavior equivalent to, or indistinguishable from, that of a human.

[19] Yale University sponsored a college symposium in December, 2013, entitled "Personhood—Beyond the Human." Animal rights groups and transhumanist leaders from Princeton and Harvard were in attendance.

[20] "Justice is turned back, and righteousness stands far away; for truth has stumbled in the public squares, and uprightness cannot enter. Truth is lacking, and he who departs from evil makes himself a prey. The Lord saw it, and it displeased him." Isaiah 59:14

Personhood in the Public Square

The most famous lines of the Declaration of Independence state:

> *"We hold these truths to be self-evident, that all men are created equal, that they are endowed by their Creator with certain unalienable rights, that among these are* ***Life****, Liberty and the pursuit of Happiness. That to secure these rights, Governments are instituted among Men..." [emphasis added]*[21]

The 5th Amendment to the United States Constitution guarantees:

> *"No* ***person*** *shall...be deprived of life, liberty, or property, without due process of law..." [emphasis added]*[22]

The 14th Amendment begins with this paragraph:

> *"All persons born or naturalized in the United States and subject to the jurisdiction thereof, are citizens of the United States and of the State wherein they reside. No State shall make or enforce any law which shall abridge the privileges or immunities of citizens of the United States; nor shall any State deprive any* ***person*** *of life, liberty, or property, without due process of law; nor deny to any* ***person*** *within its jurisdiction the equal protection of the laws." [emphasis added]*[23]

Personhood, by legal definition, endows government recognition of certain rights under the law. The foundational statement in the Declaration comports with the biblical truth that the right to life is God-given, not government-given. The 5th and 14th Amendments formally secured that right to "any person," first from the federal government,

---

[21] Declaration of Independence. (1776). An Act of the Second Continental Congress, July 4, 1776.

[22] Cornell University Law School. (2017). Fifth Amendment. Retrieved from https://www.law.cornell.edu/wex/fifth_amendment

[23] Cornell University Law School. (2017). 14th Amendment. Retrieved from https://www.law.cornell.edu/constitution/amendmentxiv

then from the state governments.[24] The Personhood movement adheres to this understanding and applies it to persons from their earliest biological beginning until natural death in all areas of public policy and law.

Personhood has been the stated objective of the pro-life movement from its inception. Every year for nearly a decade from its founding, the National Right to Life Committee adopted the Human Life Amendment, a resolution enthroning legal personhood as its premier objective. Unfortunately, they abandoned this annual resolution about three decades ago.

The Purpose of This Book

The purpose of this book is two-fold. First, it explains why a fresh approach to pro-life ministry is required. We do not want to put new wine into old wineskins[25] lest they burst and spill the past work they represent. Our intent is not to destroy, but rather to prune and nurture pro-life ministry as its cultural influence grows, rooted in biblical Christianity.

Secondly, there is an urgency to harness our present positive political realities to generate substantive attitude changes toward Personhood. These changes must translate into principled legislative strategies and actions. This cannot be accomplished without the uncomfortable exercise of "speaking truth to power," both to elected officials and pro-

---

[24] Sadly, in *Griswold v. Connecticut (1965)*, the U.S. Supreme Court used the 14th Amendment to create a "right to privacy" for birth control among married couples, which was then applied to create a woman's "right to privacy" surrounding abortion in *Roe v. Wade (1973)*.

[25] Matthew 9:17

life leaders. We must identify areas in today's pro-life movement that violate God's enduring and absolute command, "You shall not murder."[26]

Before we can expect significant change, we as a movement must confess that being severed from the biblical root of Personhood in our pro-life policies and actions is destructive to our goals. If we wrongly allow an axe to be laid to the root of Christian pro-life teaching, we should expect to hear the disturbing sound of this tree crashing to the ground.

Personhood advocates do not wish to vilify any pro-life group. Rather, we call for national repentance and for a turning away from strategy built on political pragmatism and its Utilitarian doctrine of deadly human "exceptions."[27] We cannot be faithful to the "whole counsel of God" without pointing out unholy and unjust compromises that many current pro-life leaders, politicians, and activists accept. Personhood has a proven record of accomplishment. Political and legal successes demonstrate that lethal "pro-life exceptions to life" are not required to pass protective pro-life laws.[28]

With an awareness of our own shortcomings,[29] we pray that our words reflect the spirit and manner of Christ Jesus. He loved those who had strayed from God's ways, and He spoke difficult truths with compassion that addressed the heart, revealed brokenness, and offered hope and direction. May this book be received in that spirit, manifesting

---

[26] Exodus 20:13

[27] Legalized killing of some innocent children based on their manner of conception, disability, medical prognosis, and degree of dependency.

[28] Becker, D. (2011). *Personhood: A pragmatic guide to pro-life victory and a return to first principles in politics.* Alpharetta, GA: TKS Publishing.

[29] Luke 6:41-42

true love in a tough time. And may this process yield a rich harvest of righteousness to God's glory.

Daniel Becker,
Founder and President, Personhood Alliance

SECTION I

PERSONHOOD IS THE RETURN TO FIRST PRINCIPLES

CHAPTER 1

Personhood Originates with God

By Daniel Becker, President, Personhood Alliance

"Then God said, "Let us make man in our image, after our likeness. And let them have dominion over the fish of the sea and over the birds of the heavens and over the livestock and over all the earth and over every creeping thing that creeps on the earth." So God created man in his own image, in the image of God he created him; male and female he created them."[30]

All of mankind is created by the Lord to bear His image.[31] This declaration is called the doctrine of *Imago Dei*. The doctrine of *Imago Dei* is the foundational teaching that undergirds all Christian pro-life policy and action.

Catholics and Evangelicals agree on the biblical foundations that define today's modern pro-life movement. Evangelical theologian Wayne Grudem explains:

---

[30] Genesis 1:26-27
[31] James 3:9

> *"When God says, 'Let us make man in our image, after our likeness' (Gen. 1:26), the meaning is that God plans to make a creature similar to himself. Both the Hebrew word for 'image' (צֶלֶם, H7512) and the Hebrew word for 'likeness' (דְּמוּת, H1952) refer to something that is similar but not identical to the thing it represents or is an 'image' of."*[32]

This doctrine's meaning is clear. Among all of creation, including angelic beings, we alone are designed to be His representatives. The following illustration is not intended to be complete or authoritative. It is merely to be understood that the Trinity represents three persons of the godhead and that we are somehow a physical and spiritual representative of the triune God to the rest of His creation.

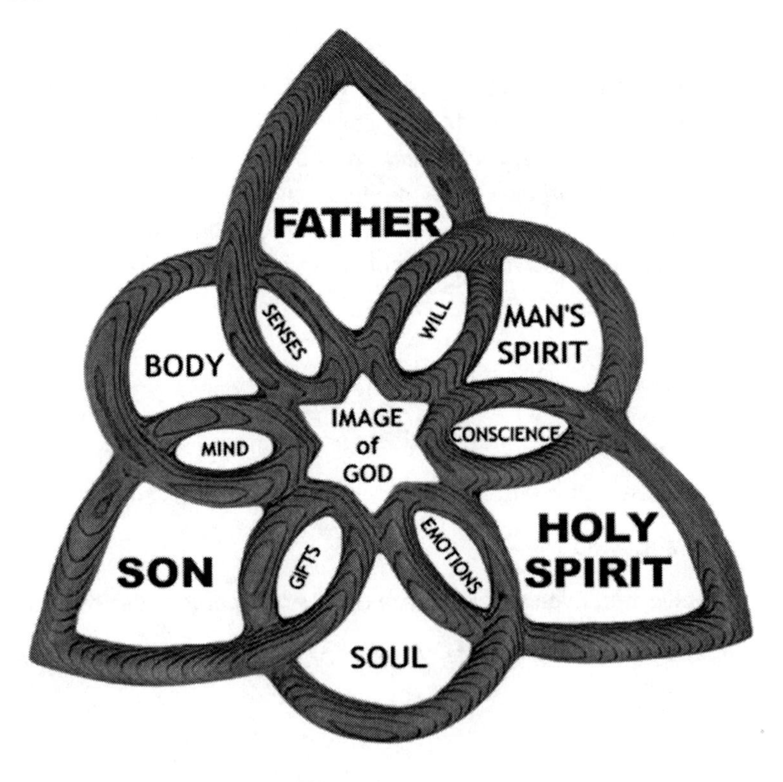

[32] Grudem, W., & Hughes, J. (2004). *Electronic Systematic Theology*. Whitefish, MO: Bits & Bytes, Inc., p. 442.

Like God, we have capacities of the mind, emotions, and will. Our consciences and gifts are expressions of His spiritual nature. We are able to experience and articulate His communicable attributes, such as love, truthfulness, and a sense of justice. Compared with other animals, only human beings encompass all of these features of His personhood. We are persons made in His image. The term "image of God" remains central to Western civilization's understanding of human exceptionalism and to the foundation of the pro-life movement.

Sanctity of Life

Human exceptionalism is God's decree. We were set apart[33] by Him from the rest of His creatures when He created us as His representatives. We call this the "sanctity of human life" or "sacredness of human life." All human life has intrinsic dignity and worth, so all innocent human life is to be protected. The Catholic Church's teaching is explicit:

> *"Human life is sacred because from its beginning, it involves the creative action of God, and it remains forever in a special relationship with the Creator, who is its sole end. God alone is the Lord of life from its beginning until its end: No one can, in any circumstance, claim for himself the right to destroy directly an innocent human being."*[34]

Marriage is Central to Being Pro-life

God commanded mankind to take dominion over His creation in our capacity as stewards. He has commanded that the means of dominion is

---

[33] This is the literal definition of the biblical term "sanctified."

[34] Congregation for the Doctrine of the Faith, Instruction on Respect for Human Life in its Origin and on the Dignity of Procreation. *Donum Vitae* (1987, February 22), Introduction, No. 5: *AAS* 80 (1988), 76-77; cf. *Catechism of the Catholic Church,* No. 2258.

the raising of godly offspring.[35] Marriage is between one man and one woman; male and female is God's design.[36] Any attack on this institution is an attack against God's intent. Marriage is an integral part of the teaching on *Imago Dei* and must hold an important position in pro-life policy and strategy.

Adam's Fall Introduced Murder

Adam rebelled against God's plan. He introduced sin into the world and the human race. Sin did not destroy the image of God in man, but it did distort it. God later reaffirmed the importance of His image in man being protected by the most severe of punishments when he spoke to Noah after the flood:

> *"Whoever shed the blood of man, by man shall his blood be shed, for God made man in His own image."*[37]

The encyclical that lays the foundation for much of present-day Catholic pro-life activism is known as *Evangelium Vitae* (the Gospel of Life). In it, Pope John Paul II said:

> *"This should not cause surprise: To kill a human being, in whom the image of God is present, is a particularly serious sin. Only God is the master of life!"*[38]

Grudem agrees:

---

[35] Malachi 2:15

[36] Genesis 1:26-27

[37] Genesis 9:5-6

[38] Pope John Paul II. (1995, March 25). *Evangelium Vitae,* par 55. *Catechism of the Catholic Church*, Nos. 2263-2269; cf. *Catechism of the Council of Trent* III, Nos. 327-332.

"Even though men are sinful, there is still enough likeness to God remaining in them that to murder another person (to 'shed blood' is an Old Testament expression for taking a human life) is to attack the part of creation that most resembles God, and it betrays an attempt or desire (if one were able) to attack God himself." [39]

Both faith streams hold that the taking of innocent life is murder:

"If such great care must be taken to respect every life, even that of criminals and unjust aggressors, the commandment 'You shall not kill' has absolute value when it refers to the innocent person. And all the more so in the case of weak and defenseless human beings, who find their ultimate defense against the arrogance and caprice of others only in the absolute binding force of God's commandment."[40]

Framing Injustice by Statute?

"Can wicked rulers be allied with you, those who frame injustice by statute?" [41]

The question that confronts the movement's anti-abortion efforts today is this: Should all preborn human beings be protected from murder, or just most of them? When otherwise God-fearing lawmakers bargain with some human lives to advance protections for others, they violate God's commandment.[42] Compromising on education or agricultural subsidies is very different from compromising on pro-life legislation. When legislators get life issues wrong—someone dies.

---

[39] Ibid., Grudem & Hughes, p. 444
[40] Ibid., Pope John Paul II, par 57.
[41] Psalms 94:20
[42] "You shall not murder." Exodus 20:13, Psalm 94:20

> *"They band together against the life of the righteous and condemn the innocent to death."*[43]

When an innocent person dies for the crimes of another, we say this is a grave injustice. When it is premeditated, it is called murder. Is this a friendly, relational thing to say? No. Is it reaching too far? I attest that it is not. International and American law handle complicity in murder very seriously. A variety of charges and penalties apply, depending on the extent of the connection to the act. What of the judges and lawmakers who create or uphold laws that permit the killing of innocent human beings? Why should they not be held to at least as much responsibility as those who carry out the laws? At the Nuremburg Trials, the leaders and policy makers of the National Socialist Party were judged as murders of the Holocaust victims. Their responsibility was deemed greater than that of the foot soldiers who carried out the exterminations.

Exceptions strategies are rooted in the false philosophy of Utilitarianism,[44] and they result in confusion and damage to our core principle of protecting all innocent human beings because they are made in God's image. Allowing the deaths of some, even the small percentage who are conceived in rape or have a disability, undercuts our argument for protecting any. We hear this refrain often, "If this bill can save 99% of the babies, it would be irresponsible not to vote for it." In this way, legislators pragmatically triage the 100 into two groups: The protected

---

[43] Psalms 94:21

[44] A relative moral philosophy espoused by Jeremy Bentham in the early 19th century, whose axiom "the greatest good for the greatest number" was intended to replace God's absolute moral code of right and wrong as reflected in the Ten Commandments

99% and the expendable 1%. But what would Jesus do? He has already answered us:

> *"What do you think? If a man has a hundred sheep, and one of them has gone astray, does he not leave the ninety-nine on the mountains and go in search of the one that went astray? And if he finds it, truly, I say to you, he rejoices over it more than over the ninety-nine that never went astray. So it is not the will of my Father who is in heaven that one of these little ones should perish."*[45]

I have lived in Israel, and I can assure you that the mountains of Judea are no place of safety for unattended sheep. Because of the deep ravines in the Judean wilderness, there is always the possibility a shepherd rescuing a sheep could find that several more had gone astray or even plunged to their deaths. If the pro-life movement will re-align itself with this principle of "saving the one,"[46] blessings and power will be released and we will witness His protection of the other 99—an end to legalized abortion.

Any Utilitarian formula applied to human life must be rejected as deeply flawed because it is rooted in evil.[47] "'The greatest good for the greatest number' is one of the most vicious slogans ever foisted on humanity,"[48] says Leonard Peikoff, a disciple of Ayn Rand. In his book, *The Ominous Parallels*, Peikoff claims that this axiom, as implemented by Germany's National Socialist Party, was the source of much human

---

[45] Matthew 18:12-14

[46] See Rebecca Kiessling's ministry www.Savethe1.com

[47] Jeremy Bentham (1748-1832) is the father of Utilitarianism who developed a relative system of morality not based on the Bible.

[48] Peikoff, L. (1983). *The ominous parallels: The end of freedom in America.* New York: Plume.

suffering and the impetus for the Holocaust. Richard Land, former chairman of the ERLC,[49] said, "When you accept Utilitarianism, you've given yourself a moral lobotomy."[50] Nevertheless, many Christian leaders and activists today defend this deadly philosophy, rather than fight to save the one along with the other 99.

The question needs to be answered once and for all: Do we promote 'murder' when we advocate for laws and politicians who find it necessary to kill some innocent human life in order, altruistically, to save others? If the womb merely houses a blob of tissue and not a human life at an early stage of development, then the answer is no. If the taking of innocent human life—be it embryonic, fetal, infant, toddler, child, adult, or elderly—really *is* murder, then what justification does any exception-inclusive politician or leader have for their Utilitarian approach? Why do these leaders fail to understand what Pope John Paul II declared, that "the absolute binding force of God's commandment"[51] is, in a word—*absolute*? Are not these laws actually allowing murder by statute?

Biblical versus Political Base

The foundational problem in today's pro-life movement is that it is not biblically, theologically, faith-based. It is politically based, and it stands on a foundation of post-modern relativism.[52] Every devout pro-life

---

[49] Ethics and Religious Liberty Commission of the Southern Baptist Convention

[50] Land, R. (2007). *The Divided States of America: What Liberals and Conservatives Get Wrong.* Nashville: Thomas Nelson, p. 184.

[51] Ibid., Pope John Paul II.

[52] Educe. (2017). Rise Up in the Truth online curriculum. Retrieved from www.educelife.org. Educe is an online education ministry whose curriculum reveals how we arrived, biblically and historically, at our current state of error in

Christian should be appalled and incensed that our biblical truth has been eclipsed by Utilitarianism's relativist philosophy,[53] masquerading as pro-life strategy.

The strategy of the Church must be grounded on the doctrine of *Imago Dei* and therefore, absolute. From a Christian standpoint, there can never be a path that includes the murder of innocent people. If we stand idly by and innocent preborn children are killed based on their manner of conception, diagnosis, disability, or degree of dependency, are we not complicit? Are we not preparing the way to declaring the elderly and infirm dispensable as well—"post-persons" in a throwaway society? As a movement, God will certainly hold us accountable for diminishing and disregarding His sovereignty by using our self-defined prudence instead of submitting to His commands.[54]

As Christians, we must demand that a true biblical standard be raised in today's corrupted landscape. The current compromised pro-life movement risks "losing its saltiness"[55] and in the words of our Lord Jesus, even being "thrown out and trampled under the feet of men."[56] Over the last 35 years, what has been accomplished? The only national law passed to curtail abortion was the deeply flawed Partial-Birth Abortion Ban Act of 2003, which even some of its most vocal champions eventually agreed

---

the Church, the culture, and the law. Educe is an affiliate organization of Personhood Alliance.

[53] The greatest good for the greatest number

[54] Proverbs 24:25-26

[55] Matthew 5:13

[56] Matthew 5:13

did not save a single life.[57] How can we expect the blessings of God when we violate His absolute command, "You shall not murder?"

In Summary

The Personhood movement calls for a return to a Christian foundation for policy and strategy. This necessitates a biblical, faith-based adherence to God's standards, as opposed to political prudence and Utilitarianism. In other words, we need to recognize that we have violated God's standards and turn around and go the other way. Only then can we be assured that the God of all creation will bless our efforts. Another pro-personhood leader, President Abraham Lincoln, said it this way:

> *"And, insomuch as we know that, by His divine law, nations like individuals are subjected to punishments and chastisements in this world, may we not justly fear that the awful calamity of civil war, which now desolates the land, may be but a punishment, inflicted upon us, for our presumptuous sins, to the needful end of our national reformation as a whole People? We have been the recipients of the choicest bounties of Heaven. We have been preserved, these many years, in peace and prosperity. We have grown in numbers, wealth and power, as no other nation has ever grown.* ***But we have forgotten God... It behooves us then, to humble ourselves before the offended Power, to confess our national sins, and to pray for clemency and forgiveness."*** *[emphasis added]*[58]

---

[57] Dobson, J., Dr. (2007, May). Focus action: A nation of prayer amidst a culture of death. Retrieved from http://americanrtl.org/files/Documents/DobsonAgreesPBAsavesnone.html

[58] Abraham Lincoln. (1863, March 30). A proclamation.

In our current cultural climate, it's the Left against the Right, Progressives against Conservatives, Democrats against Republicans, and human secularism against orthodox Christianity. Let us fervently pray that we would avoid the warning of President Thomas Jefferson when he said:

> *"God who gave us life gave us liberty. Can the liberties of a nation be thought secure when we have removed a conviction that these liberties are the gift of God? Indeed I tremble for my country when I reflect that God is just, that his justice cannot sleep forever."*[59]

[Daniel Becker is the Founder and President of Personhood Alliance. He is also the former President and PAC Director of Georgia Right to Life and a former board member of National Right to Life. He studied at L'Abri Fellowship under the mentorship of Dr. Francis Schaeffer in 1973. A widower, Daniel enjoys investing in the lives of his 26 "grand-blessings."]

---

[59] Inscribed on the third panel of the Jefferson Memorial in Washington, DC

Inscription on the third panel of the Jefferson Memorial

Washington, DC

CHAPTER 2

Why Personhood?

By Rev. Walter B. Hoye II, President and Founder of the Issues4Life Foundation, California Civil Rights Foundation, and the Frederick Douglass Foundation of California; core member of the National Black Pro-Life Coalition

"The term 'non-person' has emerged as the most far-reaching and disastrous epithet ever invoked to devalue human life in the womb. When the United States Supreme Court's Roe v. Wade decision (1973) declared that the word 'person,' as used in the Fourteenth Amendment, does not include the unborn, it sounded the legalized death knell for huge numbers of unborn humans."[60]

Personhood is a pro-life strategy that does not embrace exceptions and in my opinion, is exactly what the pro-life movement looks like victorious.

---

[60] Brennan, W., PhD. (1995). *Dehumanizing the vulnerable: When word games take lives.* Chicago: Loyola University Press, 8.; Brennan is a professor of social work at the St. Louis University School of Social Work.

Personhood in Communities of Color

Personhood allows the discussion to focus on the sanctity of life. It is a powerful and effective strategy for communicating life in communities of color. In the classroom of race-based oppression, minority communities in this country share a very painful history of lessons learned at the ultimate expense of life itself. Because we have "been there," because we understand what it is like not to be considered a person, we know exactly where the term "non-person" leads.

Personhood is rooted in truth. "Momma is with child" is a simple truth that has the power to triumphantly contend with those hiding behind socially impeccable auspices such as the pulpit, the bench, or the Resolute Desk.[61]

Personhood affords us the opportunity to address how words have been used historically to justify the vilest crimes against humanity. Personhood reminds the public that malevolent and worm-wooded words fuel violent human behavior.

Personhood is ensures Equal Protection

By design, Personhood replaces the lexicon of dehumanization with what Dr. Brennan calls a "nomenclature of life-affirming and exalted portrayals of all human beings despite their status, condition, stage of development, gender, race, age, or place of residence."[62]

---

[61] Presidential desk in the Oval Office
[62] Ibid.

If the goal of the 14th Amendment was to give legal effect to the Civil Rights Bill of 1866,[63] then the goal of Personhood is to give legal effect to a definition of personhood that includes all human beings, regardless of how they were procreated—from the preborn, to the senior citizen facing end-of-life decisions, to the disabled war veteran.[64]

Just as the U.S. Congress felt it needful to protect the fundamental rights of former slaves as United States citizens under Article IV, Section II of the U.S. Constitution,[65] proponents and those denied personhood understand how needful it is to protect all human beings by love and by the Constitution.

We Need Personhood Resolved

If Ezekiel is right, God is looking for leaders who would build up the wall and stand before Him in the gap on behalf of the land so He would not have to destroy it.[66] Could it be that abortion is still legal in America, and the needs of our women and children are still unmet, because the

---

[63] United States Congress. (1866, April 9). Civil Rights Act: An act to protect all persons in the United States in their civil rights, and furnish the means of their vindication.

[64] *Roe v. Wade*. (1973). 410 US 113; Cf. the Wisconsin abortion statute, defining "unborn child" to mean "a human being from the time of conception until it is born alive," Wis. Stat. 940.04 (6) (1969); and the Connecticut Statute, Pub. Act No. 1 (May 1972 special session), declaring it to be the public policy of the State and the legislative intent "to protect and preserve human life from the moment of conception."

[65] "The Citizens of each State shall be entitled to all Privileges and Immunities of Citizens in the several States. A Person charged in any State with Treason, Felony, or other Crime, who shall flee from Justice, and be found in another State, shall on demand of the executive Authority of the State from which he fled, be delivered up, to be removed to the State having Jurisdiction of the Crime."

[66] Ezekiel 22:30

leaders of our socially impeccable auspices are not socially impeccable themselves?

I think so.

Brothers, we need to talk.

[Rev. Walter B. Hoye II is a licensed and ordained Baptist preacher who serves as both President and Founder of the Issues4life Foundation, the California Civil Rights Foundation, and the Frederick Douglass Foundation of California. He is a core member of the National Black Pro-Life Coalition and sits on the board of The Morning Center. Rev. Hoye has been an early and insistent voice to make personhood the centerpiece of pro-life ministry within the Black community. He and the National Black Pro-Life Coalition are succeeding in that goal.]

CHAPTER 3

The Modern Personhood Movement: What is it?

By Jay Rogers, President, Personhood Florida Education

Personhood is a shift back to a Christ-centered view on the sanctity of life. This shift begins with a recognition of the dignity of the human person at all stages of development, based on the *Imago Dei.* To understand the Personhood strategy, we can simply look at three passages in the Bible, which are easy to remember: Genesis 1, Jeremiah 1, and Luke 1.

> *"Then God said, 'Let Us make man in Our image, according to Our likeness.'"*[67]

> *"Before I formed you in the womb I knew you, and before you were born I consecrated you; I appointed you a prophet to the nations."*[68]

---

[67] Genesis 1:26
[68] Jeremiah 1:5

> *"In those days Mary arose and went with haste into the hill country, to a town in Judah, and she entered the house of Zechariah and greeted Elizabeth. And when Elizabeth heard the greeting of Mary, the baby leaped in her womb. And Elizabeth was filled with the Holy Spirit, and she exclaimed with a loud cry, 'Blessed are you among women, and blessed is the fruit of your womb! And why is this granted to me that the mother of my Lord should come to me? For behold, when the sound of your greeting came to my ears, the baby in my womb leaped for joy. And blessed is she who believed that there would be a fulfillment of what was spoken to her from the Lord.'"* [69]

Personhood represents a paradigm shift in the pro-life movement. We begin with scripture and insist that the right to life is God-given. We are all created in the image of God. In fact, we were made in God's image from our biological beginning in the womb.

For the first time years ago, I heard someone say that the political end of the pro-life movement failed at its inception because it was never Christ-centered, and we cannot fight a demonic force with natural weapons. I heard the phrase, "We can't fight Goliath in Saul's armor." This means that man's efforts will fail, but God's plan for victory is according to His perfect will.

At first, I thought it was a cynical comment to impugn the pro-life movement for the devastation caused by abortion. But I eventually realized that the truth is far worse than that. Our struggle does not begin and end with abortion. Abortion is just an obvious outcropping of a deep spiritual problem we have as a culture in failing to recognize some of the most fundamental of all Biblical truths.

---

[69] Luke 1:39-45

A Brief History of the Modern Pro-Life Movement

To explain why the Personhood paradigm is much larger than just a plan to end abortion, we first need to understand a bit of history. *Roe v. Wade*[70] did not establish a women's right to choose abortion. It established a right to privacy surrounding the abortion procedure and protected doctors from criminal proceedings. That, in effect, removed protections for preborn children.

The personhood of the preborn child had already been established in many of our laws. Case in point: Ariel Castro, a man in Cleveland, Ohio, was convicted of kidnapping, enslaving, and continually raping three women over a period of years, as well as the killing of one of the women's preborn child. Castro was sentenced to life in prison. He could have been sentenced to death had he not pled guilty to first-degree murder. Ironically, he later committed suicide in prison. In this case, the law recognized the personhood of the preborn child that Castro had conceived through rape.

Charles Van Zant, a Florida state representative from Keystone Heights, likened *Roe* to establishing a loophole in the law governing murder. This assessment is a valid interpretation. In essence, we recognize forced abortion as murder, but we make exceptions for the criminality of abortion under a practitioner's supervision.

At the time *Roe v. Wade* was decided, the only large religious body that had an active plan to end abortion was the Roman Catholic Church. Most Protestant denominations were silent, and some even issued statements of agreement with *Roe*. These positions came from

---

[70] *Roe v. Wade*. (1973). 410 US 113.

progressive denominations such as the United Methodist Church, the Episcopalian Church, the Evangelical Lutheran Church of America, the United Church of Christ (Congregationalists), and the Presbyterian Church USA, as well as the unorthodox—the Seventh Day Adventists, the Unitarians, the Mormons, and so on.

Much to our shame, some evangelicals joined the chorus of briefs written in favor of *Roe*. Even the conservative Southern Baptist Convention called on all Baptists to work for abortion rights.

1971: Southern Baptists Advocate Abortion for Exceptions[71]

> *WHEREAS, Christians in the American society today are faced with difficult decisions about abortion; and*
> *WHEREAS, some advocate that there be no abortion legislation, thus making the decision a purely private matter between a woman and her doctor; and*
> *WHEREAS, others advocate no legal abortion, or would permit abortion only if the life of the mother is threatened;*
> *Therefore, be it RESOLVED, that this Convention express the belief that society has a responsibility to affirm through the laws of the state a high view of the sanctity of human life, including fetal life, in order to protect those who cannot protect themselves; and*
> *Be it further RESOLVED, that we call upon Southern Baptists to work for legislation that will allow the possibility of abortion under such conditions as rape, incest, clear evidence of severe fetal deformity, and carefully ascertained evidence of the likelihood of damage to the emotional, mental, and physical health of the mother.*

1974: Southern Baptists Reaffirm Support for Abortion[72]

---

[71] Resolution on Abortion. (1971, June). [Southern Baptist Convention proceedings].

[72] Resolution on Abortion and Sanctity of Human Life. (1974, June). [Southern Baptist Convention proceedings].

WHEREAS, Southern Baptists have historically held a high view of the sanctity of human life, and
WHEREAS, the messengers to the Southern Baptist Convention meeting in St. Louis in 1971 adopted overwhelmingly a resolution on abortion, and
WHEREAS, that resolution reflected a middle ground between the extreme of abortion on demand and the opposite extreme of all abortion as murder, and
WHEREAS, that resolution dealt responsibly from a Christian perspective with complexities of abortion problems in contemporary society;
Therefore, be it RESOLVED, that we reaffirm the resolution on the subject adopted by the messengers to the St. Louis Southern Baptist Convention meeting in 1971, and
Be it further RESOLVED, that we continue to seek God's guidance through prayer and study in order to bring about solutions to continuing abortion problems in our society.

1976: Southern Baptists Disavow Government Role in Stopping Abortion[73]

WHEREAS, Southern Baptists have historically held a Biblical view of the sanctity of human life, and
WHEREAS, abortion is a very serious moral and spiritual problem of continuing concern to the American people, and
WHEREAS, Christians have a responsibility to deal with all moral and spiritual issues which affect society, including the problems of abortion, and
WHEREAS, the practice of abortion for selfish non-therapeutic reasons only destroys fetal life, dulls our society's moral sensitivity, and leads to a cheapening of all human life, and
WHEREAS, every decision for an abortion, for whatever reason must necessarily involve the decision to terminate the life of an innocent human being.
Therefore be it RESOLVED, that the messengers to the Southern Baptist Convention meeting in Norfolk in June 1976 reaffirm the

---

[73] Resolution on Abortion. (1976, June). [Southern Baptist Convention proceedings].

> *Biblical sacredness and dignity of all human life, including fetal life, and*
> *Be it further RESOLVED, that we call on Southern Baptists and all citizens of the nation to work to change those attitudes and conditions which encourage many people to turn to abortion as a means of birth control, and*
> *Be it further RESOLVED, that in the best interest of our society, we reject any indiscriminate attitude toward abortion, as contrary to the Biblical view, and*
> *Be it further RESOLVED, that we also affirm our conviction about the limited role of government in dealing with matters relating to abortion, and support the right of expectant mothers to the full range of medical services and personal counseling for the preservation of life and health.*

Thankfully, the Southern Baptist Convention (and evangelical churches in general) greatly changed their stance on abortion as the 1970s came to a close. The Southern Baptist Convention later called upon all its members to take an active stand in support of the sanctity of human life. They should be commended on their reversal in policy. However, we should also recognize that most churches in America are still not actively engaging in a plan to end all abortion without delay or compromise, and many still outwardly support it.[74]

This complicity in the abortion holocaust is a dark stain on the evangelical movement. It ought to cause us to pause and consider that evangelicals were, in large part, responsible for it. Although most evangelical churches eventually abandoned their support of abortion, the initial confusion hurt the burgeoning pro-life movement and delayed activism. But the Catholic bishops had a plan.

---

[74] Pew Research Center. (2013). Religious groups' official positions on abortion. Retrieved from http://www.pewforum.org/2013/01/16/religious-groups-official-positions-on-abortion/

PARADIGM SHIFT 1: THE BISHOPS' PLAN

The Catholic Bishops' plan was a comprehensive strategy to pass a Human Life Amendment to the U.S. Constitution at the federal level and engage the grassroots to pass state laws and state-level constitutional amendments using the declaration of states' rights in 10th Amendment.[75]

The Bishops of the Roman Catholic Church, to their great credit, refused to compromise with the rape, incest, and health of the mother exceptions laid out in the *Roe* decision. Sadly, they did not have the support of the majority of Americans and especially of the large Protestant church denominations. The bishops' plan failed, in part, because many state and federal legislators were only willing to support a plan that had exceptions. This was the first split in the modern pro-life movement.

PARADIGM SHIFT 2: THE HYDE AMENDMENT

In 1976, Representative Henry J. Hyde (R-Illinois) sponsored an amendment to the annual budget appropriations bill for the Department of Health and Human Services. Despite opposition from pro-abortion groups, Hyde attached this amendment every year to the same appropriations bill. His amendment denied Medicaid funding for abortion unless a woman's life is endangered by carrying the child to term.[76] The Supreme Court upheld the constitutionality of the Hyde amendment in

---

[75] "The powers not delegated to the United States by the Constitution, nor prohibited by it to the States, are reserved to the States respectively, or to the people."

[76] Rovner, J. (2009). Abortion funding ban has evolved over the years. Retrieved from http://www.npr.org/templates/story/story.php?storyId=121402281

1980.[77] Because the Hyde Amendment is a budget rider and not law, its language has changed several times. For example, Congress added rape and incest exceptions in the late 1970s. These exceptions were removed in the early 80s, but reinstated in 1989.[78]

The Catholic bishops initially opposed the exceptions in the Hyde Amendment, but several evangelical groups who had begun to join the pro-life movement supported them. Although there is no question that the Hyde Amendment has saved millions of lives, Personhood advocates worry that allowing abortion in certain cases actually strengthens the pro-abortion agenda. It undermines the argument that abortion kills a child. Other life advocates argue that exceptions are necessary to save some lives, even though they only chip away at *Roe* and try to eliminate abortion incrementally and gradually.

Paradigm Shift 3: Personhood

The modern Personhood movement began in 2006 through the action of Georgia Right to Life Vice President Dan Becker.[79] Personhood received national attention when Becker's organization sought to revive the bishops' plan by passing a Human Life Amendment to the Georgia state constitution. Ironically, evangelicals lined up behind Becker's plan, while the National Right to Life Committee and the Catholic bishops opposed it. Their reasoning, as just outlined, was that any state law or

---

[77] Net Industries: Law Library. (2017). Abortion – After *Roe v Wade*. Retrieved from http://tinyurl.com/j7sh7er

[78] Ibid., Rovner

[79] Cal Zastrow also introduced a Personhood Amendment in Michigan in the fall of 2006.

amendment that did not have exceptions was unacceptable as a sound strategy to chip away at *Roe*.

In 2008, Personhood USA was established by Cal Zastrow and Keith Mason, who were working toward legislative and voter initiatives in a number of states. In every state where it has been tried, Personhood has been opposed by organizations at the national level, including Phyllis Schlafly's Eagle Forum, the National Right to Life Committee, and the U.S. Conference of Catholic Bishops. State-level affiliates and bishops have opposed Personhood legislation as well.

It is ironic that today, several conservative commentators who identify themselves as pro-life believe that exceptions are necessary in order to pass restrictive legislation—even though the *Roe* decision was framed around these very exceptions.[80] In other words, they want to reverse *Roe* but the exceptions-based legislative strategy they support actually keeps *Roe* in place. The pro-life movement now stands on its head.

This is why the growing paradigm shift in the pro-life movement is to return to its principles; to recognize that a human being is a person from his or her biological beginning, with no exceptions for manner of conception or degree of dependency. It is important to note that

---

[80] In the *Roe v. Wade* case, Justice Harry Blackmun cited exceptions as being proof that the state of Texas was not serious about banning all abortion. "When Texas urges that a fetus is entitled to Fourteenth Amendment protection as a person, it faces a dilemma. . . Neither in Texas nor in any other State are all abortions prohibited. But if the fetus is a person who is not to be deprived of life without due process of law, and if the mother's condition is the sole determinant, does not the Texas exception appear to be out of line with the Amendment's command?" Retrieved from https://supreme.justia.com/cases/federal/us/410/113/case.html#F54

overturning *Roe* will not make abortion illegal in the United States. We must work at the state level, using the Tenth Amendment for example, to nullify the Supreme Court's decision to override states' interests, but we must also use Personhood to challenge *Roe* directly and remove the restrictions on the right to life for unborn persons. We have several tasks to accomplish all at once.

Personhood's International Success

In Mexico, where abortion was recently made legal in the capital city, over half of its state legislatures have passed Personhood amendments to keep the Supreme Court from imposing abortion on the states.[81] This strategy has already worked. Poland has established that an unborn person is subject to protection.[82] Hungary has the following clause in its constitution:

> "Human dignity is inviolable. Everyone has the right to life and human dignity; the life of a fetus will be protected from conception."[83]

Personhood is a worldwide movement led by the Holy Spirit. The focus of pro-life groups in many countries around the world[84] is

---

[81] Jalsevac, J. (2011). 'Roe v. Wade' of Mexico: Mexico's highest court to decide on pro-life amendments this week. Retrieved from https://www.lifesitenews.com/news/roe-v-wade-of-mexico-mexicos-highest-court-to-decide-on-pro-life-amendment

[82] Polish Law of Jan 7, 1997 on Family Planning, Human Embryo Protection, and Conditions of Legal Pregnancy Termination, as amended, Dec 23, 1997, Article 1.

[83] SBA List. (2012). New Hungarian constitution protects the right to life. Retrieved from https://www.sba-list.org/suzy-b-blog/new-hungarian-constitution-protects-right-life

[84] In the EU (One of Us), Israel, Mexico, Netherlands, and South Africa

beginning to shift from merely regulating abortion to recognizing and protecting the God-given right to life of every human being at all stages of development.

Disagreement on Strategy and Timing—Not Policy

Pro-life advocates in our own country support Personhood philosophically almost unanimously. However, the disagreement between Personhood advocates and others in the pro-life movement is one of strategy and timing. They want to wait to stack the Supreme Court bench with conservatives in order to overturn *Roe*. We advocate for a grassroots movement right now—a movement that will bring Personhood amendments up from the state level, and concurrently, at the national level. I often tell people that if we work toward Personhood now, we will eventually get there. If we delay our obedience, we will be counted among those who opposed Personhood when our support was most needed.

Introducing Cognitive Dissonance as a Strategy

Interestingly, many pro-choice advocates are actually pro-Personhood once we remove "anti-abortion" and "pro-life" labels from the conversation. Nationally, there is a 50-50 split for and against abortion, with many in the middle advocating for some type of compromise. However, over 90 percent of college students we speak with support the position that eugenic experimentation on living fetuses should be illegal. When asked to provide the rationale for their stance, they often say that the fetus is a developing human being who has basic human rights.

For this reason, it is imperative that we seize the opportunity to create cognitive dissonance in the minds of our youth (and our older generations) who may otherwise think of themselves as pro-choice. Perhaps they identify as pro-choice under pressure to be politically correct, but are otherwise in favor of Personhood as the only alternative to Nazi-style eugenics and other abominations. From there, the mental shift toward recognizing the full Personhood of the preborn child, without exceptions, is just a few steps away.

The Biological Time Bomb

Outside of the abortion debate, there is a biological time bomb ticking. Philosophers and religious leaders have thought about the issues surrounding life, death, and immortality for thousands of years. However, the structure of the DNA molecule has been known for less than 60 years and a detailed map of this structure for less than 20 years.[85] It usually takes a generation or more for a major discovery to percolate through an entire scientific field, but due to the rapid advancement of technology, major disruptions in biological science are just over the horizon.

Medical technology will be used to save lives in a greater capacity than ever before. In a few years, a woman may be able to buy an over-the-counter fertility monitor that provides 99.9% accuracy. She may also be able to see the development of her baby in real time through a wearable ultrasound monitor. These are just a few of the technologies

---

[85] National Human Genome Research Institute. (2017). An overview of the human genome project. Retrieved from https://www.genome.gov/12011238/

we should prepare to use to save lives. However, as we are well aware, technology can also be used for evil.

The major battles that Personhood advocates will fight in the next 50 years will have nothing to do with abortion. There is a Pandora's Box of new possibilities that bring serious moral, legal, and ethical questions. Some of these technologies are already here, such as cryogenics, cloning, germline engineering, embryonic experimentation, and human-animal hybrids. Others are emerging, such as artificial wombs, advanced artificial intelligences, cyborgs, and other transhumanist technologies.[86] This might seem like science fiction, but the Millennial generation will certainly deal with the social, economic, and ethical conflicts these developments in biotechnology will inevitably cause.

[Jay Rogers is the president of Personhood Florida Education. He has been involved in political and direct action on the abortion issue since 1988. He has worked as an English teacher, writer, editor, video producer, and short-term missionary in Russia and Ukraine. A native of the Boston area, he lives with his wife Kalia in Kissimmee, Florida.]

---

[86] Anissimov, M. (2017). Top ten transhumanist technologies. Retrieved from http://lifeboat.com/ex/transhumanist.technologies

CHAPTER 4

Personhood Education: A Bridge Between Brokenness and Opportunity

By Sarah Quale, President and Founder of Educe

We are in a mess. There is no denying it. America is at a crossroads, and the pro-life movement is, too. Critical questions abound as we find ourselves caught up once again in the predictable ebb and flow on the political and cultural battlefields. Which strategies should we carry into the future? Which should we abandon? What is the best way to change hearts and minds? How can we truly heal our broken nation and bind up the divisions between us? "The pro-life movement is growing," we hear. "The Church is waking up!" It sounds exciting, but what exactly does that mean? And will this growth and awakening bring change? If so, what kind?

A Call for Restoration

It is one thing for the Church to wake up. But it is completely another for individual Christians to clean out their lives and put their focus on

God so true spiritual awakening can come to America. History shows us that revival in the culture always comes after reformation in the individual, and reformation in the individual always comes after alignment with the biblical truth.[87] When we choose to open ourselves to this truth, a powerful thing happens. Our minds get renewed. Our hearts find freedom, and our thinking and behavior transforms. We see the sanctity of life as a Jesus issue, not a political or social one. Thus, we recognize that our work must be motivated by the ways of Jesus—the work of bringing light and hope to a lost and broken world. So what is the powerful truth at the heart of the battle between life and death? It is this:

> *Every human life is valuable, from fertilization to the last breath, because every life is created by God for a specific purpose.*

This fundamental first principle not only lies at the core of the pro-life movement, but also serves as a window through which we can look to assess its health. Two words come to mind here—brokenness and opportunity.

Our current battle rises from the same ancient evil that slithered into the Garden[88]—an evil that has manifested throughout the ages and is now fiercely emboldened. The days of "safe, legal, and rare"[89] have

---

[87] Edwards, J. (1743, December 12). On the Great Awakening. [Letter to Rev. Thomas Prince]. Retrieved from http://www.nhinet.org/ccs/docs/ awaken.htm

[88] Genesis 3

[89] C-SPAN archives. (1993, January 22). Abortion rights and medical research orders by President Bill Clinton. [Video and transcript]. Retrieved from https://www.c-span.org/video/?37335-1/abortion-rights-medical- research-orders

morphed into "Care. No matter what."[90] Abortion must now be readily available, for any reason, at any time. The battle is no longer pro-life versus pro-choice; it's woman versus fetus. And the personhood of a preborn human depends solely on whether someone defines him as a person, whether it's his mother, a judge, a college professor, a member of a medical ethics board, a lab technician, or someone on Facebook.

Many long-time leaders in the pro-life movement are struggling. Some are fighting ghosts of the past, tangled up in strategies that counter our very foundation. Others are entrenched in arguments that distract and divide and are often caught up in dialogue that defames the cause of life. Meanwhile, the eugenics movement is openly advancing at a pace not seen in 120 years. It seems we need some direction here.

Perhaps the pro-life movement should seek answers in the place we find the inalienable right to life—the Creator Himself. Perhaps we should seek justice and mercy based on the teachings of Jesus, not on legal positivism.[91] Perhaps we should look at our brokenness as an opportunity to re-align with our fundamental first principle.

---

[90] O'Bannon, R. K., PhD. (2012). New logo, new slogan, same old Planned Parenthood. http://tinyurl.com/gpajlcg Retrieved on March 2, 2017.

[91] A philosophy that asserts that laws are based on measurable social standards, not moral absolutes, and are only limited by what public opinion will tolerate; law is a matter of what can be made culturally acceptable in society, not a matter of morality, preservation of individual liberty, or justice

A Challenge to All of Us

The bottom line is this: We cannot continue to allow government to define a right that has never been its right to define.[92] We must decide which path to follow:

> *"Legal protections for human life as defined by government or personhood as defined by God and legally recognized by government."*[93]

These two divergent paths define the pro-life movement today, and they have fractured it more than once. While both paths seek to end the destruction of human life as soon as possible, one path supports temporary gains that exempt certain groups of humans, and the other does not.

Although arguments for compromise and exceptions are powerful, they fail to address one of the major philosophies at the foundation of the culture of death: Utilitarianism. As discussed earlier in this book, Utilitarianism measures morality as the greatest good for the greatest number. It prefers the good of the group over the rights of the individual and values usefulness and societal contribution. Advocates for "choice" often embrace this philosophy without really knowing what it is. But it forms their justification for abortion to lessen the burden of poverty, for example, or to curb population growth, or to use aborted fetal remains for research. It also becomes the rationale for euthanizing the terminally ill, creating human-animal hybrids for the advancement of science, and

---

[92] Declaration of Independence (1776). An Act of the Second Continental Congress. (July 4, 1776).

[93] Becker, D. (2011). *Personhood: A pragmatic guide to pro-life victory in the 21st century and the return to first principles in politics*. Alpharetta, GA: TKS Publications, 32.

destroying thousands of embryos for their potential to someday treat disease.

When the pro-life movement compromises its fundamental first principle in the push to end the destruction of human life, at whatever stage, we actually embrace this same philosophy. We believe we need to create the greatest good for the greatest number in order to eventually win. We are saying the good of the group overrides the rights of the individual, and we are willing to abandon our moral fortitude because "the best is the enemy of the good."[94] Nevertheless, the ugly truth is: We are leaving tens of thousands of bodies at abortion facilities every year. We are literally sacrificing our preborn brothers and sisters for incremental gain, because they have an extra chromosome, a bleak prognosis, were conceived in rape, or simply got swept up in "life of the mother" misconceptions.[95]

We promise to go back for them, but we never do.[96]

It comes down to this: Much of our leadership, in their noble quest to end abortion, has embraced these deadly compromises. But that does not mean we have to. It does not even mean we should. To truly bring about a spiritual awakening in America (which we very much need) and to turn the lost and broken-hearted towards Jesus (which is the very mission of His Church), we must first seek reformation in ourselves. We

---

[94] Arouet, F-M. [nom de plume Voltaire]. (1764). Dictionnaire philosophique.

[95] Physicians for Life. (2016). Is abortion okay when the mother's life is in danger? Retrieved from http://www.physiciansforlife.org/is-abortion-okay-when-the-mothers-life-is-in-danger-a-new-video-has-answers/

[96] According to pro-life attorney Rebecca Kiessling, Esq., there is no known recorded case of a state or federal law having these deadly prejudices removed—*ex post facto*.

must re-align with our fundamental first principle and seek deeper understanding about the spiritual, philosophical, and cultural battle between life and death. Only then can we truly end the legalized killing of preborn children through principled strategy, policy, and activism. The starting point for this reformation is education.

Education Promotes Responsibility

There is great power in biblical truth, and as Christians, we have been given authority to speak it.[97] This means we are responsible for holding it in high regard. There is no reason to exaggerate it, misrepresent it, or alter it situationally. The truth requires us to seek information for ourselves, ask bold questions, change our long-held assumptions when necessary, and honor the great responsibility we have to carry light and life into the next generation. But we must first know what the truth is and how it fits within a broader spiritual and philosophical context in order to bring real, life-changing, culture-transforming solutions.

Good-intentioned pro-lifers mishandle the truth because they are simply not informed and often, are missing the bigger picture. This can be greatly damaging to the movement and to the authority and integrity of the Church. To break out of this pattern, we must inform ourselves so we can inform our efforts. We must learn to discern biblical truth from moral relativism, and share our knowledge in a spirit of compassion.

Education Brings Reasoned Responses

In 2 Timothy 2:14-26, Paul writes at length about the importance of correctly handling the truth, being unashamed of it, resisting quarrels,

---

[97] Matthew 16:19

and avoiding godless chatter. He writes this as a precursor to his warning about the last days, when people are lovers of themselves, without self-control, brutal, and unforgiving.[98] But what is of most significance here is that this is his final letter, scribed from a Roman dungeon shortly before his execution. It seems his warning is important. He admonishes us to gently instruct so people can come to their senses and "escape the trap of the devil who has taken them captive to do his will." Paul had a personal encounter with the resurrected Jesus, and it radically changed his perspective.[99] He transformed from a zealous persecutor to a humble follower of Jesus and as a result, altered the course of history. As vessels of the Holy Spirit, we are called to do the same.

Today, Paul is asking us to do something that is contrary to what we often feel: To actually listen and try to understand people; to be respectful and composed, but unashamed to speak truth with the hope that hearts will change. If we do not stop to recognize that the hate poured out against us is a sign of brokenness and deceit, we miss an opportunity to plant a seed. When we deliver the beautiful message about God's design in an ugly way, we can actually impede the work Holy Spirit wants to do in a person's life. In other words, our defensiveness in the defense of life does not bring life at all; in fact, it can even bring death.

So we must carry the Personhood message in a way that honors the person of Jesus, seeks to change hearts and minds, and makes injustices like abortion unthinkable. Understanding the bigger picture—the history,

---

[98] 2 Timothy 3:1-5
[99] Acts 9:1-22

the biblical context, and the strategies that come against God's design—helps us do just that.

Education Prepares the Way

1 Peter 3:15 challenges us to always be ready to give an answer for the hope that we have. What does this look like for the pro-life Christian today, particularly, the Personhood advocate? It means being prepared to speak truth in situations we encounter and being open to how God wants to use us. This involves our head and our heart. Knowledge of what the Word of God says about marriage, family, human dignity, and the sanctity of life is obviously critical. But it is just as critical for us to explore history, recognize the philosophies that set themselves up against the Word of God, and develop a perspective of compassion that comes from Jesus' ways, not the world's. The acquiring of knowledge always draws us closer to a truth about ourselves and about God's love for all people. Christians often forget that our capacity to show love and feel genuine compassion toward others, and to look through a lens of love at the evil others do, comes from experiencing this love in our own lives. It comes from our hearts. And when both heart and head are aligned, the power that comes with knowledge is intensified. Truth becomes words. Words become action, and God gets the glory.

America's moral and spiritual well-being is rapidly deteriorating. It is time to decide if we are willing to be that remnant God is seeking—the ones left standing.[100] As believers, we are called to be light in the

[100] Ephesians 6:13

darkness[101] and to demonstrate the love of Jesus in the way we live our lives.[102] Likewise, as Personhood advocates, we are called to carry the message of Personhood in the way Jesus would—honestly, graciously, and uncompromisingly—into a battered and chaotic world.

So as many politicians, leaders, and pundits try to drive the future of the pro-life movement further from the biblical standard, let us use this unique time in history to change the way we engage in the battle. Let us rediscover our values, return to our fundamental first principle, and reclaim our spiritual authority. Let us bridge the gap between brokenness and opportunity by educating, equipping, and empowering ourselves to stand in the broadest, most challenging mission field today—life.

It really is up to us.

[Sarah Quale is the founder and president of Educe (educelife.org), a non-profit organization that provides online education for the Christian pro-life movement. Sarah is an award-winning curriculum and instructional designer and a gifted facilitator. She is a busy and energetic wife, a mother of seven children (three in heaven through miscarriage), a sidewalk prayer warrior, and a redeemed child of God. Through Educe, she designs and develops online learning for numerous pro-life organizations and initiatives, as well as Educe's originally authored curricula. Sarah serves on the national board and executive committee of Personhood Alliance.]

---

[101] Ephesians 5:8-12
[102] Colossians 1:10

SECTION II

Personhood in Public Policy

CHAPTER 5

Personhood: The Image Of God In 21st Century Public Policy

By Daniel Becker, President and Founder, Personhood Alliance

"Cowardice asks the question—is it safe? Expediency asks the question—is it politic? Vanity asks the question— is it popular? But conscience asks the question—is it right? And there comes a time when one must take a position that is neither safe, nor politic, nor popular; but one must take it because it is right."[103]

Dr. Martin Luther King, Jr.

Human Slavery

In December of 2016, I met in Thailand with the founders of one of the most effective anti-slavery organizations in the world, ZOE International.[104] I was troubled to learn that the scope of child sex trafficking (slavery) is as endemic in Western countries as it is in

---

[103] King, Jr., M. L. (1968, February 6). A proper sense of priorities. [Public speech transcript]. Retrieved from http://aavw.org/special_features/ speeches_speech_king04.html

[104] Zoe (pronounced zoh-ee) is the Greek word for life.

developing countries. I was most troubled to discover that my own home of Atlanta, Georgia, is one of the top destinations for these trafficked children. In addition to rescuing these children from lives of unimaginable sexual servitude, ZOE International also engages in aiding the Thai government's public policy efforts of prevention, protection, and prosecution. They are just one of many Christian ministries demonstrating Jesus' love and compassion in action—a direct assault on the injustice of human slavery.

Using the words "human slavery" in a contemporary discussion of public policy seems anachronistic, in that it begs the question, "I thought slavery was done away with in the 1800s by reformers like William Wilberforce and Frederick Douglas?" True, the efforts of these courageous men, aided by the sacrifice of many others, led to laws assuring freedom and emancipation for all persons. How then do we explain that, according to the latest data from Global Slavery Index, there are an estimated 45.8 million slaves held against their will in the world today? [105] An estimated 20% of these slaves are children. In certain parts of West Africa, the percentage approaches 100%.[106]

In 2007, Mauritania became the last country in the world to ban slavery.[107] It has been over a decade since it was outlawed in every

---

[105] The Minderoo Foundation Pty Ltd. (2017). Global slavery index. Retrieved from http://www.globalslaveryindex.org/

[106] United Nations Office on Drugs and Crime. (2016). Global report on trafficking in persons. Retrieved from http://www.unodc.org/unodc/en/ human-trafficking/global-report-on-trafficking-in-persons.html

[107] U.S. Department of State, Bureau of Democracy, Human Rights, and Labor. (2011). Mauritania. Retrieved from https://www.state.gov/j/drl/rls/ hrrpt/2010/af/154358.htm

country of the world and still it proliferates.[108] It is alleged that the countries with the highest absolute numbers of current slaves are India, China, Pakistan, Bangladesh, and Uzbekistan.[109] Slavery is one of the oldest forms of personhood denial in the world and is a direct assault on human dignity.

Child sacrifice or infanticide is another atrocity in our modern world. In 2012, two Australian doctors published an article entitled, "After-Birth Abortion: Why Should the Baby Live?" in the UK's respected *Journal of Medical Ethics.*[110] In the article, they declared:

> *"What we call 'after-birth abortion' (killing a newborn) should be permissible in all the cases where abortion is, including cases where the newborn is not disabled."* [111]

No failure of logic here. They rightly reason that if the law deems healthy preborn children as the object of abortion, then why not healthy infants and toddlers? How do we assert that their proposal extends to toddlers? Their entire premise is based on the legal construct of personhood or, more specifically, the denial of it. Their mentor and fellow alumnus of Melbourne University, Peter Singer, has defined this version of personhood and dictated who is eligible for its rights and protections.[112]

---

[108] U.S. Department of State, Bureau of Democracy, Human Rights, and Labor. (2010). 2010 country reports on human rights practices. Retrieved from https://www.state.gov/j/drl/rls/hrrpt/2010/index.htm

[109] Ibid., The Minderoo Foundation Pty Ltd.

[110] Giubilini, A., & Minerva, F. (2012). After-birth abortion: Why should the baby live? *Journal of Medical Ethics, 39*: 261-63.

[111] Ibid.

[112] Kuhse, H., & Singer, P. (1985). Should the baby live? The problem of handicapped infants. Oxford: Oxford University Press, 143.

While attending a 2013 Yale University conference, "Personhood—Beyond the Human," I had the opportunity to sit down with Singer.[113] I confirmed that his definition of personhood does not include early stage toddlers. He also confirmed that his definition of personhood precludes those people in a persistent vegetative state, an advanced stage of Alzheimer's disease or dementia, some with mental or developmental disabilities, and all pre- and post-birth children suffering a congenital anomaly. As Singer states in his book *Practical Ethics*:

> *"If the parents want the newborn, it is wrong to kill the baby because the act deprives them of happiness. On the other hand, killing a defective newborn is not morally equivalent to killing a person."* [114]

This position is based on 19th century philosopher Jeremy Bentham's Utilitarianism, or "the greatest good for the greatest number."

21ST CENTURY INFANTICIDE

Infanticide predicated on this Utilitarian view of life leads us down a slippery slope in public policy that we have not seen advocated so blatantly since Germany adopted the policy to destroy "useless eaters" in 1920—13 years *before* the Nazis took power.[115] We know how that slippery slope progressed until it led to the horrors of the Holocaust. We must not let the Peter Singers of the world convince our governments to

---

[113] Yale University. (2013). Personhood—Beyond the Human, keynote speaker Peter Singer. Retrieved from http://nonhumanrights.net/speakers/

[114] Singer,P. (1993). *Practical ethics*. [2nd ed]. Cambridge: Cambridge University Press, 191.

[115] Binding, K., & Hoche, A. (1920). Permitting the destruction of life unworthy of living. Retrieved from http://lifeunworthyoflife.com/

accept this definition of personhood. Yet, modern-day experimentation reminiscent of Nazi atrocities abounds.

In 2008, Cornell University researchers inserted a fluorescent gene from an Australian jellyfish into a healthy preborn human at the embryonic level of development to see if successive generations of cellular division would pass on this genetic characteristic. It was a success, wherefore this young child became the world's first human-animal hybrid that, horrifically, glowed in the dark. The child was then executed under Bush-era regulations of human embryonic research.[116] In the context of the doctrine of *Imago Dei,* this experiment is blasphemous.

Lethal human research is a violation of the Nuremburg Code,[117] which was adopted by most countries in 1947. The United States was not a signatory to this legal attempt to provide ethical parameters for human experimentation until much later, when it became the basis for the Code of Federal [medical] Regulations.[118] In response to objections about the Cornell experiment, a spokesman for the National Institutes of Health (part of the US Department of Health and Human Services, which governs federally funded human subject research), said the work "would *not* be classified as gene therapy in need of federal review, because a test-tube embryo is not considered *a person* under the regulations."[119] This

---

[116] Panizzo, R., Dr. (2011). Researchers create genetically engineered human embryo. Retrieved from http://www.bionews.org.uk/page_13391.asp

[117] U.S. Government Printing Office. (1949). Trials of war criminals before the Nuremberg Military Tribunals under Control Council Law, 2(10), pp. 181-182.

[118] Code of Federal Regulations, Title 45, Part 46.

[119] Pollack, A. (2008). Engineering by scientists on embryo stirs criticism. Retrieved from http://www.nytimes.com/2008/05/13/science/13 embryo.html [Emphasis added].

experiment was a clear violation of the principles of informed consent, non-malfeasance, and beneficence that the Nuremburg Code established. A host of biotechnologies, including lethal human embryonic research, germline intervention, transhumanist enhancements, cloning, cyborgs, and human-animal hybrids challenge human dignity in chilling new attacks on human life. Artificial intelligence (AI) poses a unique threat as well.

In 2013, Bina48 became the first AI to address a college symposium.[120] Bina48 was a new form of social robot; the byproduct of SiriusXM radio's founder Martin Rothblatt[121] and his wife Bina. Bina digitally recorded her personal data onto a computer, which then simulated her real-life responses. Bina48 was a fully interactive robot with lifelike facial expressions and head movements. "She" demonstrated her abilities by engaging in a robust round of Q&A with the audience at the symposium. As an attendee, I was astounded and a little troubled[122] at how easy it was to fall into natural conversation with "her." I was sitting on the front row at the presentation and had the opportunity to ask what she thought about God? "Aaahh... the God question!" she replied, and then went into a soliloquy of the basic tenets of her beliefs, which had strong overtones of **Buddhism**. Bina48 "lives" for the day that personhood is granted to an AI.

---

[120] Ibid., Yale University

[121] Rothblatt changed his name from Martin to Martine when he had gender reassignment surgery.

[122] This particular response, called "the uncanny valley," is defined by Google Dictionary as "the phenomenon whereby a computer-generated figure or humanoid robot bearing a near-identical resemblance to a human being arouses a sense of unease or revulsion in the person viewing it."

The fight for personhood for AI is one of the main tenets of the transhumanist agenda. It was no coincidence that the U.S. leaders of the transhumanist philosophy were all present at the same personhood symposium. They see their secular and atheist constructs for legal personhood as the emerging battleground for future rights and privileges for AIs. However, no matter how close to "sentient" AIs are, they are not persons because of their self-awareness, human-like abilities, or simulation of human responses. If this were true, then some humans could be excluded—those in a temporary comatose state, those in a persistent vegetative state, extreme cases of dementia or Alzheimer's disease, and yes, perfectly normal infants and toddlers. The bar for personhood is being lowered to include human-simulated machines, but biblically based human exceptionalism rules out this allegation. We reject the transhumanist claim that we can share personhood with machines, as we assert that humans are the sole representative of the triune God.

The Crisis of Faith in Today's Pro-life Movement

It is painfully evident that the current American pro-life movement is absent from most of these fights. There is a reason for the non-engagement. The primary concern of the movement has been, and still is, *saving babies*, with some focus on end-of-life issues. I say this not to assign blame to the movement, but to share an observation. This narrowness on the part of mainstream pro-life organizations finds its root in a strategic decision made years ago—a decision to broaden the movement's base by not identifying itself as Christian. I encountered this reasoning early in my pro-life activism, in the 1980s. This shift occurred despite the fact that a vast majority of the constituents of mainstream organizations were indeed motivated by their faith in God and His view of the sacredness of life. These constituents have invested money, time, effort, education, and influence because they believe the right to life was established by God Himself. Today, the grassroots pro-life base also believes life is sacred because we are made in God's own image, as Genesis 1:26-27 declares.

My personal fight for the right to life of the preborn was what motivated my public policy involvement beginning in 1973. Through my exposure to Dr. Francis Schaeffer[123] at the L'Abri Fellowship in Switzerland, I was challenged to develop a biblical approach to social justice. He encouraged me to engage in pro-life action to achieve social justice by seeking to inform government of God's eternal and immutable teachings on the sanctity of life. It was the doctrine of the sanctity of human life (that is, the consecrated specialness) that required me not only to end abortion, but also to oppose any area where government policy allowed the destruction of innocent human life or the defacing of human dignity. As previously noted, this doctrine is taught in Christian theology as the *Imago Dei*. It is a clear declaration that all mankind is created in the "image and likeness of God."[124]

My involvement as a social justice advocate originates in my service to God. My service to God begins with researching and seeking to understand His ways as revealed throughout His Word, the Holy Bible, and the historic example of His Body, the Church. My activism, then, is faith-based, but I am motivated beyond the limited scope of abortion, euthanasia, and assisted suicide. I must oppose all threats to the sanctity

---

[123] Dr. Francis Schaeffer was the first evangelical to rise to a national leadership role in the pro-life arena.

[124] Genesis 1:25-27

of life and human dignity if I am to be truly relevant as a modern pro-life advocate. This biblical focus includes orphan care and adoption, special needs advocacy, service to immigrants and refugees, work against human trafficking, and a host of other issues regarding human dignity.

The Problem

A narrow agenda is not the only challenge at the national level. Major pro-life organizations continue to endorse elected officials as "100% pro-life" who refuse to stand up for the protection of all preborn humans. They permit and even promote abortion legislation with exceptions for those conceived in rape and children diagnosed with fetal anomalies.[125] Many of their constituents assume this is not the case. Tragically, these endorsements occur under a guise of political prudence and principled political tolerance. G.K. Chesterton said, ""Tolerance is the virtue of the man without convictions." Moreover, there is the added benefit that pro-life leaders gain or maintain friendly access to political leaders. The maxim, "access to power is power" has become the bane of principled incrementalists and seeks to justify a lack of convictions in the public square.

I recently met with Tom Minnery, former Senior Vice President of Government and Public Policy for Focus on the Family.[126] He shared that

[125] The prognosis of fetal anomalies is plagued with a high percentage of false positives, resulting in perfectly normal children being killed by abortion. Moreover, these tests are being used to eugenically remove 90% of all children with a Down Syndrome prognosis.

[126] The meeting took place at the Georgia Right to Life office in March, 2017.

he and Clarke Forsythe, President of Americans United for Life,[127] have joined forces to train pro-life legislators to be more effective, through a new Christian program called Statesmen Academy.[128] While I applauded this goal and the language used to describe the effort, I was disturbed to learn that the program embraces exceptions for rape, incest, and fetal anomaly in pro-life law and provides support for legislators who endorse this practice. This position does not uphold the sanctity of life for all human beings. Instead, it is a position that adjusts to current political realities. Nevertheless, is it true that some children must die so that the majority can be saved?

Our Answer: A Biblical Standard

Deuteronomy 24:16 declares that one should not put a child to death for the crimes of its father. This very clear command of God reveals to us His character and should inform our social justice advocacy. To back a lawmaker who advocates for the legal destruction of an innocent child based on nothing more than the crimes of her father, would, as a matter of faith, require us to vigorously oppose that politician. In like manner, pro-life organizations who advocate for exceptions, should also be called out for forsaking their role as standard bearers, while also disallowing a conscience vote for those legislators who refuse to embrace exceptions. Case in point: On January 22, 2015, the National Right to Life Committee

---

[127] Forsythe is the author of *Politics for the Greatest Good: The Case for Prudence in the Public Square*, which promotes compromise by drawing primarily on lessons in political prudence from Aristotle and natural law advocates.

[128] Family Policy Alliance. (2017). Statesmen Academy. Retrieved from http://familypolicyalliance.com/statesmen-academy/

(NRLC) issued a stern letter to all U.S. House members, warning them that anything other than a *yea* vote on the exception-laden No Taxpayer Funding of Abortion Act (H.R. 7):

> *"...**will essentially define his or her position, for or against federal funding of abortion, for the foreseeable future. NRLC will include the vote on final passage of H.R. 7 in our scorecard of key right-to-life votes of the 114th Congress** [Emphasis in the original]."*[129]

In other words, those who refused to vote for these exceptions would be blotted from the roles of the "100% pro-life" legislators, even if their consciences prohibited them.[130] From a faith-based perspective, we must ask a question: Do the supposed ends (compromising principles for incremental progress) justify the means (failing to honor the sanctity of life for all human beings)?

Michigan and Georgia are two states (one Rust Belt and one Bible Belt) that have defied this political prudence doctrine and have no rape and incest exceptions in any of their multiple pro-life laws. How did this happen? For many years, these states have rejected the prevailing strategy of political prudence and established a biblical standard to define "pro-life." Personhood-based political action does not aspire to achieve the status of *kingmakers*, but rather focuses on being *standard-bearers*. There are now 17 states with faith-based pro-life organizations

---

[129] National Right to Life Committee. (2015). NRLC scorecard letter on H.R. 7 – No Taxpayer Funding of Abortion Act. Retrieved from http://www.nrlc.org/federal/ahc/nrlc-scorecard-letter-on-h-r-7-no-taxpayer-funding-of-abortion-act/

[130] For example, former pastor Jodie Hice, a congressman from Georgia's 10th congressional district, voted "present" on the 20-Week Pain Capable Bill rather than support a bill that held these deadly compromises. NRLC reduced his pro-life score.

working toward this end.[131] The most recent additions are the critical presidential primary states of Iowa and Ohio. But, as stated earlier in this book, abortion is not the only personhood issue.

Marriage is a Pro-life Issue

Molly Smith, the president of Cleveland Right to Life, was moved by God to adopt the marriage issue as part of the *Imago Dei* mandate. Molly rightly believed that marriage and the sanctity of life are bound up in each other biblically. Damage to marriage violates God's will and causes damage to the preborn.[132]

In 2004, Ohio faced a referendum on declaring that "only a marriage between one man and one woman may be valid in or recognized by the state."[133] Molly's highly effective pro-life organization debated whether to engage the passage of this constitutional amendment, but at the time refrained, based on a limited pro-life paradigm. Fast forward nine years, and it came to the attention of NRLC that Cleveland Right to Life had criticized an NRLC-endorsed lawmaker. Cleveland Right to Life had publically challenged Ohio Senator Rob Portman's support for homosexual marriage. Under faith-based reasoning, it is clear that biblical marriage would exclude homosexual marriage. However, because the senator had voted for NRLC-sponsored pro-life legislation and was a sponsor of an NRLC-backed bill, NRLC removed the Cleveland group's

---

[131] See www.personhood.org for an updated list of these organizations.
[132] DiCaro, V. (2016). Why marriage? Retrieved from https://www.care-net.org/abundant-life-blog/why-marriage
[133] Encyclopedia of American Politics. (2016). Ohio Definition of Marriage: Amendment 1 (2004). Retrieved from http://tinyurl.com/ztpugo9

affiliation with NRLC. In a letter signed by the organization's president, Carol Tobias, the NRLC declared:

> *"By these actions, Cleveland Right to Life has violated National Right to Life policy, causing the chapter to disaffiliate itself from NRLC. We respectfully insist that you remove from your website the claim that you are affiliated with NRLC, and from this point forward, cease and desist from any representation that 'Cleveland Right to Life' is affiliated with the National Right to Life Committee."*[134]

NRLC justified their actions saying Cleveland Right to Life had:

> *"...issued public criticisms of and implicit political threats against a U.S. Senator who has supported the right-to-life position on every vote that has come before the Senate, and who is a sponsor of major NRLC-backed bills because the chapter disagrees with his position on a non-right-to-life issue."*[135]

How can this be a "non-right-to-life issue" if the same biblical passage which gives us the sanctity of life also informs us that *Imago Dei* includes advocacy for marriage between a man and a woman? It is impossible to reconcile, unless of course, you are *not* faith-based in your advocacy. Please do not misunderstand. I am not criticizing NRLC for its limited scope of advocacy. The organization is free to limit its mission statement to any degree it chooses. In the NRLC's communication to Cleveland Right to Life, NRLC stated that their mission should be specific in its scope, "to protect the right to life of innocent human beings, including those jeopardized by legal abortion, by euthanasia, and by

---

[134] LifeSiteNews. (2013). NRLC disowns Cleveland chapter for defending marriage. https://www.lifesitenews.com/news/national-right-to-life-committee-disowns-cleveland-chapter-for-defending-ma

[135] Ibid.

assisted suicide." [136] Cleveland Right to Life had engaged the *Imago Dei* doctrine in a broader scope than NRLC permitted and therefore, was summarily dismissed from the organization's membership roll.[137]

There is a happy ending to the story. Most of the 35 pro-life groups in Ohio who were troubled by the actions of NRLC realized that they needed a statewide alliance that would promote broader biblical engagement. Moreover, they wanted freedom to promote only no-exceptions legislation and to offer only no-exceptions endorsements to political candidates. In 2013, a loose alliance of like-minded groups began meeting, and on March 10, 2017, Right to Life Action Coalition of Ohio was born. This independent, statewide group does not plan to affiliate with NRLC but will work closely with Personhood Alliance on national initiatives.[138] Included in this group is former NRLC President Jack Wilke's home group, Cincinnati Right to Life.[139]

One of the additional catalysts for the Ohio alliance was the defeat of the 2013 Heartbeat Bill. Groups in the alliance viewed the bill as fatally flawed, due to the addition of the exceptions clause that moderate Republicans and leading national pro-life groups demanded.[140] The bill went down in defeat because pro-lifers were not unified in the definition used to label the bill "pro-life." The organizations and moderate

---

[136] Ibid.
[137] Ibid.
[138] The Catholic Telegraph. (2017). New pro-life coalition formed for Ohio. Retrieved from http://www.thecatholictelegraph.com/new-pro-life-coalition-formed-for-ohio/40116
[139] Ibid.
[140] A few years later, in 2015, the federal Pain-Capable Unborn Child Protection Act (H.R. 36) became one of the first instances in which all leading pro-life groups agreed to add exceptions into the *original* pre-approved filing.

politicians in Ohio who had supported the exceptions got the message loud and clear: *From this point forward, no more compromised bills.*

In 2015, the Ohio Heartbeat Bill was resurrected without any rape, incest, or fetal anomaly exceptions. Unfortunately, the NRLC successfully lobbied for "pro-life" Governor John Kasich to veto the bill. Though the bill was not Personhood compliant, due to its lack of equal protection for preborn children who did not yet have a heartbeat, it still demonstrated what a unified state group can accomplish when it seeks to advance a no-compromise agenda in the public square. Molly Smith's leadership and vision in Ohio is now extended nationally. In 2014, she accepted the role of President for National Personhood Alliance, the educational arm of Personhood Alliance, an organization of faith-based pro-life groups that promote a seamless biblical approach to the sanctity of life issues facing us in the 21st century.[141]

The Need for a New Paradigm

Human life is sacred because humans are made in God's image. Human beings are persons because He is one God in three persons. Only the concept of Personhood is large enough to encompass all life that we must protect—every innocent human being from its earliest biological beginning until natural death. At every stage of its development, a human is an image-bearer, without regard to degree of ability or disability, and in every location from laboratory to deathbed. Our legal fight is to apply the protections for persons enshrined in the U.S.

---

[141] See Appendix 2 to learn how your group can join Personhood Alliance.

Constitution and Declaration of Independence to *every* human being. This honors God's great gift of life and His right alone to end it.

It is my belief that my friends at NRLC are sincerely wrong in opposing efforts to achieve a higher standard than the one they chose to employ against Cleveland Right to Life. I do call them my friends. I served with them side-by-side for almost a decade. As an NRLC board member, I came to know them as individuals who were passionate for the cause of life and sacrificial in their dedication. I do not appreciate their detractors referring to them as part of a "pro-life industry" that seeks to propagate abortion in order to "stay in business." This is a false and baseless charge and one that I would like to see laid to rest. I also understand that their mission is more restrictive than I believe service to the biblical mandate requires. Inevitably, we agree to disagree.

A New Measure of Success

I will someday stand before the **Lord** and give an account of my actions. I will not appear before Him with a tally of how many babies I have saved. Instead, I will have to answer to Him for the difference in *how many were spared destruction* by my actions compared to *how many would have been saved* had I trusted Him more—had I been more faithful to His revealed commands and ways. It is my belief that we could have ended legal abortion decades ago. How many babies' lives have been lost in the interim?

The old pro-life scope and mission was suitable for the 20th century but is wholly inadequate for the 21st. We must address human trafficking (slavery), biomedical experimentation, the granting of personhood to non-human entities, and a host of other emerging issues by defending God's design for human dignity and exceptionalism. To do this, we must focus on human personhood as God defines it. In light of this fact, many are calling for a renewed pro-life movement that will more fully embrace the challenging times we live in. A movement that is based upon the tenets of our faith will be an effectual voice for the innocent and vulnerable. I do not wish to reduce the Gospel of Life, but to unleash its power! It gives testimony to the glory of our mighty Savior, Jesus Christ, and the kingdom of God being manifest on Earth as it is in heaven.

[Daniel Becker is the Founder and President of Personhood Alliance. He is also the former President and PAC Director of Georgia Right to Life and a former board member of National Right to Life. He studied at L'Abri Fellowship under the mentorship of Dr. Francis Schaeffer in 1973. A widower, Daniel enjoys investing in the lives of his 26 "grand-blessings."]

CHAPTER 6

Human Trafficking: Dehumanization and Personhood

By Darlene Pawlik, New Hampshire Right to Life PAC

The commodification of human beings, the trafficking of persons, and the buying and selling of their body parts should not be taken lightly as some infrequent occurrence. It is one of the fastest growing commercial enterprises on the Earth today, with an estimated annual market of $32 billion dollars.[142]

Before we look at exactly what trafficking in persons actually is, how it relates to personhood, and how you can spot it, I would like to share my experience.

---

[142] United Nations Office on Drugs and Crime. (2005). Fact sheet on human trafficking. Retrieved from http://www.unodc.org/documents/ human-trafficking/UNVTF_fs_HT_EN.pdf

123 Main St., Anytown, USA

I was conceived during rape. My mother's assailant convinced her that no one else would ever want her. When she realized she was pregnant with me, she married her rapist. After two years of brutality, she left him. As a toddler, I had witnessed this brutality, but I was also his victim. I lived a double life, enduring unspeakable violations in the darkness and burying them so deep that, if you asked me, I would not tell you what happened.

As I grew, I refused to go to visits where our abuser would be, but staying alone after my mother's second divorce was no better. We were very poor and I sought drugs regularly, not just while being hurt. After an uncle also molested me, I started running away, skipping school, and hanging in the neighborhood. Then a man came around befriending kids in the area. It was not long before I was in his car. Soon, I was in his bed. I was 13. He said I could have anything I wanted. He said that if I ever needed anything to call him and he would fix me up with someone who could get it for me. He sold me to men for sex. It was often brutal and sickening.

It was as though I was floating downstream in a life I did not own, in a world that I had no control over. I had no identification, no accountability, no one looking out for me. I was an implement for use, not a person.

I was 17 when I was sold to one buyer as a house pet. From city councilmen and police, to painters and bachelors, I was purchased in cars, vacant buildings, college housing, family homes, and rented rooms. I suffered atrocities in silence, just the way I had been taught.

I had attempted suicide numerous times, but when I got pregnant, he said he would kill me if I did not abort. My life did not matter to me, but I knew a baby was involved. I made the appointment. I cried myself to sleep that night, and I had a dream of the abortion procedure from the perspective of the womb. I saw a tiny face, a little hand, and part of a ribcage. I woke up in a panic. I literally threw my hands into the air and said, "God, if you are real, I need you to show up." I remembered a social worker from when I was a runaway, and I reached out to her. She contacted a maternity home and helped me plan my escape. I had to have dinner with him after the appointment. He was well-connected in the community, with the police, and to illegal activity as well. So I was sure that he would find me if I ran. He let me go after I convinced him that I had gone through with the abortion and would never come back.

Mine is just one story among millions. Many others have been denied the basic right of personhood.

Modern Day Slavery Denies People Their Personhood

Modern day slavery, or human trafficking, is a direct result of denying the basic human rights afforded by natural law in order to use people as commodities for labor, for sex, or to harvest their body parts. Too many Americans think slavery is a thing of the past; that it ended with the Emancipation Proclamation in 1863. Almost a century prior, our founders gave us the Declaration of Independence. In it, we see certain universal truths. The Declaration begins by establishing the great cause these men were undertaking, which would change the course of history forever.

> *"When in the Course of human events it becomes necessary for one people to dissolve the political bands which have connected*

> *them with another and to assume among the powers of the earth, the separate and equal station to which the Laws of Nature and of Nature's God entitle them, a decent respect to the opinions of mankind requires that they should declare the causes which impel them to the separation.*
>
> *We hold these truths to be self-evident, that all men are created equal, that they are endowed by their Creator with certain unalienable Rights, that among these are Life, Liberty and the pursuit of Happiness."*[143]

Pregnancy and the Succession of Rights

These rights set forth in the Declaration are consecutive, not concurrent. One cannot have liberty without life, and there can be no pursuit of happiness when a person is in bondage. Life is first. Therefore, a pregnant woman's right to absolute liberty is superseded by her baby's right to life.[144] In the past, the medical profession called the due date "the estimated date of confinement." Women were expected to confine their activities to those that would ensure the proper welfare of their preborn children.

This confinement is limited and temporary. It is limited to anything that would cause direct harm to her child. Otherwise, she is free to engage in any lawful activity. Some abortion advocates argue that her confinement constitutes slavery. This is simply not true. It may inhibit her or limit her physically. Some women are impacted to a greater degree than others, but most maintain autonomy throughout pregnancy.

---

[143] The U.S. Declaration of Independence. (1776). An Act of the Second Continental Congress (July 4, 1776).

[144] This is also true of *in vitro* fertilization. A woman's privilege to parent must never supersede her child's right to life.

Abortion advocates say this is unfair, and it may seem to be, especially regarding sexual assault. But the same natural law holds true, even in the case of rape. She is a victim, but her child is no less a victim. Her confinement is in no way due to her decisions, but neither is the innocent child to be held accountable. She is still limited to conducting herself in a way that protects and nurtures both her baby and herself. The confinement is still temporary, though obviously much more complex. When two lives are so entangled, as they are in cases of rape, both victims need to be cared for. Working through the trauma of rape will need to happen. Working through the trauma of abortion does not need to happen. Pregnancy does not constitute slavery.

Slavery and Human Trafficking

Real slavery in the form of human trafficking is a massive problem in our modern world. The liberty of millions of people is being infringed—right now. Men, women, and children are enslaved. Their right to life may be intact, but their right to liberty and subsequently, their right to the pursuit of happiness, are violated. This is contrary to the Declaration of Independence and ultimately, contrary to natural law.

Human trafficking happens by force, fraud, or coercion all over the world. The particular category of trafficking in persons varies. Agricultural areas may experience more labor trafficking and child labor. Areas with a lot of sports and entertainment could see more sex trafficking. Wealthy areas might see more domestic servitude, restaurant labor, or the trafficking of body parts. Very poor communities are especially vulnerable. That is not to say that any form is exclusive or segregated. Child and juvenile sex trafficking happens everywhere as well.

Labor trafficking, or forced labor, is what we usually think of when we hear the word "slavery." This means forcing people to work without payment and without the freedom to leave or make choices about their own lives.[145]

"We do not pay them.
They are part of the land."[146]

Amadou, Maurianian slaveholder[147]

Forced labor may be agricultural. In this case, property owners bring in people and promise them a new start where they can earn money and build a better life, but they are defrauded. The trafficking victims—men, women, and children—are brought to unfamiliar territory without identification or knowledge of the native language. They may receive no compensation or insufficient pay, even when the commissary on site and housing fees are exorbitant. They may be encouraged to become more indebted by borrowing against future pay as well. The living conditions are poor. They are unable to escape.

There are reports of children ages 5 to 17 who labor long hours in granite quarries in Burkina Faso; children who cultivate coffee and raise cattle in Costa Rica, sugarcane in Cambodia, and tin mining in Indonesia. There are reports that children ages 10 to 17 harvest sand in Kenya and 7 to 17 year olds who produce bricks in Iran. Children as young as 7 mine gold in Uganda, and as young as 8 mine gold in Nigeria. Ten-year-old

---

[145] U.S. Department of Justice. (1999). Worker exploitation and trafficking in persons task force handbook. Washington, D.C.
[146] U.S. Department of State. (2016). Trafficking in persons report 2016. Retrieved from https://www.state.gov/documents/organization/258876.pdf.
[147] Pseudonyms are used for all survivor quotes.

children mine gold in Sudan. This is very dangerous work. Evidence reveals that children ages 5 to 17 grow cashews, manufacture footwear, produce furniture, engage in fishing and fish processing, process leather, cultivate rice, tea, pepper, and tobacco, and process timber and textiles. Their childhoods are stolen.[148]

Refugees in war-torn countries also become easy prey for labor traffickers. Warlords often force refugee boys and young men into labor, and even combat. About 40% of labor trafficking victims are men.[149] The impact on these men spans generations who are unable to assume their equal station.

> *"We slept on the ground. We had to loot villages to eat. We were drugged to remain obedient. We were forced to kill. When I was in the armed group, I committed violence and crimes. I lost my childhood, my friends, and my mother."*
>
> *Martin, former child soldier in the Democratic Republic of the Congo*

Other trafficking markets include begging, construction, domestic work, fishing, mining, or restaurant labor. Thankfully, there is attention now on places like Lake Volta, where young boys were sold to work on fishing boats for long hours with no pay under horrendously abusive conditions. This denial of their inherent right to liberty, as they were imprisoned in extremely dangerous conditions, cost many young boys

---

[148] Bureau of International Labor Affairs, US Dept. of Labor. (2016). List of goods produced by child labor or forced labor, TVPRA 2005.

[149] Anti-trafficking Independence Project. (2014). Male labor trafficking: The invisible 40%. Retrieved from https://antitraffickip.wordpress.com/2014/02/13/male-labor-trafficking-the-invisible-40/

their lives. Similarly, diamond and precious metal mines are extremely harsh environments, wrought with constant violence.

TRAFFICKING OF BODY PARTS

The human body has been used for education and research since the 4th century BC. For many decades now, people have made the ethical decision to bequeath their bodies to science in order to provide better medicine to future generations. On the other hand, the highly unethical practice of murder for the procurement of body parts exists as well. For example, David Daleiden's Center for Medical Progress exposed Planned Parenthood's role in trafficking the body parts of aborted children in 2015.[150]

Thankfully, we do have laws against trafficking body parts, but appropriate consent for organ donation continues to be a problem. India is taking a preventative approach by implementing *Poochna mat bhoolo* (Do not forget to ask), a campaign to encourage medical professionals to ask patients if they would like to be organ donors.[151] If organs are available ethically, then trafficking by force, fraud, or coercion will not be as prevalent.[152]

---

[150] The Center for Medical Progress. (2015). Human capital. Retrieved from http://www.centerformedicalprogress.org/human-capital/

[151] Srivastava, R. (2017). India launches organ donation awareness drive to check black market trade. Retrieved from http://news.trust.org/item/20170110102123-gz4ml/

[152] Perry, P. (2016). What you need to know about human organ trafficking. Retrieved from http://bigthink.com/philip-perry/what-you-need-to-know-about-human-organ-trafficking

The U.S. Definition Of Trafficking In Persons

Human trafficking is not an event, but a process and the results of the process. The United States defines trafficking in persons as:

> ***The action of*** *recruitment, transportation, transfer, harboring, or receipt of persons* ***by means of*** *the threat or use of force, coercion, abduction, fraud, deception, abuse of power or vulnerability, or giving payments or benefits to a person in control of the victim* ***for the purposes of*** *exploitation, which includes exploiting the prostitution of others, sexual exploitation, forced labor, slavery or similar practices, and the removal of organs.*
>
> ***Consent of the victim is irrelevant*** *where illicit means are established, but criminal law defenses are preserved. The consent of a victim of trafficking in persons to the intended exploitation is irrelevant, if the victim is a child. A "Child" shall mean any person under eighteen years of age.*[153]

Three Elements of Trafficking

Trafficking can be broken down into three elements: criminal acts, the means used to commit those acts, and the goals or forms of exploitation. Here is an example of how these three elements work together: Babies and toddlers are used as props for adult beggars. As soon as the children can talk, they are forced to beg long hours under the watchful eye of their handlers. They do not attend school or learn any other way of life.

In another example, children may be purchased from severely impoverished families under the guise of adoption agencies that promise to place the children in loving homes. Some traffickers do adopt the

---

[153] U.S. Department of State. (2000). Victims of trafficking and violence protection act of 2000. Retrieved from https://www.state.gov/j/tip/laws/ 61124.htm

children out, but usually charge exorbitant fees. Sadly, many of these children are sold for sexual exploitation. Child sex tourism is a horrific problem in some areas of the world where a sense of anonymity keeps mainly white, affluent American men coming back for more of this demonic practice.

Trafficking's Assault On Identity

Human trafficking denies the human right of personhood. We have witnessed this in cases throughout modern history, such as Dred Scott and his wife,[154] the Jews of the Holocaust,[155] and more recently, the nearly 60 million unborn victims of *Roe v Wade* and *Doe v Bolton*.[156] But let us consider this on a more intimate, personal level.

Boys and girls, without any understanding of what their true identity is, are suffering right now as you read these words. The core violation of child sexual abuse will never leave them, if they live to adulthood. The essence of the human spirit is to love and be loved. Being used and abused distorts their young minds. Pain and trauma delays their ability to develop decision-making capabilities and social skills. Many children are physically injured. They may die of their injuries or live unable to control elimination or other normal bodily functions. Of the estimated 20-30

---

[154] Missouri Digital Heritage. (2017). Dred Scott case, 1946-1957. Retrieved from https://www.sos.mo.gov/archives/resources/africanamerican/scott/scott.asp

[155] University of South Florida, College of Education. (2005). Holocaust documents. Retrieved from https://fcit.usf.edu/holocaust/resource/document/document.htm

[156] *Roe v. Wade*. (1973). 410 US 113, No. 70-18.; *Doe v. Bolton*. (1973): 410 US 179, No. 70-40.

million people enslaved worldwide, about half are children, many of whom are exploited commercially for sex.[157]

My story at the beginning of this chapter alludes to numerous risk factors for juvenile sex trafficking in the United States—things like domestic violence, child sexual abuse, a broken home, poverty, and a transient lifestyle. Shared Hope International has an annual scorecard and recommendations for improving such risk factors for individual states.[158] However, there are no barriers, no absolute safety nets, and no guarantees that any child will not fall prey to traffickers. Many of the perpetrators who participate in child trafficking were likely influenced by their involvement in pornography, which is a key driver of buyers.[159] The dehumanization and commodification of people engaged in pornography is highly destructive to the innate value we have as human beings.

The modern push for transgender and alternate body type recognition is, at its base, similarly an assault on the very identity our Creator gave us. There are people who have altered their bodies, some disabling themselves by amputation or self-inflicted trauma, in order to identify as anything other than their perfect human selves. This identity marring is often a set up for trafficking or a result of trafficking and other severe abuse.

---

[157] DoSomething.org (2017). 11 facts about human trafficking. Retrieved from http://tinyurl.com/zanm372

[158] Shared Hope International. (2017). Report cards. Retrieved from http://sharedhope.org/what-we-do/bring-justice/reportcards/

[159] Nolot, B. (2012). Who buys sex? Linking porn and human trafficking. Retrieved from http://www.covenanteyes.com/2012/10/18/why-human-trafficking/

Our bodies are ours, and we have free will to do with them as we please. However, when we recognize that our identity is in Christ, we see that our bodies are a living sacrifice.[160] We are admonished to take care of our bodies and not inflict self-harm or engage in identity-destroying sexual behaviors. Conversely, when our bodies have been misused, our identity in Him is harder to accept. Of course, there is awesome power in the Word of God to restore, heal, and redeem.

Conveying the message of personhood is therefore essential. The natural right of people to be free to choose life, liberty, and the pursuit of happiness includes the right to salvation. God created people because He is Love. It is for souls to receive the Gospel that we work.[161]

What Can We Do?

What can we do about the epic crisis of human trafficking? We can think globally, but act locally. You and I can look for information about the country of origin of the products we purchase and make sure to buy slave-free. There is a supply chain. We can interrupt that chain. We can make a difference in small, simple ways or we can jump in with both feet. Take a look at the issues. Evaluate your unique gifts, talents, and abilities. Figure out how you can help change the world within your sphere of influence. Respect the gifts our Creator gave you, and use them wherever you can. Let us look at some examples.

---

[160] Romans 12:1-2
[161] Genesis 1:26, John 3:16, 1 John 4:8, 1 Corinthians 3:9, 2 Corinthians 5:20

Philanthropy and Fundraising

Perhaps you are a philanthropist, a fundraiser, or are involved in donor relations for a non-governmental organization. You can provide or procure financial support for actions that restore personhood to human trafficking victims. For example, you can support education and other preventative measures in your community or help survivors of trafficking by donating to aftercare programs, scholarships, and restorative or trauma-informed housing. You can help elect legislators that will advocate for personhood rights for every human being. Rescue organizations are everywhere. As you would with any investment, look into these organizations carefully and make certain that the money you or your donors provide is achieving your giving goals. You can do this by examining the efficacy of education and prevention programs, for example, or by monitoring rescue-housing outcomes. You can also make a difference by enabling and equipping those on the front lines who are rescuing and re-establishing personhood for survivors of human trafficking.

Be aware, however, that anti-trafficking organizations often advocate for abortion or even the decriminalization of prostitution. Biblical personhood acknowledges the innate dignity of all people from conception to natural death and recognizes that both abortion and prostitution are inherently destructive to the dignity of a person.

Communication and Leadership

If you are a dynamic communicator, a political activist, or a group leader in your church, there are many ways you can help promote personhood. Testify before the legislature on bills that recognize the preborn as persons and acknowledge slaves and prostituted youth as trafficking victims. Let legislators know that exceptions in pro-life laws make trafficking victims targets of the abortion industry. Communicate recommendations from organizations that work toward restoring personhood, and help those organizations in your area bring awareness to the community by exposing the atrocities that go on every day. Write letters to the editor or engage others through social media and direct mail campaigns to support the logic of Natural Law.

Marketing

If marketing is your gift, you could work on an awareness campaign or join a rescue organization to help them with exposure. You see things differently than many other people. You understand the subtle inferences depicted in a meme and can point them out. You can convey emotional hooks to draw people into a post that will wake up their minds about the dehumanization of trafficking and abortion. You are sensitive to the way our brains process images. This is very important when we think about pornography and the link to sexual exploitation. It is clear that we need to present an expanded view of the people involved. You can show their humanity in ways many of us cannot.

Research and Education

Perhaps research is your forte. You could gather resources that fit the demographics of your area and provide them to law enforcement, churches, emergency responders, laundromats, pregnancy resource centers (PRCs), or schools. Law enforcement and other first responders are often in the same proximity to the problem. Potentially, medical personnel, teachers, and social workers have intimate communication with victims, too. We should present the topic of trafficking in the same way we discuss domestic violence among these stakeholders.

Pregnancy Resource Centers

Perhaps you work or volunteer for a PRC. PRCs have a unique opportunity to fight the injustice of human trafficking. This is because some traffickers want children to be born to the women they hold in labor trafficking or sex trafficking. One reason is leverage. Traffickers will be able to threaten their children to ensure the mother's compliance. Another reason is to build up the supply of future slaves. Traffickers may also want to appease their victims. By allowing women to have their children, they seem like the good guys, making it less likely the women will run away.

Trafficking victims lack autonomy. A PRC client may come in with a handler. Allowing a client to bring their companion seems caring, but it is often hard to tell if the companion is actually an advocate or a handler. Here, communication is essential. If there is a potential for language barriers in your area, recruit a volunteer or staff member who can do the intake or interpret.

Prayer

We are all needed. Maybe you are a stay-at-home parent. Perhaps you homeschool or foster small children and think you have no time to contribute at all. There is one thing that even the busiest of us can do, and that is to pray. Obviously, this is no small issue, so it is hard to know where to begin. There are prayers from numerous advocacy groups online that you can print and put on your fridge or in your journal. I have a photo that reminds me to pray. Ultimately, we can all pray for a world where personhood is extended to every human being, where dignity and honor is restored, and where the value of all human life is rightly acknowledged.

Keep Your Eyes Open

Anyone can be a trafficking victim. Adopt this mindset, and you might save a life. In your interactions with others, look for signs of abuse like bruises, cuts, and burns. Does the person have inappropriate clothing for the weather, very expensive clothing or jewelry, or does he or she appear to be destitute? We often see people who are stressed out or depressed, but is this person withdrawn or "checked out"? He or she may be exhausted, strung-out, or poorly nourished; maybe even distressed or terrified. Does the person have a handler—a man or woman nearby who will not leave them alone, who answers questions for them or holds their identification? Some victims have tattoos that signify ownership, like a name or a bar code. Some are even branded.

During your conversations, listen for clues to the truth of how they spend their time. Are they consistent in their answers? Are they hesitant? Watch for a change in tone while they speak, and note if they look away when answering. True responses show on our whole face. Blocking movements, like crossing arms or leaning toward a handler, are also signs of distress.

Language barriers hinder any conversation, but most trafficking victims would not identify themselves as victims if they could because of the complexity of the definition. Asking the right questions the right way can make all the difference. If you notice any signs of trafficking, you might ask if they get paid to work. Ask if there are locks on the doors that they do not have keys for. Ask if they carry identification with them when they are out. Question whether they are free to eat when they want to and if they can come and go at will. Ask if they feel safe.

If the person is a pregnant minor, ask how old her boyfriend is. Ask if he asks her to help pay the bills. Sometimes it is possible to ask directly if she is prostituting. If she is under 18, she is automatically a trafficking victim. If she is older, ask her if she can stop if she wants to, and ask her if stopping is what she wants. She may be looking for a way out. Of course, if a handler is present, you will have to limit what you ask for safety reasons.

Trafficking victims are under the control of their traffickers. They are slaves by force, fraud, or coercion. They may be on drugs or engaged in other harmful activities. They may have issues related to extreme trauma. Your compassionate responses may be the only kindness they know, but be careful. They live in a world of pain and fear.

Even if you are not responsible for evaluating the risk to the person, you can communicate what you see to someone who can decide how to proceed. In many settings, like a school, PRC, or hotel, someone can casually direct them to brochures about trafficking, leaving it to them to discover whether their situation fits. In other cases, it might be appropriate to direct them to a safehouse immediately. There is also a National Human Trafficking Hotline you can call at (888) 373-7888, or you can text HELP or INFO to 233733.[162] More segments of society are becoming educated and equipped to handle this issue, from first

---

[162] The Polaris Project. (2017). Human trafficking hotline. Retrieved from https://humantraffickinghotline.org

responders and hotel clerks to truck stop staff and transit operators. Each situation is different, as are the appropriate actions to take.

Human trafficking victims are people, and we must treat them as unique individuals with dignity at all times. Think about this: When our children, grandchildren, and great-grandchildren look back in history, we want them to find a heroic heritage—a legacy of valiant advocacy for the personhood of all people everywhere.

[Darlene Pawlik is a wife, mother of five grown children, and grandmother of two. She served her home state of New Hampshire for 25 years in various positions at New Hampshire Right to Life (NHRTL), including terms as President, chair of the Educational Trust, and chair of the Political Action Committee. She currently serves as a member of the NHRTL PAC, an affiliate of Personhood Alliance. Darlene is Vice President of Save the 1, a global ministry concerned with protecting the people often referred to as the 'hard cases' in the abortion debate, and is a writer and speaker at TheDarlingPrincess.com, which seeks to provide educational support to anti-human trafficking efforts.]

CHAPTER 7

The Antithesis of the Planned Parenthood Worldview

By Les Riley, President, Personhood Mississippi; Executive Director, The Morning Center (Memphis)

"You say you are against abortion, but all you really care about is legal protection for the fetus and controlling women through politics. What are you doing to take care of mothers with unwanted pregnancies?"[163]

Some variation of this straw man argument has been used against those who seek to ensure equal protection for preborn persons. It is an illegitimate charge on a number of fronts, and I will not take the time or effort to refute it here. But there are a couple of points worth commenting on before I share how we at the Memphis Morning Center are working to build a comprehensive response to the culture of death. The Memphis Morning Center stands as a compassionate, Christ-centered, life-affirming answer to this red herring.

[163] A common charge abortion advocates bring against pro-life ministries

Let Us Not Dignify the Challenge

First, Planned Parenthood and others willing to deny equal human rights, including the right to not be dismembered, experimented on, or discarded, have no moral high ground to challenge us to "do more" so that they somehow achieve credibility in the eyes of those who see abortion as a primary freedom. This is similar to those who participated in the Rwandan Genocide claiming, "If you really cared about the Tutsis, you would fly them all to another country and give us their property" or the Nazis on trial at Nuremberg indignantly asking, "What are you doing for the Jews in your country?" This challenge by abortion advocates is simply a deflection to avoid addressing the God-given dignity and unique worth of every human being and the inherent right to legal protection as a person.

Secondly, Christian pro-life activists have done plenty, but they do not care to take credit or use their service to others as a means to score points. Love for God and love for others is the driving force. These are the motivations behind the hundreds of Christian-charity medical clinics across the United States. For example, Christ Community Health Fellowship has 360 affiliates in 40 states. Many more groups exist. Christians that serve in refugee camps in war-torn regions, start orphanages and schools in the developing world, run homeless shelters and feeding programs, or foster and adopt children are not going to rush to speak at a Planned Parenthood convention or call up MSNBC to tout their work.

Once, during the campaign to pass a Personhood Amendment in Mississippi, I was interviewed by a pro-life reporter who commented, "You don't just talk pro-life, you've adopted an African American son haven't you?" While I was not upset with him, I was offended by the whole mentality behind the question. I simply told him I did not adopt my son to exploit him or to appease those who believe it would have been otherwise okay to kill him in the womb.

In reality, when the mainstream media and those who call themselves pro-choice say, "If you are really concerned about abortion, what are you doing to help mothers and their babies?" what they really mean is, "Are you going to support the expansion of government social welfare programs?"

I have worked in inner-city ministry and have come to love the victims of these government programs. I have seen how counter-productive and destructive they have been to the lives, families, and communities they claim to help. So the answer is an emphatic NO! I care about the poor, so I oppose socialism and government social welfare programs. Nevertheless, a critical question remains: If not government programs, then what?

A Christian Alternative to Social Welfare

The answer is very simple. We are going to live out the two great commands—to love God and love our neighbors—by declaring and living the Gospel, which is what followers of Christ have been doing for 20 centuries. Who cared for the poor before the government?

The Morning Center is a very new and unique concept in our post-modern, humanist world. The president of the aforementioned Christ Community Health Fellowship said he did not know of anyone doing what the Morning Center is doing in the way we are doing it. But in another sense, the Morning Center is a return to a very old model of care for the underserved. So what is The Morning Center? How is it the antithesis of the Planned Parenthood worldview, and what does any of this have to do with personhood?

The Memphis Morning Center exists to provide high-quality, comprehensive maternity care, including delivery, absolutely free, in the name of Jesus to women in underserved areas.[164] It sounds simple; so simple that, at first glance, it does not seem unique. In fact, when most people in the pro-life movement hear of our mission, they respond by saying, “The pregnancy center in our town does that,” or, perhaps, “There is a free clinic in our city doing that.” A further clarification is, therefore, in order.

In the Memphis area, we do partner with and get referrals from pregnancy resource centers (PRCs). The work of PRCs and the level of relationship-based, individual care they give to mothers in unplanned or crisis pregnancies is tremendously needed. In addition, their work dispels (again) the lie that people who seek to offer legal protection to persons do not offer practical help for moms.

The Morning Center fills the next need on the continuum of care, in that PRCs, mercy ministries, and word-of-mouth referrals bring patients to us. The Morning Center’s medical staff of doctors, nurses, practitioners, sonographers, and others—all paid, full-time missionaries—provide comprehensive obstetrics and maternity care in one of our neighborhood clinics for 6 to 9 months. Then, our medical staff either performs the delivery or we cover the cost at a local hospital. This care is all free of charge, and we do it while building a relationship

---

[164] The Morning Center. (2017). Mission. Retrieved from https://www.morningcenter.org/about/mission

with the patient and working with local churches and partnering ministries to holistically address the mom's spiritual and social needs.

Our relationship with PRCs could be likened to the interdependent components of addiction treatment. The PRCs are like detox and emergency shelters that, for the first 24 to 72 hours, are there for addicts who need immediate help. The Morning Center is akin to a halfway house, where an addict stays during rehab to heal from drug dependency and to work toward a productive life. The focus on the individual is key.

A Name, Not a Number

The abortion industry, and too often, well-meaning pragmatists in the pro-life movement, reduce the debate over the killing of children in the womb to a Utilitarian numbers game. We talk about how many abortions there are and how many can be saved through this regulation or that incremental bill. To abortionists, a preborn child is just a blob of tissue, and a mother in crisis is simply one in a long line of desperate customers that can generate a few hundred dollars of easy cash. Former abortion clinic director, Carol Everett, has detailed how women are exploited and treated like profit centers:

> *"We had a whole plan to sell abortions called 'Sex Education': Break down their natural modesty, separate them from their parents and their values, become the sex expert in their lives; so they'd turn to us and we'd give them a low dose birth control that they'd get pregnant on; or a defective condom, because we didn't provide the most expensive condoms, we bought the cheapest*

> *condoms. Our goal was 3 to 5 abortions from every girl between the ages of 13 and 18."*[165]

Infamous Communist dictator Joseph Stalin is reported to have said this about the Ukrainian holomodor (or, genocide by starvation) that he directed: "If only one man dies of hunger, that is a tragedy. If millions die, that's only statistics."[166] Before we further explore the work of The Morning Center, it is valuable to contrast Stalin's immoral view with the story of April, one mom whose life trajectory was transformed through the love of Jesus that was shown to her as a Morning Center patient.

April and her children were second- and third-generation residents of Section 8 housing. April's mother had grown up and lived in the now-closed Warren Apartments where the Morning Center operated a clinic in partnership with the Red Door missionaries.

When the Morning Center opened here, Memphis was named the "most dangerous city in America," and the Warren Apartments had the highest violent crime rate in the city. Drug dealing, prostitution, shootings, gang violence, and the absence of fathers and positive male role models were endemic. Poverty and welfare dependency were the normal environment that the residents of this community had lived in for generations. The Red Door, a ministry of suburban Faith Baptist Church, operated a mission that conducted a ladies' Bible study and offered practical aid and a refuge of peace in an apartment in the middle of the

---

[165] TAH, LLC. (2012). Blood money: The business of abortion. [Film]. [Zipp, J., Producer, & Kyle, D. K., Director]. Available at www.bloodmoneyfilm.com

[166] Lyons, L. (1947, January 30). Loose-leaf notebook [p. 9], *Washington Post* interview. Washington, D.C.

complex. The Morning Center opened a free maternity clinic in this apartment.

April's mother had come to faith in Christ. She participated in the Monday Bible study with the women from Faith Baptist and helped operate the Red Door. April came to the Morning Center with her sixth baby, as well as her seventh. She had fallen into a destructive pattern. April's last four children had the same father, but April and the father had not married and had a very rocky relationship.

As April attended the ladies' Bible study and The Morning Center team gave her care and ministered to her, she heard the Gospel. There was a gradual, but dramatic change in her life over this time. One of the men from the Red Door also began to disciple the father of the four children.

Shortly after April's seventh child was born, HUD closed the Warren Apartments. Most of the residents received vouchers and moved into similar situations, but not April. On a Friday night in the spring of 2016, April married the father of most of her children. The following Sunday, they were both baptized. Shortly thereafter, they purchased their first home and are both working good jobs.

The Morning Center is no longer just a great-sounding idea. The first baby delivered through The Morning Center in Memphis was born in January of 2014. By January of 2017, over 300 babies had been delivered—all free to the mother, all funded through private charity without taxpayer money, all with holistic, comprehensive, high-quality care, and all wrapped in Gospel love. Hundreds more moms have received some level of care at The Morning Center. However, as stories like April's show, the Morning Center and the biblical personhood ethic that undergirds this work is about much more than numbers.

To the abortion industry, the welfare state, and opportunists on both sides of the political pendulum, April, her husband, and her precious children are just numbers—just statistics, just nameless faceless tools to be used to advance an agenda. However, to us, each mom, each dad, each baby, and each friend or extended family member who comes across our path is a unique image bearer who has unique needs. We are compelled by the love of Christ, therefore, to stop and look at their faces and care about their lives. In turn, we invest our lives in addressing their unique situation through service and love.

The Antithesis of the Planned Parenthood Worldview

Much of the focus of the pro-life movement in the arena of ideas and politics points toward the abortion giant, Planned Parenthood, and for good reason. This entity has been around for 100 years and is now a multi-billion dollar global entity. Planned Parenthood operates hundreds of surgical abortion facilities and referral clinics, where they distribute both contraceptives and chemical abortifacients. In keeping with the vision of its eugenicist founder, Margaret Sanger, the vast majority of Planned Parenthood locations, and most surgical abortion facilities in general, are located in minority neighborhoods. Planned Parenthood kills over 320,000 children every year, along with other services that generate hundreds of millions of dollars in revenue.[167] They also generate revenue

---

[167] Planned Parenthood Federation of America. (2015). Planned Parenthood 2014-2015 annual report. Retrieved from

through the sale of aborted fetal body parts[168] and, up through 2017, received hundreds of millions of taxpayer funds annually. Planned Parenthood uses these funds to sexualize children through public education programs that keep their flow of customers coming.[169] They also use these funds to influence politicians, fund massive propaganda campaigns, and oppose pro-life legislation of any sort.[170] For example, in 2011, Planned Parenthood affiliates from around the country funneled over $1 million into Mississippi to defeat a Personhood Amendment through a massive campaign of lies and confusion. Planned Parenthood does not even operate a surgical abortion business in Mississippi.

As of this writing, in early 2017, there are bills in Congress and several state legislatures to defund Planned Parenthood, at least temporarily. This push is the culmination of many years of pro-life activists' work. Personhood advocates believe Planned Parenthood should not only immediately be defunded, but closed down and its leaders investigated for crimes against humanity. But we also recognize that Planned Parenthood is not the only problem.

---

https://www.plannedparenthood.org/files/2114/5089/0863/2014-2015_PPFA_Annual_Report_.pdf

[168] Sekulow, J. (2016). House panel on infant lives: Defund Planned Parenthood. Retrieved from https://aclj.org/pro-life/house-panel-on-infant-lives-defund-planned-parenthood

[169] Live Action. (2017). Sex ed: Planned Parenthood's dangerous sex advice for kids. Retrieved from https://www.plannedparenthoodexposed. com/sexed/

[170] Center for Responsive Politics. (2017). Planned Parenthood PAC: 2016 contribution data. Retrieved from http://www.opensecrets.org/pacs/lookup2 .php?strID=C00314617

Hundreds of other surgical abortion facilities exist in America,[171] and major pharmacy chains sell abortifacient drugs over the counter.[172] Legal abortion must be abolished and the legal personhood of all humans recognized from the moment of biological beginning until natural death. Christians should labor to see all of our image-bearing neighbors protected in law and in love.

Why do I refer to the Morning Center as "the antithesis of the Planned Parenthood worldview"? For our purposes, the term *planned parenthood* is to be understood here as shorthand for the comprehensive, anti-Christian worldview that the Planned Parenthood organization was founded upon and consistently carries out. This worldview has built and now undergirds the entire abortion industry. For example, in my native state of Mississippi, it is not Planned Parenthood but the notorious "pink house" two miles north of the state capital that kills thousands of children annually through surgical abortion. In addition to a large Planned Parenthood clinic in Memphis, Tennessee (where The Morning Center operates), the recently rebranded Choices facility exists. After killing tens of thousands in Memphis since the 1970s, Choices is attempting to become the first in Tennessee (and only the second in the country) to open a midwife-run birthing center to deliver babies under the same roof where others are killed by abortion.

---

[171] Guttmacher Institute. (2017). Fact sheet: Induced abortion in the United States. Retrieved from https://www.guttmacher.org/fact-sheet/induced-abortion-united-states

[172] Szabo, L. (2013). FDA Approves Over-the-Counter Sales for Plan B. Retrieved from http://www.usatoday.com/story/news/nation/2013/ 04/30/fda-plan-b-over-the-counter-emergency-contraception/2125131/

The Morning Center Origins

In 2011, James Lansberry, Elysse Baumbach, and John Creath, who were all working at Samaritan Ministries International (SMI), birthed The Morning Center vision. SMI is a major Christian medical cost-sharing ministry based in Peoria, Illinois. The concept was to address the abortion issue and work to replace counter-productive government social welfare programs with a return to a Gospel-centered biblical charity. It began as a monumental vision to operate free Christian, pro-life maternity hospitals in every city in America, without seeking or accepting any funds from the government. When the incredulous question came, "How are you going to do this without taking any money from the government?" James's reply has become a mantra of sorts: "We have to get over the idea that government's resources are unlimited."

I heard of this vision while working on the campaign to pass the aforementioned Personhood Amendment in Mississippi in 2011, and I reached out to get involved. I began working with another early founder, Burt Stouffer, after Memphis was chosen as the pilot location. I started as a volunteer in 2012 as the groundwork was being laid, and in 2014, I was hired as executive director.

Strategic Location

Memphis' selection as the pilot location is another example of The Morning Center's worldview as the antithesis of Planned Parenthood. The effort was launched in Memphis for the same reason that Planned Parenthood chooses the locations they do, but with the opposite end goals. Memphis is a regional abortion hub where children from West Tennessee, East Arkansas, and North Mississippi are killed. Memphis has a long history of race problems and a high minority population. The city has some of the highest poverty, infant mortality, and maternal mortality rates in the country. In addition, a culture of multigenerational welfare dependency has contributed to loss of work ethic, dignity, and hope; family breakdown; and fatherlessness—all of which fuels gang activity, high violent-crime rates, drug use, prostitution, and human trafficking.

The Morning Center stepped into this difficult and heartbreaking world and opened its first inner city clinic in the building of Leawood Baptist Church, a long-standing congregation that stayed when many others moved to the suburbs. Leawood is in an old neighborhood sandwiched between a largely African-American community on one side and a largely Hispanic community on the other. There is also a significant population of international refugees and immigrants in the area. In fact, the Memphis Morning Center has served mothers from at least 28 countries, from Latin America to Eastern Europe, Asia, the Middle East, and Africa.

A Eugenic Reality

Planned Parenthood's founder, Margaret Sanger, would have despised the thought of a Christian ministry helping people from these various "races" deliver more children and seeking to restore these communities. Even though she saw the suffering and poverty in inner city communities and third-world countries, Sanger was a eugenicist who had a vision to improve the world by reducing populations of "unfit" ethnicities.[173] Like her associates in Nazi Germany, Sanger announced her

---

[173] Sanger followed the eugenic premise that Charles Darwin first suggested in his book, *On the Origin* of *Species by Means of Natural Selection, or the*

genocidal intentions to the world. Calling people of color "human weeds" and other pejoratives, Sanger sought to use birth control as a eugenic means to greatly reduce certain populations, including the African-American one.[174] She put this vision into action in part through her hallmark campaign called "the Negro Project."[175]

Far from seeing the breakdown of the family as a bad thing, Sanger actively sought the destruction of the family and pushed for sexual liberation, which the Christian worldview recognizes as the slavery to ensnaring, soul-destroying sin. Unlike The Morning Center's commitment to relationship-based private charity, Sanger's ideological descendants in the culture, along with those who now operate and lead the organization she founded, do not build relationships and provide free care. Rather, the abortion industry sells its grisly service to a desperate mother, takes her money, kills her child, and then tosses her aside for the next customer. Planned Parenthood uses this money, along with donations from pro-abortion organizations and taxpayer contributions, to build its organization and advance Sanger's agenda worldwide.

The Morning Center has established a beachhead in Memphis that opposes this destructive worldview—and it is spreading. In 2017, a second Morning Center city, Atlanta, is moving forward. Places like Jackson, Mississippi, and other cities around the country are in the works. In addition, a similar project, Luke 52, now operates in Detroit.

Preservation of Favoured Races in the Struggle for Life—a title that speaks volumes.

[174] Sanger, M. (1922). *The pivot of civilization.* [e-book version]. http://www.gutenberg.org/files/1689/1689-h/1689-h.htm

[175] Hoye II, W. B., Rev. (2010). The negro project: 1939-1942. Retrieved from http://www.issues4life.org/blast/2010242.html

The Morning Center vision is not only to expand this work to other cities, but also to help other organizations with similar aims in different places. Our motto is: "We don't care who gets the credit, as long as it's Jesus."

But surely, one or two medical charities delivering babies and helping underserved women in a few cities is not accomplishing much. After all, we face an abortion industry that kills millions, a culture that accepts it as normal, and a political system that supports it as a basic liberty. The answer to this charge is two-fold.

First, we do not as the Bible says, "despise our day of small beginnings." We believe, as Jesus told us, that the Kingdom of God is like a tiny mustard seed that grows to fill the whole field. Planned Parenthood has grown into a billion-dollar international entity, but it began with only one location and Margaret Sanger's commitment to her twisted eugenic beliefs. In contrast, we have a greater faith that encompasses a greater worldview, and we follow a God who is greater than any earthly system.

Secondly, we are not attempting to build a Utopian Tower of Babel on the shifting sand of a destructive worldview, nor are we trusting in human schemes or temporal riches. The Morning Center, like the different local entities of the Personhood movement, is simply putting our pushpin on the map. The Morning Center partners with a number of great PRCs, mercy ministries, and medical clinics focused on other components of care. We join forces with a mentoring ministry called One-by-One, restorative discipleship ministries like Families Matter, adoption agencies, and many others to care for moms and babies as individuals.

Ultimately, we are laboring for the eternal—to see individuals pointed to Christ, to see His Kingdom advance in this fallen world, and to bring the transforming, restoring power of the Gospel brought to bear against the culture of death and despair. In this, we believe that it is the Church, not solely parachurch ministries or political efforts, that will ultimately prevail. Therefore, we want to see those we serve, and even those who oppose us, come to saving faith in Jesus Christ. This salvation will bear the fruit of healthy families and healthy local churches. As these restored individuals in healthy families and healthy churches live out their redemption—communities are transformed.

Therefore, The Morning Center seeks to partner not only with parachurch ministries, but also with and through churches in the communities we serve. The Morning Center is, at its core, merely a conduit—a means for the Church of Jesus Christ and individual Christians to serve "the least of these."[176]

Personhood's Orthopraxy

Perhaps one more story will illustrate this vision. On her second visit to The Morning Center, Marquita was no longer living in South Memphis with the father of her preborn child, but in a homeless shelter across the river in Arkansas with her two-year-old son, fathered by a different man. All of the worldly possessions that this articulate and intelligent young woman had for herself and her children fit into a couple of Walmart bags. Having grown up with abusive parents and now in a cycle of abusive men

[176] Matthew 25:40

and homelessness, Marquita was replacing her hopes and dreams with cynicism and a survival mentality.

First Baptist West Memphis had been working to help her. The pastor of a smaller Baptist church, who is a sidewalk advocate outside Planned Parenthood, along with a neighboring Presbyterian pastor, got a car seat and brought Marquita and her children to a Morning Center appointment at Bellevue Baptist's Frayser campus. Our *Hannah's Closet* baby store at Leawood Baptist had just received two vanloads of donated items from a coalition of churches in Illinois, Alabama, Mississippi, and Tennessee. Vicki, a woman from our ministry team, provided Marquita with new clothes, a pack-and-play where the little boy could sleep, and even a few toys from the coalition's donations. After the appointment, Camille, The Morning Center's manager, took them home and made a place for them to live in a garage apartment for the remainder of the pregnancy and a few months after. Camille's family and church cared for and discipled her. Eventually, Marquita moved to Virginia where a program through another church helped her find a place to live, get a job, and receive continued mentoring and training.

The Power of Personhood

The Planned Parenthood worldview, and the abortion industry that carries it out, harms mothers like Marquita and kills children by the millions. People on both sides of the abortion debate talk of numbers and seek to advance agendas, either through cultural revolution or political pragmatism. But the Kingdom of God is advanced through the redemption and regeneration of individual souls. The Personhood movement is about valuing and protecting individual lives. In Marquita's case, many individuals from eleven churches, in three different denominations, and in six states, all came together to serve one mother, her two-year-old little boy, and her preborn child.

> *"The light shines in the darkness, and the darkness has not overcome it."*[177]

[Les Riley is the Founder and President of Personhood Mississippi and the Executive Director of The Morning Center in Memphis. Les has been involved in pro-life, pro-family, pro-liberty, gospel, worldview, and mercy ministries in Mississippi, inner city Memphis, and Uganda, Africa. He is a sinner saved by grace and has been abundantly blessed by his wife Christy of 31 years and their 10 children and 9 grandchildren.]

---

[177] John 1:5

CHAPTER 8

Personhood and Unnatural Death

By Nancy Elliott, Chairman, Euthanasia Prevention Coalition USA, and former New Hampshire House State Representative

Euthanasia and assisted suicide deny the personhood of an individual in the most permanent way. The practices imply that people are disposable; that as soon as a person is no longer "productive," they should be removed from society.

The Church's Role

Recently, in an area where a battle was raging for assisted suicide, a pastor responded to my request for help by saying that he did not want to get involved in a political matter. While I generally use secular arguments when publicly discussing this topic, I firmly believe this issue belongs to the Church. This pastor had a view of where the Church should stand on assisted suicide and euthanasia that was not rooted in the Word of God.

Scriptural Insights

To correct this view, I would like to address the issue from a biblical perspective and use five points to explain why this is important to the Church. First, consider the Ten Commandments. Assisted suicide violates at least two of these commandments. The first is honor your father and mother. [178] Honor implies supporting and taking care of. When assisted suicide is on the table, it is our seniors—our mothers and fathers—who become its victims. Assisted suicide also violates the commandment: You shall not murder.[179] A doctor (or anyone, for that matter) who supplies poison, along with directions on how to commit suicide, is an accessory to murder.

Second, Jesus said, "Love your neighbor."[180] Is helping our healthcare system end the life of your neighbor really loving her?[181]

Third, the whole premise of suicide results in a rejection of God, in that a human decides to override the plan God has for him.[182] Suicide steals the last chance for repentance of the unbeliever.[183] It steals the legacy (and witness) of the person committing it, whether a believer or not.

Fourth, John 8:44 tells us that the devil is a murderer and a liar. Assisted suicide laws come from the Father of Lies. We know this because the assisted suicide movement engages in deception to justify the murder of humanity (Satan's enemy) and make it palatable. What

---

[178] Exodus 20:12
[179] Exodus 20:13
[180] Matthew 19:19
[181] Romans 13:10
[182] Jeremiah 29:11
[183] Hebrews 9:27

advocates are proposing is so ugly that they are forced to use poetic language and euphemisms to portray it. But they are selling death, not life.

Fifth, Christianity and Judaism have traditionally condemned suicide and murder as morally wrong. If you believe that it is morally wrong to kill the preborn, to kill a disabled child, or to give a gun to a suicidal teen, you must also concede that it is morally wrong to assist a suicide or engage in euthanasia. Christian morality originates in the Church. No other entity on Earth can decide what is moral or not, apart from the revelation of God in Scripture. The Church must not allow men like Peter Singer and George Soros to set the moral compass for our nation because we are not willing to stand for truth and respect innocent human life. The Church must call out euthanasia and assisted suicide as sin, or we will be culpable. To be neutral or do nothing is to aid this sin, just as being neutral to the message of the Gospel is to perish.

Deceptive Euphemisms Mask Evil

Before we examine the euphemisms used to mask these practices, let us define and differentiate them. *Assisted suicide*, which is legal in several states and often interchangeable with the term physician-assisted suicide, involves a doctor "knowingly and intentionally providing a person with the knowledge or means or both [that is] required to commit suicide, including counseling about lethal doses of drugs, prescribing such lethal doses or supplying the drugs."[184] *Euthanasia* is "knowingly and

---

[184] Canadian Medical Association. (2007). Euthanasia and assisted suicide. Retrieved from https://web.archive.org/web/20111219230512/ http://policybase.cma.ca/dbtw-wpd/Policypdf/PD07-01.pdf

intentionally performing an act that is explicitly intended to end another person's life."[185] The three types of euthanasia are voluntary (the patient consents), non-voluntary (patient consent is unavailable), and involuntary (against the patient's will).[186] Put simply, in assisted suicide, a doctor gives his patient the means to takes her own life. In euthanasia, the doctor, or someone else in assistance, takes the patient's life. Assisted suicide and euthanasia are considered morally equivalent, but these practical definitions, as well as their legal distinctions, make them different.[187]

In the United States, euthanasia is illegal. By comparison, assisted suicide is legal in five states, as of 2017: Oregon, Washington, Vermont, California, and Colorado. It is not legal in Montana, however, a court ruled that a doctor who performs it there may use a patient's request for assisted suicide as an affirmative defense if charges are brought against him. Here are some of the deceptions used to legalize assisted suicide in America:

- Assisted suicide is not murder, but death with dignity or aid in dying.
- The procedure is pain-free.
- It is an act of courage and bravery.
- Only religious people are opposed to it.
- There are adequate safeguards in place to protect patients.
- Assisted suicide is self-determined; there is no coercion.

---

[185] Ibid.

[186] Wreen, M. (1988). The definition of euthanasia. *Philosophy and Phenomenological Research, 48*(4): pp. 637.

[187] Ibid., Canadian Medical Association

- It is about choice.
- The patients are mentally sound.
- Assisted suicide gets government out of health care.
- Assisted suicide will not lead to euthanasia.

Moreover, many countries are beginning to reach beyond assisted suicide, into the realm of euthanasia. The following statements reflect an increasing call for death, even in American culture:

- Euthanasia exalts mercy and personal choice.
- People are valuable in terms of their contribution to society.
- "Quality of life" should be the determining factor in medical treatment.
- Legalization of voluntary euthanasia is underpinned by a raft of safeguards.
- Physicians should be authorized to end the suffering of incurable patients.
- Euthanasia is a humane social policy.

These statements are not drawn from today's headlines, however, but from advocates of Nazi Germany's *Aktion T-4 Euthanasie Programme* (Action T-4 euthanasia program), carried out from 1939-1941.[188] Consider this reasonable-sounding standard of care from Germany's Ministry of Justice in 1933:

> *"Overseeing security and ensuring that the safeguards for the patients were strictly adhered to, the only patients affected were*

---

[188] Jewish Virtual Library. (2017). The Nazi euthanasia (T-4) program: Background & overview. Retrieved from http://www.jewishvirtuallibrary.org/background-and-overview-of-the-nazi-euthanasia-t-4-program

> *those who, after the most careful examination, a series of four tests carried out by at least two physicians, were considered incurable. A painless death would be a merciful release from an intolerable existence, the patient himself shall 'expressly and earnestly' ask it, or in case the patient no longer is able to express his desire, his nearer relatives, acting from motives that do not contravene morals, so request."*[189]

An Ominous Parallel

Upon visiting the United States Holocaust Memorial Museum in Washington D.C., I was overcome by profound sadness. The pure evil that is euthanasia permeates as you walk through. I noticed the exhibit on euthanasia of the disabled. It was eerily similar to the practices and goals of today's advocates. There were pictures of children mercilessly euthanized in the name of humane treatment. Yet it was a disabled child, Gerhard Kretschmar in 1939, whose death ushered in the Holocaust.[190] Gerhard was born blind, missing a leg and parts of an arm. At 5 months old, his parents wrote to Hitler's office asking for their son to be euthanized. Three weeks after Gerhard was killed, Hitler issued a decree to begin euthanizing all disabled children. It was not long before he moved on to disabled adults.[191]

> *"[People were] more ready to accept the extermination of the sick, than execution for political reasons. It was for that reason*

---

[189] Ohio Right to Life. (2000). Nazis plan to kill incurables to end pain; German religious groups oppose move. Originally published in *New York Times*. (1933, October 8). Retrieved from http://www.pregnantpause .org/euth/nyt33.htm

[190] Zoech, I. (2003). Named: The baby boy who was the Nazis' first euthanasia victim. Retrieved from http://www.telegraph.co.uk/education/ 3319981/ Named-the-baby-boy-who-was-Nazis-first-euthanasia-victim.html

[191] Quarmby, K. (2011). *Scapegoat: Why we are failing disabled people*. Granta Books.

> *that the first exterminations of the later (political) group, were carried out under the guise of sickness."* [192]

This acceptance of extermination was rooted in the drastic scientific and cultural changes happening in Germany in the late 18th and early 19th centuries.[193] Nationalist ideas had taken hold and even permeated the Christian Church. Nationalism was met with the poverty and unrest created by World War I, the sharp rise in anti-Semitism post-war, and the social-Darwinist thinkers of that time.[194] Germany and her Church were ready and willing to accept eugenic extermination as an opportunity to fix their failing society and a means to cleanse the human population of "useless eaters."[195]

The Log in Our Own Eye

The United States has its own dark history as well. During the Progressive era and the few decades that followed, the US passed state-level eugenics laws to prevent those with disabilities and other "unfit" traits from reproducing.[196] We euthanized those in mental institutions[197,

---

[192] Ibid., The Life Resources Charitable Trust

[193] Crew, D. F. (1994). "The genesis of the 'final solution' from the spirit of science". In Nazism and German Society, 1933–1945. London: Routledge. pp. 274–299.

[194] Projetaladin. (2009). The roots of the Holocaust: Anti-semitism. Retrieved from http://www.projetaladin.org/holocaust/en/history-of-the-holocaust-shoah/the-roots-of-the-holocaust.html

[195] United States Holocaust Memorial Museum. (2017). Children during the Holocaust. Retrieved from https://www.ushmm.org/wlc/en/article.php?ModuleId=10005142

[196] Cold Spring Harbor Laboratory. (2017). Image archive of the American Eugenics Movement. Retrieved from http://www.eugenicsarchive.org/eugenics/list2.pl

[197] Black, E. (2003). The horrifying American roots of Nazi eugenics. Retrieved from http://historynewsnetwork.org/article/1796

[198] and employed forced sterilization laws, even into the 1970s.[199] This Darwinian mindset[200] tells us that, because a human is just another animal, it is OK to kill him. It becomes important to selectively breed him, or reduce his capacity to breed, for the betterment of the species. Nazi Germany actually followed the lead of the American Eugenics Movement.[201] Today, our own culture, like Germany's before the Holocaust, is ripe for the acceptance of extermination by assisted suicide and euthanasia.

It Begins with A Right to Die

Some would say that, because we have a right to life, we should also have a right to die. We are all going to die. But it is not a right—it is our destiny. Our right to life is universal. It applies to all people, young and old, sick and well. If we agree that someone with 6 months to live has a right to a poison prescription, we must also conclude that, because rights are for all, that a well person or even a well child, should also have a right to a poison prescription. As this is not where most people are willing to go, we must conclude as our ancestors did before us—that there is no right to die.

---

[198] Van Wagenen, B. (1912). Preliminary report of the committee of the eugenic section of the American Breeders' Association to study and to report on the best practical means for cutting off the defective germ-plasm in the human population. *Buck v. Bell* documents. (2009). Paper 74. Retrieved from http://readingroom.law.gsu.edu/cgi/viewcontent.cgi?article=1073&context=buckvbell

[199] Curators of the University of Missouri. (2017). Eugenics and sterilization. Retrieved from https://library.missouri.edu/exhibits/eugenics/sterilization.htm

[200] Darwin, C. (1876) *On the Origin of Species by Means of Natural Selection, or the Preservation of Favored Races in the Struggle for Life.* New York: D. Appleton & Co.

[201] Ibid., Black

HOLLYWOOD'S CONTRIBUTION: A DUTY TO DIE

The use of movies to spread "right to die" propaganda is very evident. The 1916 silent film, *The Black Stork*, dramatized the mercy killing of a disabled infant, which was based on the true story of Dr. Harry Haiselden's contributions to the American Eugenics Movement.[202] In the 1941 film, *Ich Klage an (I Accuse)*, produced by the Nazis' Ministry of Propaganda, an attractive woman suffering from multiple sclerosis was gently killed by her loving doctor-husband.[203] We have seen this theme repeated over and over throughout modern history; that the disabled do not want to live and should not, for the sake of suffering and society.[204] In a more recent film, *Me Before You*, a young, handsome quadriplegic succumbs to the siren call of assisted suicide and leaves all his money to his beautiful caregiver.[205] These movies soften the population to accept assisted suicide and euthanasia. People with disabilities want to live, and they have every right to. But Hollywood's message is, "If one is seriously disabled—one has a *duty* to die." This message then progresses to cultural enforcement—the belief that we have a duty to die once our social usefulness enters its waning years. From here, it is just a few steps to involuntary death through state-mandated euthanasia.

The legalization of assisted suicide gives the government the right to decide who is deserving or worthy of death, particularly when healthcare

---

[202] Pernick, M. (1996). *The Black Stork: Eugenics and the death of "defective" babies in American medicine and motion pictures since 1915*. New York: Oxford University Press.

[203] Ministry of Propaganda. (1941). Ich Klage An. [Film]. [Liebeneiner,W., Director].

[204] Ibid., Pernick, M.

[205] MGM Studios. (2016). Me Before You. [Film]. [Sharrock, T., Director].

cost-containment is considered. Assisted suicide laws currently target three groups of people: The infirm, the disabled, and the elderly.

The Infirm

Most assisted suicide bills state that the patient must have 6 months or less to live. In Oregon's law, for example, *terminal disease* is defined as "an incurable and irreversible disease that has been medically confirmed and will, within reasonable medical judgment, produce death within 6 months."[206] While this definition brings images of people who are at the very end of their lives, this is not necessarily the case. In Oregon, this definition has broadened to cover people who, without the assistance of medication, have less than 6 months to live.[207] This law has already been applied to people with chronic lower respiratory disease, heart disease, and those who are terminal *only* without the assistance of treatment,[208] in cancer patients like Jeanette Hall, for example.[209] Jeanette had voted for the Oregon law that authorized assisted suicide. When her doctor diagnosed her cancer, the fear that naturally arose led her to choose assisted suicide. Her doctor did not believe in killing his patients and instead, encouraged her to live for the sake of her son. She decided to

---

[206] Oregon Health Authority. (2017). Oregon revised statute: 127.800 s.1.01. Definitions. (12). *Terminal illness*. [1995 c.3 s.1.01; 1999 c.423 s.1]. Retrieved from http://tinyurl.com/h796e2

[207] Ibid.

[208] Oregon Public Health Division. (2016). Oregon Death with Dignity Act: 2015 data summary. Retrieved from https://public.health.oregon.gov/ProviderPartnerResources/EvaluationResearch/DeathwithDignityAct/Documents/year18.pdf

[209] Choice is an Illusion. (2016). If my doctor had believed in assisted suicide, I'd be dead. Retrieved from http://www.choiceillusion.org/2016/10/ if-my-doctor-had-believed-in-assisted_21.html

seek treatment. It was a success. Sixteen years later, Jeanette is happy to be alive.

Doctors can now treat many medical conditions that were deemed untreatable in the past, and the miracles of modern medicine continue to expand. Diseases themselves are unpredictable, and prognosis is far from an exact science. Case in point: I was at a hearing on assisted suicide in Massachusetts in 2012 when John Norton testified about his ALS diagnosis as a young man. Had assisted suicide been legal at that time, he noted, he would have opted for it. But a few years into the disease's progression, it just stopped. Now in his late 70s, John enjoys his life with his children and a grandchild.[210]

Misdiagnosis is also a critical consideration. When doctors make mistakes and assisted suicide is on the table, those mistakes can turn to tragedy and lead to injustice. Assisted suicide laws often contain a protective caveat that empowers doctors, not patients.[211] If a doctor misdiagnoses a condition and the patient takes his life by assisted suicide—the doctor is immune from prosecution. For example, in Italy, a man received an incorrect terminal diagnosis and traveled to Switzerland

---

[210] Mass Against Assisted Suicide. (2012). John Norton: A cautionary tale. Retrieved from http://www.massagainstassistedsuicide.org/2012/ 09/john-norton-cautionary-tale.html

[211] Valko, N. (2017). Physician-assisted suicide empowers doctors, not patients. Retrieved from http://www.nationalrighttolifenews.org/news/ 2017/03/physician-assisted-suicide-empowers-doctors-not-patients/#.WNbRqMs2xMs

to legally end his life. However, an autopsy later revealed the misdiagnosis.[212] He forfeited his life based on a mistake.

Assisted suicide laws also affect those who do not want to end their lives. The cases of Barbara Wagner and Randy Stroop illustrate the dangers.[213] Both were diagnosed with cancer and prescribed medication as part of their treatment protocol. Both received letters from Oregon's Medicaid program announcing denial of coverage for the cancer drugs, but availability of coverage for a lethal dose of medication to end their lives. A young woman in California, where assisted suicide became legal in 2015, faced a similar situation. She was denied insurance coverage for the cancer-treating drug her doctor prescribed. But when she inquired about assisted suicide coverage, she learned the co-pay was just over a dollar.[214] When death is the treatment for certain diseases, alternatives are no longer sought. If assisted suicide were ever to become a national policy, would cures be sought as vigorously? Would our healthcare system pursue even further this "give up at first fight" mentality?

The Disabled

The second group of people that assisted suicide laws target is the disabled. Advocates are quick to claim this is not about disability, but about people who are dying. Are they being truthful? Most people that

---

[212] Schadenberg, Alex. (2014). Switzerland, assisted suicide, and death clinics. Retrieved from http://alexschadenberg.blogspot.com/2014/08/switzerland-assisted-suicide-and-death.html?m=1

[213] Smith, W. (2009). 'Right to die' can become a 'duty to die.' Retrieved from http://www.telegraph.co.uk/comment/personal-view/4736927/Right-to-die-can-become-a-duty-to-die.html

[214] Center for Bioethics and Culture. (2016). Compassion and choices denied. [Documentary film]. Official trailer. Retrieved from https://youtu.be/hwLs3D062Vk

qualify for death under assisted suicide law have a disability. Anecdotal evidence and my years of experience as a life advocate have shown me that those with long-term disabilities have been labeled all their lives as terminal. Without medication, treatment, and assistance, they would not survive. Assisted suicide laws, and the propaganda that supports them, encourage these people to end their lives. Compare this to attempts to prevent suicide among young, non-disabled persons. An entire support network of suicide hotlines, specified counseling, awareness campaigns, and other preventative measures exists to save lives. Why is the approach different for the disabled? Are assisted suicide laws, then, a form of discrimination?

Our disabled veterans must also be considered. The rate of suicide among recent-war veterans is 50% higher than the non-military civilian population with similar demographics.[215] Yet in 2009, controversy arose upon discovery of a Department of Veterans Affairs' end-of-life planning booklet, written by a prominent assisted suicide advocate, that asked veterans to consider such questions as, "Is my life worth living?" and "Am I a burden to my family?"[216] Why are we, as a society, validating our veterans' desire for death, especially those injured in combat? Are we going to forego counseling, physical therapy, and PTSD treatment and instead, push suicide—after all of the sacrifices they have made? When the government has a cost-containment motivation, the answer may be difficult for us to accept.

---

[215] Zarembo, A. (2015). Detailed study confirms high suicide rate among recent veterans. Retrieved from http://www.latimes.com/nation/la-na-veteran-suicide-20150115-story.html

[216] Levi, M. (2009). A "death book for veterans"? Retrieved from http://www.cbsnews.com/news/unplugged-a-death-book-for-veterans/

THE ELDERLY

Let us look at the third group of people targeted by assisted suicide laws—the elderly. Seniors can easily fall victim to coercion, and the process of assisted suicide is vulnerable to abuse. For example, there are many front-end requirements put in place to prevent abuse, such as repeated meetings with the prescribing doctor and built-in waiting periods. However, in most states, heirs to an elderly person's estate can be there for the medication request and even speak on behalf of the patient. Once the prescription is written, the safeguards in the process all but vanish. Anyone can pick up the lethal dose, even the heir. Once the prescription is in the house, no one can know whether the dose was voluntarily self-administered. No witness is required. It is also not required that death certificates list assisted suicide as the method of death but rather, the certificate must reflect a natural death caused by the underlying disease. All the information is sealed, unavailable to the public.[217]

Coercion is not only present from family members who may benefit from the death of their elderly relative, but from doctors as well. Kathryn Judson, a woman from Oregon, reported she had attended a doctor's appointment with her seriously ill husband. She was feeling and looking visibly exhausted from caring for him. Her ears perked up as she heard the doctor begin to pitch assisted suicide to her husband. "'Think

---

[217] Dore, M. (2009). 'Death with dignity': What do we advise our clients? Retrieved from https://www.kcba.org/newsevents/barbulletin/BView.aspx ?Month=05&Year=2009&AID=article5.htm

of what it will spare your wife. We need to think of her," he persuaded. They left and never came back. Her husband lived for another 5 years.[218]

Prominent author Ezekiel Emanuel, President Obama's special healthcare advisor for the Affordable Care Act (ACA), was featured on the front cover of the October 2014 issue of *The Atlantic* magazine, which featured his article, "Why I Hope to Die at 75: An Argument That Society and Families—and You—Will Be Better Off If Nature Takes Its Course Swiftly and Promptly."[219] In the article, he argued for death when one's social utility begins to wane. Emanuel also co-created the Complete Lives System, a set of decision-making principles for the ACA's Independent Payment Advisory Board to use to allocate scarce resources, like vaccines, organs, and medical treatments.[220] The system calculates a priority curve that favors younger people who have not yet lived a complete life, but also incorporates prognosis, what actions would save the most lives, a person's social usefulness, and even a lottery.[221] So what happens to the outliers—the very young, the disabled, the terminally ill, and the elderly—who fall outside of the prioritized distribution of resources? We need to look no further than the provisions within the

---

[218] Judson, K. (2011, February 15). Assisted suicide? I was afraid to leave my husband alone again with the doctors and nurses. [Letter to the editor]. *Hawai'i Free Press*. Retrieved from http://hawaiifreepress.com/ArticlesDaily News/tabid/65/ID/3647/February-2011-Letters-to-the-Editor.aspx

[219] Emanuel, E. (2014). Why I hope to die at 75: An argument that society and families-and you-will be better off if nature takes its course swiftly and promptly. Retrieved from https://www.theatlantic.com/magazine/archive/2014/10/why-i-hope-to-die-at-75/379329/

[220] Persad, G., Wertheimer, A., & Emanuel, E. (2009). Principles for allocation of scarce medical resources. Retrieved from http://www.ncpa.org/pdfs/PIIS0140673609601379.pdf

[221] Ibid.

ACA that require Medicaid to cover end-of-life consultations. These provisions were authored by the assisted suicide advocacy organization, Compassion & Choices (formerly, the Hemlock Society).[222] Hemlock Society founder, Derek Humphry, openly admitted the cost-containment motivation:

> *"A rational argument can be made for allowing PAS [physician-assisted suicide] in order to offset the amount society and family spend on the ill...There is no contradicting the fact that since the largest medical expenses are incurred in the final days and weeks of life, the hastened demise of people with only a short time left would free resources for others."*[223]

Apart from targeting specific groups and the eugenic and financial motivations for the laws themselves, suicide contagion is a broader societal factor that also must be considered in discussions of assisted suicide.

SUICIDE CONTAGION

When my daughter was in high school, a classmate committed suicide. She was despondent and so were all of her friends. The school brought in counselors from all over who, for a week and a half, worked with the students directly. They knew from experience that when one student in a school commits suicide, others are in danger of following. Multiple suicides can also plague generations in individual families. Even the news and social media can greatly influence incidents of suicide. This

---

[222] Smith, W. (2009). Obamacare: Compassion and Choices seeking to become Planned Parenthood of death. Retrieved from http://www.nationalreview.com/human-exceptionalism/324843/obamacare-compassion-and-choices-seeking-become-planned-parenthood-death

[223] Humphry, D., & Clement, M. (2000). *Freedom to die: People, politics, and the right-to-die movement.* New York: St. Martin's Griffin.

phenomenon is known as *suicide contagion*.[224] Incidentally, suicide rates in Oregon have increased almost 50% since assisted suicide was legalized in 1997.[225] Oregon has a suicide rate that is 41% higher than the nation as a whole.[226] This rise is consistent with suicide contagion.

SELF-ADMINISTRATION: THE SLIPPERY SLOPE TO EUTHANASIA

Recall that, in assisted suicide, a doctor gives his patient the means to take her own life. In euthanasia, the doctor, or someone else in assistance, takes the patient's life. Euthanasia is illegal in the US, while assisted suicide is permitted in some states. However, most of our assisted suicide laws actually allow for euthanasia, in that the laws state that the patient *may* self-administer, which also means they may choose not to.

In Colorado, legislators brought the concept of *standard medical practice* into the assisted suicide statute. Standard medical practice permits a parent to administer medication to a child. In the statute, a grown child is permitted to administer medication to a parent. If the grown child administers a prescribed lethal dose, this becomes euthanasia by definition. But the law simultaneously rejects that

---

[224] U.S. Department of Health and Human Services. (2017). What does "suicide contagion" mean, and what can be done to prevent it? Retrieved from https://www.hhs.gov/answers/mental-health-and-substance-abuse/what-does-suicide-contagion-mean/index.html

[225] Associated Press. (2013). Report: Oregon's suicide rate higher than the nation's. Retrieved from http://www.oregonlive.com/health/index.ssf /2013/05/report_oregons_suicide_rate_hi.html

[226] Ibid.

euthanasia is its goal, while also claiming that nothing done in accordance with the law is euthanasia.[227] This is double-speak.

The slip from assisted suicide to euthanasia often comes in the challenges inherent in self-administration of the medication. This is because, in practice, there are more and more situations like Betsy Davis's in California. Betsy had invited her family and friends to her farewell party—a practice that is becoming increasingly prevalent.[228] When it was time for Betsy to commit suicide, she was too weak to finish the dosage of lethal medication. Her caregiver held the cup for her, with the agreement of an unidentified doctor at the scene.[229] This is euthanasia by definition, which is illegal. The California Board of Medicine and other medical experts agreed. But the director of the Compassion & Choices state affiliate, Matt Whitaker, did not: "[It] does not mean they couldn't hold a cup that a person is drinking out of. That would be fine."[230] We continue to see that, where assisted suicide is legal, troubling issues are emerging from the thin line between current practices and the dangerous realities of euthanasia.

---

[227] Colorado General Assembly. (2016). Proposition 106: End of Life Options Act - Access to medical-aid-in-dying medication. Retrieved from http://www.leg.state.co.us/LCS/Initiative%20Referendum/1516initrefr.nsf/b74b3fc5d676cdc987257ad8005bce6a/99fbc3387156ab5c87257fae00748890/$FILE/2015-2016%20145bb.pdf

[228] Associated Press. (2016). Terminally ill are saying goodbye with assisted suicide parties. Retrieved from http://nypost.com/2016/08/11/ terminally-ill-are-saying-goodbye-with-assisted-suicide-parties/

[229] Munson, K., & Clayworth, J. (2016). Suicide with a helping hand worries Iowans on both sides of 'right to die'. Retrieved from http://www.desmoinesregister.com/story/news/investigations/2016/11/25/too-weak-kill-herself-assistance-legal/92407392/

[230] Ibid.

Belgium: An International Warning

At an international level, euthanasia is legal in the Netherlands, Belgium, Luxembourg, and Canada. Belgium in particular has had major challenges since euthanasia was legalized. Here, children can be euthanasia patients, which begs the question: How could a child have the mental or emotional capacity to consent to his or her own death? Belgium's law also goes beyond the terminally ill and allows for euthanasia of people suffering from depression. [231] My friend's mother met this fate in Belgium. Doctors did not even notify the family of her intent until she had already been euthanized.

We see people with Alzheimer's disease, dementia, autism, anorexia, borderline personality disorder, chronic-fatigue syndrome, partial paralysis, blindness coupled with deafness, manic depression, and recently, alcoholism being euthanized.[232] Like children, some of these people do not have the ability to consent to their own death. A 2014 study found that almost 32% of the euthanasia deaths in Belgium were performed without the patient's request. And in some areas, as much as 47% of the deaths went unreported.[233]

Euthanasia is also being linked to organ donation initiatives. In Belgium, the default position is that every patient is an organ donor. In 2007, just under a half percent (0.49%) of deaths were via euthanasia, and yet these deaths accounted for 23.5%, or almost one quarter, of all

---

[231] Lore, K (2014). Euthanasia already out of control in Belgium. Retrieved from http://guardianlv.com/2014/02/euthanasia-already-out-of-control-in-belgium/
[232] Ibid.
[233] Ibid.

lung donations.[234] This connection is ripe for abuse and could lead to increases in euthanasia where there are decreases in organ availability.[235]

In Summary

We are already experiencing a slippery slope here in America: From the right to die to the duty to die, and from healthcare cost-containment to insurance coverage for end-of-life counseling. Those who society judges to be too elderly, ill, or disabled are the victims of a system built on a foundation of deception.

Everyone fears natural death to some degree, and we must recognize that some people want assisted suicide for themselves. However, we must also consider that many organizations exist to convince the elderly, ill, and disabled that suicide is their only hope, that death can be experienced with dignity, not fear, and that death is somehow the ultimate human right. But these organizations sprung forward from the same eugenic root as the abortion industry, who presents death as empowering and compassionate. Death is neither of these things, and taking one's own life by means of the government is a tragic and alarming symptom of our cultural decay. Death is knocking on America's door. It is time for the Church to wake up.

---

[234] Schadenburg, A. (2013). Euthanasia statistics in Belgium. Retrieved from http://alexschadenberg.blogspot.com/2013/12/euthanasia-statistics-in-belgium.html

[235] Ibid.

[Nancy Elliott was a three-term State Representative in New Hampshire (2004-2010). While serving on the Judiciary Committee in the New Hampshire House of Representatives, she worked to defeat HB 304, an Oregon-style physician-assisted suicide bill. As a private citizen in 2011, she was instrumental in defeating a similar bill, HB 513. Nancy has worked with grassroots organizers in Montana, Connecticut, and New York in the fight against assisted suicide and has testified in opposition to assisted suicide in New Hampshire, Massachusetts, New Jersey, and Rhode Island. She is an international speaker, serves on the leadership team for Euthanasia Prevention Coalition, International, and is the chair of Euthanasia Prevention Coalition USA.]

CHAPTER 9

WHY HUMAN DIGNITY IS A PRO-LIFE CONCERN

By Darlene Pawlik, New Hampshire Right to Life PAC; Vice President, Save the 1

As elsewhere in this book, where human dignity is discussed, it is imperative to recognize that our inherent human dignity is unique in that, we alone—of all of creation—were fashioned in the similitude of God Himself.[236]

HUMAN DIGNITY

The attributes locked up in our DNA are expressed as we grow and change and explore and develop—physically, mentally, and spiritually. We are creative, dynamic, and fragile. We are absolutely interdependent. As illustrated by the cross of Christ, we are designed to have a solid relationship vertically with our Creator and horizontally with one another.

---

[236] Genesis 1:27

Although we are designed to love and nurture one another, it is also within our capacity to brutalize and torture others, even unto death. This is the mystery of free will. Our eternal being is spirit, we have a soul, and we live and interact with our physical bodies. Our soul is made up of our mind, will, and emotions, and this triune attribute generates our behavior.

In the beginning, the first human beings were perfect, covered in glory and purity. By deceit, they chose to separate themselves from God, thereby establishing a barrier between themselves and the Creator that was passed down through all generations.[237] It is this metaphysical barrier that has the whole world in a state of chaos. Unless we are born again,[238] we cannot relate to our Creator and therefore, cannot love and nurture one another with His perfect love.

People operate under the false assumption that our bodies are the highest part of our beings when, in reality, they are the least. We have come to believe that our physical needs drive us; that our bodies control our lives. If we are hungry, we eat. If we are cold, we seek shelter. If we are in pain, we find relief. If we desire pleasure, it becomes our focus. On the surface, there is nothing wrong with meeting our basic physical needs, but these needs make us easy prey for the devourer.

Our enemy, the devil, roams around like a lion seeking whom he might devour.[239] Our vulnerability to the devourer is the fallout of the disconnection between our spirit and our Creator. Human beings have free will to choose what leads them. We can choose to submit to God

---

[237] Genesis 3
[238] John 3:3
[239] 1 Peter 5:8

and His way, or we can choose to submit to our animalistic drives. Abuse, abortion, slavery, sex trafficking, and violence are the direct result of this submission. They are the consequences of a society devoid of love.

The Preservation of Human Dignity

Preserving the dignity of other humans is one of our highest callings. Anyone anywhere can do it, but it is a conscious choice. The pro-life community has long known this to be true, but often, people focus on activism at the doors of abortion facilities, debate on public policy, or efforts to influence legislation. These are truly of utmost importance, but they are not the entirety of the calling.

We must rescue those drawn toward death.[240] By standing at the doors of abortion facilities, we save the lives of unborn children. We protect women from harm, and we preserve the future of families. As the days become more evil and assisted suicide spreads across the country, we will need to be there as well.

Public debate and discussion must ensue. Ethical justifications for abuse and murder will always be with us. People will continue to deny the intrinsic value of human beings, as long as they are not wholly dedicated to acknowledging the Divine nature of human dignity.

We must be involved in the enactment of legislation as well. The law is a teacher. It is by the law that children and adults appreciate external controls for their behavior.[241] Both punishments and rewards are found in the law. Protections for the weak and vulnerable establish a contrived

---

[240] Proverbs 24:11

[241] All law, by its nature, legislates someone's (the lawmaker's) morality over someone else's. Our prisons are full of people who deny someone else's morality.

respect. Not by nature, but by fear do we pay our taxes, refrain from stealing, and drive by the rules of the road. No law will stop the truly corrupt. Here, the law is only a stopgap and a way of retribution.

Exceptions for Human Dignity?

Laws with exceptions for certain humans do not consistently support human dignity and create loopholes for subversion, whether they apply to abortion, assisted suicide, or freedom of speech and religion. Therefore, we must work toward laws that uphold protection for all. For example, right now in America, there are hundreds of thousands of children and adults being sold into slavery, used and abused sexually, trafficked, and taken to abortion facilities to be further traumatized. Laws that exclude them from protection are the height of demoralization for these victims. At the same time, these laws perpetuate a deeper social stigma. By setting this segment of the population up as targets for the abortion industry, their captors and buyers are enabled and emboldened. We acknowledge that abortion is bad for women, so why would we expect it to be the inverse for a woman or a girl who is already deeply wounded?

Exceptions in law tend to expand, not contract. We see this in abortion law, but also in other areas. For example, assisted suicide laws typically focus on the terminally ill, but exceptions might exist for people diagnosed with depression who do not find relief after a specific period of time. What protection is that? Depression is treatable with a variety of means and may wax and wane throughout the years. Logic requires consistency.

Why Consistency Is Paramount

Valid law is applicable at all times and in all situations. Like gravity, lift may counteract it, but the law is always operating. A law prohibiting murder should always prohibit murder. Even if the retribution may be mitigated, the prohibition stands in every case.

Pro-life laws vary in scope and consequence. They do not merely prohibit abortion, but actively promote protection from other harms as well. From adoption to safeguarding regulations for healthcare facilities, many laws seek to protect human beings from imposed death. It is our duty to expand the definition of pro-life to include the active participation in protecting every human being divinely entrusted to us. We must be present at abortion facilities when we can. We must engage in debate and discussion about the value of human life at every opportunity and help enact pro-life laws and policies locally and nationally.

Although each of these pro-life endeavors is essential, it is important to remember that not everyone has the capacity to participate in all of them. We are unique in our gifts and abilities, in our ages and stages of life, and in the environments in which we live. We may be involved in any one of these efforts at any point in our lives. However, promoting a life-affirming culture is incumbent upon every single one of us.

We can promote a culture of life by being kind to orphans and shut-ins, feeding the hungry, assisting the disadvantaged, respecting everyone with no regard to their economic or social status, caring for the sick, and practicing self-control in every situation—even remaining calm in traffic. When we allow the Spirit of our loving Creator to guide us, we recognize the multitude of opportunities we have to engage in promoting the pro-life ethic. And our efforts, whatever they may focus on, can simply flow from love.

[Darlene Pawlik is a wife, mother of five grown children, and grandmother of two. She served her home state of New Hampshire for 25 years in various positions at New Hampshire Right to Life (NHRTL), including terms as president, chair of the Educational Trust, and chair of the Political Action Committee. She currently serves as a member of the NHRTL PAC, an affiliate of Personhood Alliance. Darlene is Vice President of Save the 1, a global ministry concerned with protecting the people often referred to as the 'hard cases' in the abortion debate, and is a writer and speaker at TheDarlingPrincess.com, which seeks to provide educational support to anti-human trafficking efforts.]

SECTION III

PERSONHOOD AND MEDICAL ETHICS

CHAPTER 10

PERSONHOOD PROTECTS THE MOST VULNERABLE

By Brad and Jesi Smith, Personhood Michigan; founders of Keeping Our Faith; speakers at Save the 1

Our youngest daughter, Faith, has Trisomy 18, a chromosome abnormality that we were told was "incompatible with life." Trisomy 18, or Edwards Syndrome, carries a difficult prognosis— 90% of children born alive with Trisomy 18 do not reach their first birthday. We are thankful to report that, today, Faith is a happy, beautiful, eight-year-old little girl living and thriving with disability. Yet, it was not always this way. Our journey to this point has been a battle.

Right from the beginning, when doctors found indications of disability during a routine ultrasound, we encountered many medical professionals who believed our daughter had a life unworthy of living and thus, refused to treat her. We, on the other hand, were medical novices. We chose our four older children's doctors by looking to see if their office plants were living. We were in for a crash course in the midst of a medical field, and a society, that deems only some worthy of care. As we learned to advocate for our daughter, new terms became a part of our vocabulary, like lethal neglect, slow code, and the phrase, "denying my child access to care."

This experience has dramatically impacted our lives. Our journey in fighting for Faith's care has led us on a mission to create a more transparent medical field that gives parents and their children, regardless of prognosis or disability, honesty from medical professionals regarding treatment options and care.

Slow Code: Hastening the Death of the Disabled

At this time, Faith was 2 ½ years old and began to have some serious illnesses that almost took her life several times. We thought they were helping. Every time we took Faith to the hospital for breathing distress and bronchial issues, they would nurse her back to health. The hospital provided the basic care that we assumed any other child would receive. However, we had an opportunity to meet Senator Rick Santorum whose little girl Bella also has Trisomy 18. Rick gave us advice that we had never heard from a single doctor. At first, we were somewhat skeptical as he shared a list of things that we should be doing to advocate for Faith's care. His honest and straightforward advice convinced us that, if we did not do these things, we were going to lose our daughter.

When we showed the list to the doctors, their response was, "Nobody does this!" We were shocked. We pushed to get them to help us, but after Faith's third hospital visit for the same problem and a near-death experience, we finally figured it out. The doctors were not going to treat her. We had returned again and again because we expected the doctors to help us. We trusted them without realizing that trust must be earned.

During this journey, we researched many medical journals on Trisomy 18, and this is where we first stumbled upon the term slow code. In *slow code*, medical providers either restrict treatment options they offer, or they offer the appearance of treatment, but knowingly administer it so slowly that it is useless to the patient. Obviously, this is not care, but lethal neglect or intentional death—otherwise known as murder. We realize this may sound crazy, like something we might make up. We assure you, it is real. In one article we found in the *Journal of Perinatology*, a pediatric ethics committee discussed slow code as a possible solution for an infant with a poor prognosis in the neonatal intensive care unit. The parents had been offered CPR as a treatment option, but this option was later withdrawn through a do not attempt resuscitation (DNAR) order the doctors placed on the infant's record. The ethics committee debated the placement of the DNAR order, but only in terms of whether CPR should have been offered in the first place.[242] Ultimately, the committee decided that, in this case, it was deceitful to use slow code, but the fact that it was considered a legitimate option is troubling.

We not only learned about the theory of slow code from reading industry journals, but we experienced it for ourselves in practice, in our struggle to treat our daughter. Faith had severe sleep apnea, which went untreated. She had a small jaw that caused dangerous complications, but no one would correct the problem. At that time, however, we were

---

[242] Mercurio, M. (2011). The role of a pediatric ethics committee in the newborn intensive care unit. *Journal of Perinatology, 31*: 1-9. Retrieved from http://tinyurl.com/2vny4g2

novices. We were not even aware that these problems had solutions. We were not even offered what we now know to be basic treatment.

All we wanted was for the medical professionals we encountered to deal with us in good faith. We made appointments and paid our medical bills believing that if they could not or would not treat our daughter, they would be transparent with us. Hidden hospital policies and personal biases against the disabled denied vital medical care for Faith—almost taking her life. Due to our experience with multiple hospitals, we began a journey to change Michigan law in order to stop this deadly bias.

Our Push to Protect the Vulnerable

In June, 2013, the Medical Good-Faith Provisions Act[243] was signed into law to require medical facilities to provide information about life-sustaining treatments they are willing and unwilling to offer patients. Beyond our work to give Michigan families the transparency they deserve, we speak as part of Save the 1.[244] We share our story and talk about the dangerous path our country is headed down when it comes to medical ethics for the disabled and the preborn. We are also actively engaged in the creation of a trisomy clinic to help children like Faith not only survive, but thrive. While on this journey in our own family and on behalf of others, we began to realize that many in the pro-life movement were willing to compromise on protections for the disabled.

---

[243] Medical Good-Faith Provisions Act. (2013). State of Michigan 97th legislature. S.B. 165: Public Act 57. See: http://www.legislature.mi.gov/documents/2013-2014/publicact/pdf/2013-PA-0057.pdf

[244] Founded by Rebecca Kiessling, herself conceived in rape, Save The 1's mission is to "educate everyone on why all preborn children should be protected by law and accepted by society, without exception and without compromise." See: http://www.savethe1.com/about/

Pro-Life or Discriminatory?

In May of 2016, many in the pro-life community celebrated as the South Carolina House voted 79-29 to pass the South Carolina Pain Capable Unborn Child Protection Act.[245] This bill protects preborn children from abortion after 20 weeks, due to their ability to feel pain—except for those with "severe fetal anomalies."

Rejecting through law the disabled child's equal humanity and right to life is far from a victory. Where is the disabled child's equal protection under the law? Children with disability feel pain, too. There is no master race, no superior group of people, no elite class that alone deserves to be protected by the law, while the disabled are considered less than human and administered death as if it were a cure. Only by declaring ourselves something more can we treat a child with disability as something less.

We applaud those legislators who fight the good fight for life, not compromising on equal protection for the disabled, but we also remember the victims in this battle. They suffer more than just legislative defeat—they suffer death.[246] These children, unoffending, innocent, and beautiful, are most often abandoned twice—once by those who want to prevent them from entering society in the first place and secondly by

---

[245] South Carolina Pain Capable Unborn Child Protection Act. (2016). State of South Carolina. 121st session. (A183, R196, H3114). See: http://www.scstatehouse.gov/sess121_2015-2016/bills/3114.htm

[246] In 2013, the Georgia legislature inserted deadly exceptions for fetal anomaly in their 20-week pain capable bill. In the waning hour of the last day of the session, five Senators added a lethal bias against those with fetal anomalies. Georgia Right to Life, the sponsor of the bill, withdrew their endorsement and instructed their PAC to expose the senators. At the time of this writing, four of the five senators no longer serve in the Georgia Senate.

those who claim victory while removing protections for the most vulnerable.

If we point out that South Carolina's bill is an abandonment of disabled children, will we be branded as disloyal to the pro-life cause? Probably, but no person of integrity that wishes to save the lives of our most vulnerable citizens can remain indifferent when the law holds the lives of the disabled in contempt. They alone were singled out for legal destruction. South Carolina must not let them be forgotten.

It is important to remember that "exceptions" to equal protection under the law were the method by which abortion was first justified and eventually, made legal. In 1962, the American Law Institute (ALI) released the final version of its Model Penal Code, which provided legal recommendations on various criminal, civil, and social issues to the states.[247] This code recommended the legalization of abortion in cases of fetal anomaly, rape and incest conception, and mental and physical health of the mother.[248] When states began to decriminalize abortion in 1967, they cited the ALI's code as the foundation for their legislative efforts.[249]

Targeting the most vulnerable and the least wanted was the way abortion advocates decriminalized this abhorrent practice in the first place. Only by rescuing these targeted children and declaring their

---

[247] Robinson, P.H., & Dubber, M.D. (2012). An introduction to the model penal code. Retrieved from https://www.law.upenn.edu/fac/phrobins /intromodpencode.pdf

[248] Tinnelly, J. T., CM. (2016). Abortion and penal law. Retrieved from http://scholarship.law.stjohns.edu/cgi/viewcontent.cgi?article=1254&context=tc l

[249] Ibid.

absolute, natural, God-given right to life will we end it. As G.K. Chesterton warned, "Evil always takes advantage of ambiguity." [250] Legislators must not be ambiguous. Instead, they must be clear in their intentions to stand by the most vulnerable and not betray them.

Jonah's Story

The story of Jonah illustrates the targeting of the disabled, both inside and outside the womb. Jonah was diagnosed *in utero* with Trisomy 18's "severe fetal anomalies." His parents, Heather and Greg, did not abort but could have, given South Carolina law. They quickly learned that, not only would they battle Trisomy 18 to save their son, but they would also battle the hospital to keep him alive. Even after Heather and Greg found a hospital willing to help Jonah, they had to fight the insurance company who refused to pay for a potentially life-saving heart surgery. Tom Lockhart, a man unknown to the family, donated $39,000 to help Jonah get the necessary surgery.[251] What Tom did for a little boy he did not know should be a clarion call to legislators to stand up for the least among us. What about the doctors themselves? Does their patient advocacy change when a disability is present?

---

[250] Chesterton, G. K. (1922). *Eugenics and other evils*. London. ISBN: 153539238X.

[251] Deiters, B. (2016). $39K donation to send baby to Ohio for surgery. Retrieved from http://woodtv.com/2016/05/18/39k-donation-to-send-baby-to-ohio-for-surgery/

PHYSICIAN-ASSISTED DEATH FOR CHILDREN WITH POOR PROGNOSES

In 2016, the *Journal of Medical Ethics* published a survey conducted among practicing neonatologists.[252] The survey revealed that 76% of neonatologists thought it was ethically permissible to issue a DNAR order without asking or notifying an infant's parents when they "felt it impossible" for the child to survive. 61% of the neonatologists said a DNAR without parental consent was permissible when survival was "unlikely."[253] Let us look at this in practice.

Lane Hauber's first few days of life in the hospital were difficult, but staff had been optimistic about his upcoming heart surgery. Everything changed on the third day when Lane was diagnosed with an extra 18th chromosome. Lane's father, Alex, arrived in the Neonatal Intensive Care Unit for a visit and found a DNAR order in the paperwork attached to his son's crib. When Alex and his wife, Alisha, asked who had put the DNAR in his file, they were ushered into a private room with the doctor and told the hospital could make the decision to place a DNAR on a patient without the parent's approval.[254] Alisha explained:

> *"We were devastated...Not only did we get the shock of the diagnosis, but now we were being told that we had zero rights in making medical decisions for our son. The hospital sent us home*

---

[252] Murray, P.D., Esserman, D., & Mercurio, M. (2016). In what circumstances will a neonatologist decide a patient is not a resuscitation candidate? Journal of Medical Ethics. Retrieved from http://tinyurl.com/zkhg7sd

[253] Symons, X. (2016). Unilateral 'do not resuscitate' orders: What do doctors think? Retrieved from http://www.bioedge.org/bioethics/unilateral-do-not-resuscitate-orders-what-doctors-think/11807

[254] Smith, J. (2016). Shock study: 76% of doctors say it's OK to put DNR on disabled baby without telling his parents. Retrieved from http://www.lifenews.com/2016/03/24/shock-study-76-of-doctors-say-its-ok-to-put-dnr-on-disabled-baby-without-telling-his-parents/

> *with zero information, zero support, and told us that we might have a week at most with our son."*

Lane is now eight years old and lives with unrepaired holes in his heart. His parents question what kind of life their son could have had if given equal treatment and rights as a patient.

> *"We felt lied to by the hospital, and angry about our child not being treated like a human being. Why is it ok to take away parental rights? Aren't we the ones that have to live with the consequences of our decisions?"*

When a neonatologist neglects a patient based on many unknowable qualities and capacities at birth, that care can neither be called scientific nor compassionate.

VIOLATION OF INFORMED CONSENT

Lane's parents initially assumed the doctors were acting in good faith toward their son eight years ago. As revealed in the neonatologist survey, however, the vast majority of doctors would treat Lane the same way today.[255] Their chilling admission shows that, by and large, these doctors do not see informed consent as an important professional responsibility, particularly with their most vulnerable patients. It is reminiscent of the infamous Tuskegee Study of Untreated Syphilis in the Negro Male.[256] In this experiment, which began in 1932, doctors never informed participants that the study's purpose was to show the consequences of untreated syphilis in black men in the rural South. Doctors also did not

---

[255] Ibid., Murray, Esserman, & Mercurio

[256] Tuskegee University. (2017). About the USPHS syphilis study. Retrieved from http://www.tuskegee.edu/about_us/centers_of_excellence /bioethics_center/about_the_usphs_syphilis_study.aspx

inform the men of the consequences of treatment or non-treatment and how that would affect their families. Even when penicillin became a standard treatment for syphilis during the 40 years of the study, the men were never informed. Many died over the course of the study, and their wives and children became infected.

Any patient whose standard medical care is deliberately and secretly withheld is being treated as less than human. Whether this lack of ethical behavior is a reflection of the attitude in society or in the medical professional, or both, it should elicit a huge outcry from those who advocate for vulnerable patients. Thankfully, a class action lawsuit filed on behalf of participants and families, awarded $9 million in 1973. President Bill Clinton apologized to the victims in 1997:

> *"The people who ran the study...diminished the stature of man by abandoning the most basic ethical precepts. They forgot their pledge to heal and repair."*[257]

But where is Lane's apology? If neonatologists cannot be trusted to treat and be transparent, where are children like Lane to go? To neglect the patient's right to standard treatment and informed consent, based on subjective assessments that are little more than one doctor's best guess at the moment, is not just ethically unjustified, it is evil.

THERE IS HOPE

At the opening of this chapter, we shared the statistic that 90% of children born with Trisomy 18 will not reach their first birthday. Sadly,

---

[257] CNN. (1997). Clinton apologizes to Tuskegee experiment victims. Retrieved from http://www.cnn.com/ALLPOLITICS/1997/05/16/tuskegee.apology/

most medical professionals encourage parents to abort children diagnosed with Trisomy 18, not even giving them a chance at birth. Even more sadly, the vast majority of these parents end up killing their own children. The outlook seems desperately grim, but there is hope.

Dr. Glenn Green, who is Faith's ENT, has helped her live by simply treating her airway. He has become a leading physician for Trisomy children. We have referred numerous families to him because of his great care, and he now has over 20 Trisomy 18 patients. Dr. Green's dedication to caring for the disabled has resulted in a 90% *survival rate* in children reaching their first birthday. Most of his Trisomy 18 patients are living well beyond this milestone. These children, when given the help they deserve and need, not only survive, but thrive. They are filled with joy and make the people around them better and more compassionate human beings.

[Brad and Jesi Smith are the parents of five children. In 2013, they testified and helped secure unanimous votes in the Michigan House and Senate to pass the Medical Good Faith Act, named after their youngest daughter Faith who has Trisomy 18, to require transparency for the sick and disabled in medical facilities. They actively speak around the country as members of Save the 1, a global group that seeks to protect the 'hard cases' in the abortion debate. They both serve on the Mott Children's Hospital Patient and Family Centered Care Board, and Brad also serves on the Personhood Alliance board as the Michigan delegate.]

CHAPTER 11

Personhood and the Life of the Mother

By Dr. J. Patrick Johnston, D.O., Director, Association of Pro-Life Physicians; President, Personhood Ohio

There is a pro-life rebellion afoot—a rising movement that distinguishes itself from the mainstream pro-life factions by its unwavering stance on biblical personhood. State-level Personhood amendments, the movement's major strategy, define *person* to include preborn children in an attempt to end abortion without waiting for the Supreme Court's permission to do so. Opponents of these Personhood amendments not only include abortion advocates, but also, unfortunately, most mainstream pro-life organizations, though for strikingly different reasons.

What has precipitated this schism in the pro-life movement, whose divisions are increasingly at odds with one another? Over one million people have signed Personhood petitions in state ballot initiatives, and states have brought Personhood amendments to the ballot box three times, largely without the support of mainstream pro-life organizations.

Some pro-life leaders have gone so far as to officially oppose and actively work against the very measures with which they claim to agree in principle. Why?

First, pro-life leaders embrace the myth of judicial supremacy—that is, they believe our obligation to submit to the judiciary is unconditional, even as the judiciary defies the law of God and the laws of the land.[258] These leaders would rather oppose Personhood Amendments and other total abortion bans than risk losing the case in the Supreme Court.[259] Ignoring the troubled history of Republican judicial appointees over the last five decades,[260] they continue to shut their eyes and cross their fingers, hoping for that elusive pro-life majority on the High Court. However, after 44 years and 59 million dead, Republican political leaders throw us no more crumbs than that which are necessary to gain our support.

Secondly, mainstream pro-life leaders oppose Personhood amendments and other total abortion bans because they do not include exceptions. In 2006, for example, President George W. Bush opposed South Dakota's abortion ban because it did not include exceptions in cases of rape, incest, and maternal health.[261] Likewise, many pro-life leaders today would rather avoid political fallout and wait for "the right time" than protect all preborn children from abortion.

---

[258] The myth of judicial supremacy is addressed thoroughly elsewhere in this book.

[259] Johnston, P., Dr. (2006). National Right to Life: The Judas of the Preborn. Retrieved from https://www.newswithviews.com/Johnston/ patrick.htm

[260] American Right to Life. (2015). Has Judge Gorsuch ever said... Retrieved from http://americanrtl.org/judge-neil-gorsuch-anti-abortion-qualifications-unproven

[261] Ibid., Johnston

Answering the Exceptions

The exceptions of rape, incest, and fetal anomaly are addressed thoroughly elsewhere in this book. However, I must point out here that we should never abandon our principles in our response to even the most difficult, heart-wrenching scenarios. These exceptions can and should be answered without shame or hesitation from the unshakeable foundation of these two indisputable premises:

1. Human life begins at fertilization.
2. It is always wrong to intentionally kill an innocent human being.

Scientific fact proves the first premise conclusively.[262] Nothing *after* fertilization makes you any more human or any more alive than the moment *of* fertilization.[263] Scripture tells us that Rebecca's twins "struggled together within her."[264] Mary was "great with child."[265] Job spoke of "a man child [who] was conceived," not a blob of tissue.[266] David said he existed in his mother's womb. He was not something else that became him later on.[267] Exodus 21:22-23 prescribed a "life for a life" penalty for killing a preborn child through negligent carelessness. What more evidence do we need to prove that God values the preborn lives He knits together in the womb?[268]

---

[262] Princeton University. (2017). Life begins at fertilization. Retrieved from https://www.princeton.edu/~prolife/articles/embryoquotes2.html
[263] Sarfati, J. (1998). Abortion: The answer's in genesis. Retrieved from http://creation.com/abortion-the-answers-in-genesis
[264] Genesis 25:22
[265] Luke 2:5
[266] Job 3:3
[267] Psalm 51:5
[268] Psalm 139:13

The exceptions of rape, incest, fetal anomaly, and maternal health, when evaluated, are really just smoke and mirrors. If I held an infant in my arms and informed a crowd of pro-abortion advocates that the child was disabled and conceived through rape and that the mother was extremely depressed that the child was still living, would any of them propose that the infant be killed? Of course not. The circumstances surrounding conception are irrelevant. Making such justifications for abortion are insincere attempts to distract from the true point of contention in the debate: *When does life begin*? The justification of abortion for the life of the mother seems most difficult to uproot from pro-life policies and as such, that is the subject I would like to address.

Exceptions in the Bible

Some have argued that the intentional killing of a preborn baby to save the life of the mother is justified in Scripture.[269] The mother, it is argued, has the right to lethal force in self-defense of her property (her body), and if there is no malice, her act of killing another is innocent. But does abortion for the life of the mother meet the biblical criteria for justified killing?

In God's law as well as our laws, the non-malicious killing of a person—accidental killing and killing in self-defense or defense of another—is not murder. Biblical statutes for justifiable killing, however, were governed carefully in Israel's God-penned criminal code, as they are in our modern laws, and for good reason. For example, imagine if a

---

[269] Christ Covenant Church. (2015). Abortion due to mother's health risk. Retrieved from http://christcovenant.org/who-we-are-section/gya-momhealthrisk.htm?

criminal intentionally ran over an innocent person, claiming he lost control of his vehicle, or if a homeowner shot a teenager who stepped off the sidewalk and trespassed onto his land a few feet. To avoid such usurpations, the following principles govern justifiable killing in God's Word:

1. If a person is killed accidentally, in order to be blameless, the act must not be pre-meditated. It must genuinely be accidental and non-malicious.[270]
2. No carelessness can be associated with the act that resulted in the death. Driving under the influence of controlled substances, or texting and driving, for example, would make the act criminal, even if non-malicious.[271]
3. Justifiable homicide only applies to force used against a person who is in the process of committing a crime, in self-defense or in defense of another, and is not pre-meditated. Moreover, no more force can be applied than what is safely and reasonably necessary to stop the crime and protect the innocent.[272]
4. Whether the death is accidental, or whether it is intentional and justified, the person who killed another was to travel to the nearest "city of refuge," and if he or she was caught outside of the city of refuge, the loved one of the dead victim could kill that person and be guiltless. Within the city of refuge, however, they were safe until the trial.[273]

---

[270] Exodus 21:12-14; Deuteronomy 19:4-13
[271] Exodus 21:22-23, 28-29
[272] Exodus 22:2-3
[273] Deuteronomy 19

God's Priority Is Life

These principles reveal to us God's priority of preserving life. Even if killing another person was truly unintentional and non-malicious, to avoid execution, the person had to uproot his family and travel to the city of refuge with haste. Killing a person, even by accident, is a serious matter. Criminal justice in God's law errs on the side of protecting the innocent, not on the side of the person who non-maliciously kills another. Applying these biblical principles to our subject matter, two questions arise:

1. Is the intentional killing of the innocent preborn child reasonably necessary to save the mother's life?
2. Are there other ways to protect the mother besides intentionally killing the child?

Since I began to write on this subject, many pro-life women have tearfully informed me of life-threatening illnesses during their pregnancies that justified their therapeutic abortions. Sadly, these women adhere to these justifications based on demonstrably false information given to them by their physicians. In my 16 years as a family practice physician and pro-life speaker, I have never heard of one case in which the intentional killing of a baby was necessary to save the mother's life. Other physicians, and even former abortionists, concur.[274]

---

[274] U.S. House of Representatives. (2013, May 23). Testimony of Dr. Anthony Levatino before the Subcommittee on the Constitution and Civil Justice. Retrieved from http://judiciary.house.gov/_files/hearings/113th /05232013/Levatino%2005232013.pdf

WHAT ABOUT CANCER TREATMENT?

In 2013, Answers in Genesis, a well-respected Christian apologetics ministry, published an article titled, "Is Abortion Ever Justifiable?"[275] In this article, the physician author justified abortion to save the life of a mother with aggressive leukemia who required immediate chemotherapy treatment "that is virtually certain to kill the unborn child." If postponing chemotherapy is too risky for the mother, the author argued, the doctor is justified in advising "immediate abortion."[276] Is this justification compatible with scientific fact?

The chemotherapy necessary to save the life of the leukemia patient in this scenario would be *just as effective* whether the patient were pregnant or not. Moreover, a 2012 study reported in *The Lancet Oncology* found little evidence of negative health effects on the infants of breast cancer patients who underwent chemotherapy during pregnancy.[277] Delay of cancer treatment did "not significantly affect disease-free survival" for the women in this study, and chemotherapy was found to be relatively safe after the first trimester.[278]

Almost all physicians recommend an abortion before they will prescribe chemotherapy. This is not to save the mother's life, however, but to protect the physician from litigation. I have witnessed physicians

---

[275] On February 26, 2013, as printed in *Answers* magazine, Dr. Tommy Mitchell, a physician and AIG speaker, authored the article, "Is Abortion Ever Justifiable?" The article has since been removed from online access.

[276] Johnston, P., Dr. (2013). With the compromise of Answers in Genesis, a giant has fallen. Retrieved from http://www.newswithviews.com/Johnston /patrick146.htm.

[277] Loibl, S., MD, et al. (2012). Treatment of breast cancer during pregnancy: An observational study. *The Lancet Oncology, 13*(9): 887–896. Retrieved from http://tinyurl.com/8p5kqlw.

[278] Ibid.

withhold life-saving care from a pregnant mother unless she agrees to an abortion, not because the abortion was necessary to save her life, but because they feared the treatment they planned to prescribe would harm the baby and therefore, lead to a lawsuit.

What About HELLP Syndrome and Chorioamnionitis?

HELLP syndrome is a pregnancy complication that occurs mostly in the third trimester and is considered to be a variation of preeclampsia.[279] *Chorioamnionitis* is a bacterial infection of the *chorion* (outer membrane) and *amnion* (fluid-filled sac) that can affect the amniotic fluid, placenta, and the baby itself.[280]

The medical literature declares that, in chorioamnionitis and HELLP Syndrome, "facilitating delivery" may be necessary to save the life of the mother.[281] Can a doctor facilitate delivery without dismembering the baby? Absolutely. Granted, the premature delivery may inadvertently result in the death of the child, but the physician should do everything in his power to save the mother and the baby. If the mother's life is truly threatened, the premature delivery may be the best way to save the baby, not just the mother, because if the mother dies, so does the baby. If through the doctor's careful treatment of the mother's illness the preborn baby inadvertently dies or is injured, this is a tragedy, not an abortion. If the death is unintentional and not careless, it is consistent

---

[279] Preeclampsia Foundation. (2015). HELLP syndrome. Retrieved from https://www.preeclampsia.org/health-information/hellp-syndrome

[280] Tita, A.T., MD, PhD, & Andrews, W.W., MD, PhD. (2010). Diagnosis and management of clinical chorioamnionitis. *Clinical Perinatology, 37*(2):339-354. Retrieved from https://www.ncbi.nlm.nih.gov/pmc/articles /PMC3008318/

[281] Ibid.

with the Hippocratic Oath and the law of God. The intentional killing of a preborn baby through abortion, however, is a grievous violation of both.

In an extensive conversation with the physician author of the Answers in Genesis article and another doctor on staff at the ministry, I learned that HELLP Syndrome and chorioamnionitis were also justifications for abortion. These physicians asserted that if the premature delivery resulted in the death of the baby, then the outcome was the same: The baby died, just as if an abortion was performed. Therefore, they argued, we should do what is best for the mother, even if that means aborting the baby. Let us look closer at this claim.

Outcomes and Moral Equivalence

First, the outcome is not necessarily the same. If a baby is delivered prematurely, the baby may survive. The earliest surviving premature infant, Kenya King of Orlando, Florida, was born at 21 weeks.[282] Consider that due dates could be incorrect as well, and the baby may be further along than expected. However, if a baby Kenya's age is dismembered (as in dilation and evacuation abortion) or she is injected with a drug to stop the heart (as in induction abortion), what are her chances of survival then? The outcomes are not always identical. Just because the baby may die through a natural delivery or survive only for a short time does not justify an intentional killing.

Consider the burning building analogy. If a rescuer ventures into a burning building to try to save two trapped occupants and is only able to

---

[282] Ditlev-Simonsen, C. (1985). Baby who beat odds finally heads home. Retrieved from http://articles.sun-sentinel.com/1985-10-04/news/8502140900_1_healthy-baby-dimples-plantation-general-hospital

save one, is he justified in shooting the one he was unable to save? Of course not. We have the technology and expertise to provide quality healthcare to a pregnant woman without intentionally killing her preborn child, regardless of the severity of her disease.

Secondly, it is self-evident that intentionally killing a preborn child is morally different than delivering a baby prematurely (to save the life of the mother *and* the baby) only to have the baby die in spite of a physician's care. Trying to save a baby's life and failing is not morally equivalent to deliberately taking the baby's life. An abortion violates God's law because it intends to kill an innocent person, whereas premature delivery does not. One is violent and cruel, the other heroic and compassionate.

Pennsylvania abortionist Kermit Gosnell was found guilty in the deaths of born-alive infants who survived his late-term abortion procedures.[283] A friend of mine recently miscarried and, in spite of the physician's efforts, the baby died peacefully in her parents' arms. In both of these cases, children died. The outcomes were the same, but the acts were not at all morally equivalent.

Redefining What It Means to be Pro-Life

Many pro-life and Christian medical groups concur that abortion is never necessary to save the mother's life, including:

- The Association of Pro-Life Physicians
- The American Association of Pro-Life Ob/Gyns

---

[283] Associated Press/Fox News. (2013). Doctor Kermit Gosnell found guilty of murdering infants in late-term abortions. Retrieved from http://www.foxnews.com/us/2013/05/13/jury-split-on-2-counts-in-trial-abortion-doctor-kermit-gosnell.html

- The Christian Medical Association
- The Catholic Medical Association
- Personhood Alliance and its many state affiliates
- American Right to Life
- Georgia Right to Life
- Colorado Right to Life
- The Dublin Declaration on Maternal Healthcare[284]

Former Surgeon General C. Everett Koop held that abortion was never needed to save the life of the mother. "In my 36 years in pediatric surgery," he said, "I have never known of one instance where the child had to be aborted to save the mother's life."[285] Congressman and obstetrician Ron Paul concurred, saying he never saw an abortion that was medically necessary.[286] Even Planned Parenthood's Dr. Alan Guttmacher acknowledged:

> *"Today it is possible for almost any patient to be brought through pregnancy alive, unless she suffers from a fatal illness such as*

---

[284] "As experienced practitioners and researchers in obstetrics and gynecology, we affirm that direct abortion – the purposeful destruction of the unborn child – is not medically necessary to save the life of a woman. We uphold that there is a fundamental difference between abortion and necessary medical treatments that are carried out to save the life of the mother, even if such treatment results in the loss of her unborn child. We confirm that the prohibition of abortion does not affect, in any way, the availability of optimal care to pregnant women." See http://www.dublin declaration.com/

[285] Bohon, D. (2013). Former U.S. Surgeon General remembered for his pro-life stand. http://tinyurl.com/zjhlcs4 Retrieved February 15, 2017.

[286] Paul, R., MD. (2007). Statement of faith. Retrieved from http://www.covenantnews.com/ron-paul-statement-of-faith-ron-paul-statement-of-faith/

> *cancer or leukemia, and if so, abortion would be unlikely to prolong, much less save, life."*[287]

What About an Ectopic Pregnancy?

In an ectopic pregnancy, the embryo attaches to the mother's body in a place other than the *endometrium* (the inner lining of the uterus). Complications include hemorrhage and tubal rupture, in which the mother can lose vital amounts of blood. Ectopic pregnancies are, without a doubt, serious tragedies that can result in the death of the mother and the preborn child, but is the intentional killing of the child really necessary to save the mother's life? The aforementioned physicians at Answers in Genesis asserted that it is. Let us look at the scientific evidence.

There are several cases in the medical literature where preborn children have survived ectopic pregnancies. You can hear the testimony of a survivor in a powerful documentary, *Pro-Life Without Exception.*[288] Cases in which embryos naturally unattach from the fallopian tube and reattach elsewhere are well-documented.[289,290] Procedures to surgically remove the embryo from the fallopian tube and implant it into the uterus

---

[287] Guttmacher, A. F. (1967). *The case for legalized abortion now.* Berkeley, CA: Diablo Press.

[288] Humphrey, K. [Director]. (2014). Pro-life without Exception. [Documentary film]. Retrieved from https://www.amazon.com/Life-Without-Exception-Keith-Humphrey/dp/B00K5EJF3Y

[289] Fortenberry, B. (2015). Ectopic personhood. Retrieved from http://www.personhoodinitiative.com/ectopic-personhood.html

[290] Fortenberry, B. (2015). Successful ectopic pregnancies. Retrieved from http://www.personhoodinitiative.com/successful-ectopic-pregnancies.html

have also been successful.[291] There is at least one American physician who is willing to perform embryo transplantation to try to save these preborn children.[292]

Several large studies have confirmed that expectant management of ectopic pregnancies, which is appropriate in cases where the risk of tubal rupture is low, can lead to spontaneous regression of the tubal ectopic pregnancy the vast majority of the time.[293] One historic study documented a 57% spontaneous resolution rate of tubal ectopic pregnancies, with rates in other studies varying from 48% to 100%.[294] In all of these cases, informed consent and close observation throughout pregnancy is critical. If physicians are to be governed by evidence-based medicine, we cannot deny this evidence and claim that abortion is necessary to save the life of the mother in cases of ectopic pregnancy.

It is important to note that, if expectant management fails and the ectopic pregnancy does not spontaneously resolve, surgery may become necessary to save the life of the mother, particularly in the case of tubal rupture. However, it is likely at this point that the embryo has already overgrown his or her blood supply and succumbed to death. Nevertheless, with the mother's life imminently threatened by hemorrhaging, a removal of the embryo may be necessary to save the life of the mother. Autotransfusion, in which the mother's hemorrhaged

---

[291] Shettles, L. (1990). Tubal embryo successfully transplanted in utero. *American Journal of Obstetrics and Gynecology, 163*: 20-26. Retrieved from http://tinyurl.com/jzpub2e

[292] Dr. Patrick J. Baggott, M.D., 3020 Wilshire Blvd. Ste. 219, Los Angeles, CA 90010

[293] Tulandi, T., MD. (2017). Ectopic pregnancy: Expectant management. http://www.uptodate.com/contents/ectopic-pregnancy-expectant-management

[294] Ibid.

blood is suctioned from the pelvic cavity, filtered, and reinserted via venous access, had a success rate in one study greater than the surgical remedy for ruptured ectopic pregnancy.[295] In each case, the physician should do everything possible to save the preborn child as well as the mother.

Contrary to the evidence presented, physicians often recommend a chemical abortifacient, methotrexate, in women with early tubal ectopic pregnancies in order to decrease the chances of hemorrhage or a surgical alternative being necessary later. I have found this to be an unnecessary risk to human life. I offer the following case to demonstrate this point.

A Pro-Life Tragedy

One of my patients was diagnosed with a tubal ectopic pregnancy by her obstetrician. He informed her that they were fortunate to have made the diagnosis early and that she should have a methotrexate abortion. The patient was strongly pro-life and did not want to take the medicine, but the physician insisted. The baby was not going to survive, he argued, and a chemical abortion now could prevent the need for a surgical procedure later. The chemical abortion would lessen her chances of a life-threatening rupture of her fallopian tube and could better preserve future fertility than surgical removal of the embryo later. Feeling like she had no other reasonable alternative, and facing the thought of her three daughters motherless, she took the methotrexate. There was an unfortunate complication.

---

[295] Selo-Ojemea, D.O., Onwudea, J.L., & Onwudiegwu, U. (2003). Autotransfusion for ruptured ectopic pregnancy. *International Journal of Gynecology & Obstetrics*, *80*(2): 103-110. Retrieved from https://www.ncbi.nlm.nih.gov/pubmed/12566181

Two weeks later, she continued to experience marked vaginal bleeding and pelvic discomfort. A repeat ultrasound confirmed the physician's worst fears: There was a dead child in the uterus. Either the patient had twins, one in the fallopian tube and one in the uterus, or the embryo in the fallopian tube unattached and reattached in the uterus prior to the chemical abortion. If there were twins, expectant management could have resulted in spontaneous resolution of the tubal pregnancy or surgical removal of the tubal pregnancy when the embryo had likely already died. In both cases, the child in the uterus would have survived. If there were not twins, the embryo that dislodged and reattached in the uterus would be alive today, and the mother would not have suffered such guilt and potentially life-threatening complications.

In Summary

There are no exceptions to the Divine ordinance against intentionally killing innocent people. To embrace exceptions is to usurp God's rule and set up a counterfeit moral standard modeled after Lucifer's example. Too many Christian leaders have abandoned the solid rock of God's Word for the quicksand of relative morality. They have surrendered "Thus saith the Lord" to the father of lies. They may call themselves "pro-life," but if they are willing to justify the intentional killing of one innocent child, I beg to differ.

We should never be swayed from the unshakable foundation of God's law by raw emotional appeals that admittedly swell our eyes with tears. Truth, compassion, and the fear of God should prevent us from this deceitful, fatal compromise.

Personhood

[Dr. Patrick Johnston is a family practice physician and the father of ten home-educated children. He has authored ten novels, including *The Reliant*, which he has produced as a full feature film starring Kevin Sorbo, Brian Bosworth, and Eric Roberts. He also directs ProLifePhysicians.org and Personhood Ohio, but marrying the love of his life, Elizabeth, aka "The Activist Mommy," is his claim to fame.]

SECTION IV

PERSONHOOD AND THE LAW

CHAPTER 12

PERSONHOOD IN VIEW OF *WHOLE WOMAN'S HEALTH V. HELLERSTEDT*

By Gualberto Garcia Jones, Executive Director, International Human Rights Group; Vice President and National Policy Director, Personhood Alliance

"[T]he purpose of the Bill of Rights is to withdraw certain subjects from the vicissitudes of political controversy."

Justice Stevens, citing WVBE v. Barnette in Thornburgh v. ACOG (1986)[296]

The pro-life movement is divided into two general spheres. In one sphere, pro-life lawyers craft legislative strategies to try to unravel an increasingly complex knot of pro-abortion precedent. In the other sphere, pro-life activists talk of saving babies from abortion and engage in educational efforts and crisis pregnancy counseling.

[296] *Thornburgh v. American College of Obstetricians and Gynecologists* (1986). 476 US 747, No. 84-498.

The goals of both spheres are undoubtedly the same, and for decades, pro-life activists have entrusted the legal sphere with the task of ending legalized abortion. Yet, because of the convoluted nature and twisted logic of abortion jurisprudence, pro-life lawyers repeatedly find themselves arguing cases around the edges, never challenging the fundamental assumptions that deprive the child in the womb of legal protection. Some of the most influential pro-life organizations even actively oppose legislation that aims to challenge the central holding of *Roe v. Wade*.[297, 298]

Taking the Preborn Out of the Abortion Equation

When archliberal Justice Stevens voted to invalidate an informed consent law in 1986, he noted that certain "subjects" must be removed from the political process. He was referring to the subject of fundamental rights.[299] Yet, a more accurate reading of the word subject would be the one ascribed to a slave; a person who is under the dominion of another. I conclude that the *Whole Woman's Health v. Hellerstedt* opinion[300] relegated the preborn child to a subject who is under the dominion of another and whose interests and very existence have been removed, not only from the political process but also from the legal one. Here, I will

---

[297] National Right to Life Committee, the nation's most politically influential pro-life organization is opposed to challenging Roe v. Wade and actively works against laws that do so. See: Thomas More Law Center. (2004). NRLC role in defeat of South Dakota legislative effort to ban abortion and challenge Roe v. Wade. Retrieved from http://tinyurl.com/hma9kds

[298] *Roe v. Wade*. (1973). 410 US 113, No. 70-18.

[299] Ibid., United States Supreme Court

[300] United States Supreme Court. (2016). Whole Woman's Health, et al v. Hellerstedt (2016). No. 15-274. Syllabus. Retrieved from https://www.supremecourt.gov/opinions/15pdf/15-274_p8k0.pdf

endeavor to analyze the *Whole Woman's Health v. Hellerstedt* decision and place it within the context of the pro-life movement's goal to protect the right to life of preborn[301] children.

THREE PHASES OF ABORTION LAW

Modern abortion jurisprudence has gone through three phases.[302] The first phase started with *Roe v. Wade* and *Doe v. Bolton* as "an exercise of raw judicial power."[303] During this phase, the court unapologetically legislated from the bench in favor of abortion as a fundamental privacy right. This initial phase saw its apogee in *Thornburgh v. ACOG* (1986)[304] and was driven by Republican-appointed justices Blackmun and Powell.

In 1992, the abortion tide changed, and a new era was ushered in with *Planned Parenthood v. Casey.*[305] Suddenly, states were given more leeway to regulate abortion and as professor Charles Rice predicted, "make it inconvenient"[306] not prohibited. Republican-appointed justices O'Connor and Kennedy captained this second phase, which reached its

---

[301] The term preborn is used instead of the more commonly used unborn to emphasize that the preborn child is not deficient in any way.

[302] Prior to *Roe v. Wade,* there were legislation and court cases that set the stage for *Roe*, but that is beyond the scope of this analysis.

[303] *Doe v. Bolton*. (1973). 410 US 179, No. 70-40. 221-23.

[304] In *Thornburgh*, the court struck down informed consent laws arguing that fetal development may not be relevant to a woman's decision to abort and thus, advances no legitimate interest. The decision also invalidated standard of care regulations and a requirement for a second physician to be available to provide life-saving care after a failed abortion.

[305] *Planned Parenthood of Southeastern Pennsylvania et al v. Casey*. (1992). 505 US 833, No. 91-744.

[306] Rice, C. (1973). The Dred Scott case of the twentieth century. *Houston Law Review*. Retrieved from http://scholarship.law.nd.edu/law_faculty _scholarship/780/

maximum expression in *Gonzalez v. Carhart* in 2007,[307] the Supreme Court's upholding of the Partial-Birth Abortion Ban Act of 2003.[308] The second phase came to an abrupt end in 2016 with the *Hellerstedt* decision, which returned full circle to Blackmun's vision of the court as the protector of the abortion industry. Alarmingly, the *Hellerstedt* decision saw the interests of the child eviscerated from the Constitution to an even greater extent than in *Roe v. Wade* and *Doe v. Bolton*.

A Return to First Principles

Let us examine *Hellerstedt* from the position of the preborn child as a member of the species homo sapiens, or to put it in more classical language, the preborn child as man. That the preborn child is a human being from conception is a scientific fact that embryology has amply proven[309] and should be accepted without great exposition.

This is primarily a legal analysis, and yet as the legal standards constantly evolve, and as laws vary from state to state, the central questions involved in abortion jurisprudence remain the same and are universal. The central core of *Roe v. Wade*'s holding—which is the absolute relegation of the preborn child to "an inferior order ... so far inferior" as to possess "no rights which the" the rest of society "is bound to respect"—strongly resonates with the central holding of *Dred Scott v. Sandford*, which 150 years ago, attempted to relegate people of African

---

[307] *Gonzales v. Carhart*. (2007). 550 US 124, No. 05-380.

[308] Civic Impulse. (2017). S. 3 — 108th Congress: Partial-Birth Abortion Ban Act of 2003. Retrieved from https://www.govtrack.us/congress/bills/ 108/s3

[309] Terzo, S. (2011). When does life begin? Quotes from many sources. Retrieved from http://www.epm.org/resources/2011/Apr/27/when-does-life-begin-quotes-many-sources/

descent to a second class of human beings.[310] The life and death battle that has constitutionalized abortion resonates far beyond its original boundaries. The battle overflows from the field of law to the fields of political and legal philosophy, to our culture, and to the very roots of social justice.

Where do our most fundamental rights come from? And what can we do when these fundamental rights are denied by man-made law? The answers to these two questions construct a frame of reference for analyzing *Hellerstedt* in the context of personhood.

Two Types of Law

Professor Hadley Arkes and other legal philosophers posit that there are two basic types of laws, both of which are binding. There are man-made laws that facilitate the administration of benefits, such as the rules for group membership or even the rights exclusive to citizens of one country. There is a second, higher law, which applies to all human beings regardless of their membership in a particular group, and which governments are bound to respect if they are to remain legitimate. Thus, to paraphrase an example given by Professor Arkes, when a British citizen arrives at a U.S. airport, he does not have a right to vote in U.S. elections or get a work permit, but he does have a right to be protected by the police from physical assault, even if no man-made law obligates the police to act. The difference between man-made rights versus natural-law rights is recognized in the Declaration of Independence's

---

[310] *Dred Scott v. Sandford*. (1857). 60 U.S. 393 at 407.

reference to the Creator (a higher authority than the British monarch) as the source of inalienable rights.[311]

Man-made law is fairly straightforward and in its purest constitutional sense, is limited by the text of the Constitution. However, the second type of law is more complicated, for inalienable or natural-law rights are not only inherent to man, but also built in to the Constitution. To understand this, simply examine the selective use of the word "person" versus the word "citizen" in the 14th Amendment.[312] In *Roe*, the 14th Amendment became the constitutional source of the putative right to abortion. It states that all persons[313] born in the United States are citizens, and one state cannot deny some of its citizens the privileges enjoyed by citizens of other states. However, the 14th Amendment goes on to state that, regardless of whether he is a citizen, no *person* can be denied the right to life, liberty, or property without due process of law. Clearly, the Constitution distinguishes between man-made rights or privileges, which must be available to all *citizens,* but may

---

[311] The Declaration of Independence. (1776). An Action of the Second Continental Congress. (July 4, 1776).

[312] It should be noted that the words human being are never used in the text of the Constitution or Bill of Rights, although they were commonly used in the floor debates and speeches at the time of the passage of the 14th Amendment.

[313] An argument that is often made by abortion advocates is that the Constitution only recognizes citizenship after birth, and therefore does not contemplate the preborn. However, this argument actually undermines the pro-abortion position, for the word "person" is used to describe the broader group of potential citizens. It is only citizens that must be born or naturalized, but the broader term "person" and not citizen is the one used to describe the group whose right to life must be protected. Recently, presidential candidate Hillary Clinton, an avid abortion advocate, stated her opinion that "The unborn person doesn't have Constitutional rights." By admitting that the preborn is, in fact, a person, she was placing the preborn squarely within the protection of the 14th Amendment.

be denied non-citizens, and the natural-law rights that cannot be denied to any *person* whether citizen or not.

The drafters of the 14th Amendment had an unambiguous understanding that the word person was synonymous with the word human being. In fact, they used the two words interchangeably.[314] To these men, the denial of the deep fundamental rights protected by natural law would have been impossible. After all, they had just fought a civil war over the interpretation of the inalienable right to liberty.

ABOLITION OF MAN

Hellerstedt stands for nothing less than the abolition of natural law through the abolition of man himself.[315] The fact that the majority opinion in *Hellerstedt* failed to mention, even once, the existence of the preborn child or even consider an interest in the "potential life of the fetus" as a legitimate governmental interest is indicative of the devastating results of a legal system that has rejected its own foundations. By failing to give any weight to the life of the preborn child, the Supreme Court removed the thorny problem of competing rights by pulling up the root. If there is no child, there is no conflict and no controversy.

---

[314] "...a State has not the right to deny equal protection to *any human being* under the Constitution of this country in the rights of life, liberty, and property." From the speech of Hon. John A. Bingham of Ohio, father of the 14th Amendment, titled "One country, One Constitution, and One People," given in the House of representatives, February 28, 1866.

[315] "Abolition of Man" is the title of C.S. Lewis' great work defending natural law against moral subjectivism.

THE IMPORTANCE OF HELLERSTEDT

The *Hellerstedt* decision is also important for other reasons. It was the first abortion decision by the Supreme Court in almost a decade. It was the first abortion decision of President Obama's judicial appointments, and the first decision in almost 30 years without the distinctive voice of Justice Antonin Scalia.[316] *Hellerstedt* was also the first abortion case in modern history where Republican appointments did not make up a majority of the court.[317] Most importantly for the future of the pro-life movement, *Hellerstedt* radically redefined the level of scrutiny that abortion legislation must meet to be considered constitutional. In so doing, *Hellerstedt* destroyed the strategy of the mainstream pro-life movement of chipping away at *Roe* through abortion-limiting regulations. Let us now turn from the philosophical to the legal context of *Hellerstedt*.

TWO STANDARDS OF JUDICIAL REVIEW

For those readers who are not trained in law, a short explanation of constitutional standards of interpretation is in order before I analyze the holding of the *Hellerstedt* decision.

Modern courts often determine whether a challenged law is constitutional by using tiers of right-specific balancing tests.[318] As Justice

---

[316] Justice Antonin Scalia died on February 13, 2016.

[317] Including the *Hellerstedt* opinion, there have been 38 opinions on abortion by the Supreme Court. Prior to *Hellerstedt,* the high court never had more than three Democratic appointees at any one time. In fact, over 75% of the votes cast on abortion cases in the Supreme Court, all of them affirming *Roe v. Wade*, have belonged to Republican judicial appointees.

[318] Justice Scalia famously decried this modern tendency to apply policy-preference-sensitive balancing tests as a path that inevitably leads to judicial

Thomas pointed out in his dissent in *Hellerstedt*, reliance upon these judicially constructed balancing tests is a fairly recent phenomenon that became prevalent in the 1960s. At the heart of the balancing tests is an initial value judgment that measures the weight or importance of contested rights. The tests usually involve balancing an individual right with the government's power to interfere with that right.

On the one end of the spectrum of balancing tests is the strict scrutiny review, under which almost all laws that conflict with fundamental rights enumerated in the Bill of Rights and the 14th Amendment are struck down. On the other end of the spectrum is the rational basis review. Here, almost all laws that are reviewed are upheld, so long as the government can come up with a hypothetical application of the contested law that would constitute a legitimate exercise of its power.

Traditionally, the strict scrutiny review protected fundamental rights, not because of the justices' personal policy preferences, but because these rights are specifically written in the text of the Constitution. *Griswold v. Connecticut*[319] and *Roe v. Wade* were the first cases to apply the strict scrutiny review to due process rights that are not specifically written in the Constitution. Since that time, substantive due process has

---

activism. In fact, Justice Thomas closed his dissent in *Hellerstedt* by lending his own voice to echo the late great Justice Scalia on this very point. "The majority's embrace of a jurisprudence of rights-specific exceptions and balancing tests is a regrettable concession of defeat — an acknowledgement that we have passed the point where 'law,' properly speaking, has any further application." Scalia, A. (1989). The Rule of Law as a Law of Rules, 56 U. Chi. L. Rev. 1175, 1182.

[319] *Griswold v Connecticut* found that forbidding the use of contraceptives violates the right of marital privacy, which is within the penumbra of specific guarantees of the Bill of Rights. *Griswold v Connecticut*. (1965). 381 US 479, No. 496, at 481-486.

allowed the court to expand judicial oversight in many areas of the law, such as abortion and homosexual marriage, effectively allowing judges to free themselves from the constraints of the Constitution's text. In other words, strict scrutiny review is like putting the government in a strait jacket, out of which none of its legislation normally escapes. Rational basis review, then, is like giving the government a free night on the town.[320]

In addition to the two end points of review standards, several standards lie in between and are used by the court to review the putative right to abortion, discrimination based on a person's sex, commercial speech, gun ownership, gender identity, and other social activities. These standards are called by different names, but the most subjective and vague standard of all—the undue burden test—was applied to abortion after the *Planned Parenthood v. Casey* decision.

The novel aspect of the *Hellerstedt* opinion is that, for all intents and purposes, the court moved beyond interpreting the 14th Amendment to fit its own ends to reinventing the abortion-specific undue burden test established in *Casey*, making it a strict scrutiny test by another name.[321]

---

[320] Justice Thomas, in his dissent in *Hellerstedt,* calls into question the application of the standard by pointing out how "easily the Court tinkers with levels of scrutiny to achieve its desired result." Justice Thomas notes that while racial discrimination triggers strict scrutiny, the court routinely allows racial discrimination for purposes of affirmative action to pass constitutional muster by asserting such aspirational goals as the cultivation of leaders.

[321] "This case also underscores the Court's increasingly common practice of invoking a given level of scrutiny—here, the abortion-specific undue burden standard—while applying a different standard of review entirely. Whatever scrutiny the majority applies to Texas' law, it bears little resemblance to the undue-burden test the Court articulated in *Planned Parenthood of Southeastern Pa. v. Casey*, 505 U. S. 833 (1992), and its successors. Instead, the majority

To understand the implications of the *Hellerstedt* decision, let us pause for a moment and analyze the evolution of judicial review standards as applied to abortion.

EVOLUTION OF JUDICIAL REVIEW STANDARDS IN ABORTION JURISPRUDENCE

Before the court adopted the undue burden standard in *Casey*, abortion was examined under a shifting standard that Justice Blackmun developed and defined as the trimester framework in *Roe*. This standard turned out to be exceedingly similar in effect to the strict scrutiny standard, because Justice Blackmun made the decision, contrary to existing legal precedent,[322] that the child in the womb was not a person. If the preborn was not a person, then the interest or the right the court would examine in abortion cases was not the preborn child's right to life, but the woman's right to access an abortion without government interference. According to the trimester framework, the child's right to life was nonexistent in the first trimester and before viability in the second. The framework acknowledged the child's right to life after

---

eviscerates important features of that test to return to a regime like the one that *Casey* repudiated." Justice Thomas' Dissent in *Hellerstedt* (p. 2). Retrieved from https://supreme.justia.com/ cases/federal/us/579/15-274/dissent5.html

[322] In *Stenberg v. Brown* (1970), a three-judge federal district court upheld an anti-abortion statute, stating that privacy rights "must inevitably fall in conflict with express provisions of the Fifth and Fourteenth Amendments that no person shall be deprived of life without due process of law." After relying on the biological facts of fetal development, the court stated that "those decisions which strike down state abortion statutes by equating contraception and abortion pay no attention to the facts of biology." "Once new life has commenced," the court wrote, "the constitutional protections found in the Fifth and Fourteenth Amendments impose upon the state the duty of safeguarding it."

viability and in the third trimester, but *Doe*'s extremely expansive health-of-the-mother requirement trumped it. Except for laws that denied the public financing of abortion, the only laws to survive *Roe*'s trimester framework from 1973 to 1992 (when *Casey* was decided) were those laws that included ready-made loopholes for the abortion industry to circumvent any protection of the preborn child.[323]

For two decades, Justice Blackmun and his trimester standard of review reigned supreme. Justice Blackmun became the unelected head of what one legal expert called the "National Abortion Control Board." [324] Early on, in *Colautti v. Franklin*[325] and *Thornburgh v. ACOG*, Justice Blackmun deprived the preborn of legal status by authoring opinions that statutes cannot "'trade-off between the woman's health and fetal survival," and insisting that "maternal health be the physician's paramount consideration."[326] In other words, the child's very right to exist had to, by law, subserve the woman's paramount right to an abortion. Clearly, the balancing test was not justly balanced but was, in fact, prejudiced to always rule in favor of abortion. Under this strict scrutiny standard that masqueraded as a trimester framework, restrained laws like parental consent, informed consent, 24-hour waiting

---

[323] A trio of cases in 1983 struck down costly hospitalization requirements: *City of Akron, PP of Kansas City v. Ashcroft, and Simopoulos v. Virginia.*

[324] Burke, D. M. (2016). Supreme Court disavows precedent, refusing to protect women for abortion industry abuses. Retrieved from http://www.scotusblog.com/2016/06/symposium-supreme-court-disavows-precedent-refusing-to-protect-women-from-abortion-industry-abuses/

[325] *Colautti v. Franklin* (1979), 439 U.S. 379, No. 77-891.

[326] Ibid.,*Thornburgh* at 768-9, Blackmun quoting *Colautti v. Franklin* (1979), 439 U.S. 379.

periods, and preserving the life of an abortion survivor were all deemed unconstitutional.

Writing to justify his logic for striking down informed consent laws in the *Thornburgh* case, Justice Stevens wrote, "The purpose of the Bill of Rights is to withdraw certain subjects from the vicissitudes of political controversy."[327] Apparently, Justice Stevens did not see the irony of his own words. He was not only advocating the absolute protection of certain rights, but also, coincidentally, the withdrawal of an entire class of human beings from the protection of the law. Likewise, Justice Powell, in striking down parental notification without judicial bypass in *Belloti v. Baird (1979),*[328] wrote that "a child, merely on account of his minority, is not beyond the protection of the Constitution." Justice Powell also did not see the irony in standing up for the rights of one minor child by denying the rights and the very existence of another.

Throughout the 1980s, as Blackmun's abortion decisions continued to shape a judicially created national policy of abortion-on-demand, with no acknowledgment or concern for the right to life of the preborn child, a few dissents began to express a desire to reconsider *Roe*'s trimester framework. In *Akron v. Akron Center for Reproductive Health*[329] and *Planned Parenthood v. Ashcroft,*[330] Reagan's appointee, Justice Sandra Day O'Connor, voiced concern about the application of the trimester framework that she worried did not recognize an "interest in protecting

---

[327] Ibid.
[328] *Belloti v Baird*. (1979). 433 US 622, No. 78-329.
[329] *Akron v. Akron Center for Reproductive Health*. (1983). 462 US 416.
[330] *Planned Parenthood of Kansas City v. Ashcroft*. (1983). 462 US 476.

potential human life [that] exists throughout the pregnancy."[331] In his last abortion opinion, Chief Justice Warren Burger wrote a stinging dissent to Justice Blackmun's *Thornburgh* opinion, in which he asserted that *Roe v. Wade* did not stand for abortion-on-demand and if it did, he would not have joined the majority opinion.[332]

To the surprise of most, the increasing uneasiness with the radicalism of Justice Blackmun's opinions, along with a Supreme Court composition that boasted of eight Republican-nominated judges, resulted not in the overturning of *Roe,* but in the affirmation of Blackmun's decision and the adoption of O'Connor's undue burden standard. The level of division within the court was at an all-time high, as were the social tensions surrounding a vigorous civil disobedience movement led by Operation Rescue. Four of the judges, including Chief Justice Rehnquist, Justice White, Justice Scalia, and Justice Thomas voted to overturn *Roe v. Wade* in *Casey*. Justice O'Connor and four others voted to affirm it, replacing the trimester framework with the new undue burden standard in *Casey*. In her opinion in *Casey*, Justice O'Connor explained that an entire generation had come of age relying on *Roe*'s concept of liberty. The irony of Justice O'Connor's words, which condemned another generation of innocent preborn children, escaped her, just as much as it had escaped other justices before her.

Under the undue burden standard of review, a regulation or law would be struck down as unconstitutional, wrote O'Connor, if "its purpose or effect was to place substantial obstacles in the path of a

---

[331] Ibid., *Akron*, O'Connor at 461
[332] Ibid., *Thornburgh*

woman seeking an abortion before the fetus attains viability." The majority ruled that Pennsylvania's spousal notification law was an undue burden because it might act as a *de facto* veto over the woman's decision to abort. However, a plurality held that informed consent and parental consent and notification laws could stand, thus overturning *Thornburgh*.

In effect, Justice O'Connor had opened the door to the regulation of abortion and given hope to those who would seek to chip away at *Roe v. Wade*. Yet, 20 years earlier, Notre Dame law professor, Charles Rice, had foreseen this turn of events and warned against this strategy in a comparison of *Roe* with *Dred Scott*. Rice wrote:

> *"The desirability of enacting other state laws restricting abortion within the confines of the Supreme Court rulings - e.g., requiring that abortions be performed by doctors, that the father of the child consent, that efforts be made to save aborted babies who are born alive, that mothers undergo counseling before abortions, will depend on whether those restrictive laws will save the lives of children in the womb. Generally, they will condone abortion and cause some opponents of abortion to relax their efforts, but whether a particular provision will actually prevent abortions will have to be decided in each instance. In general, the Supreme Court has left no room for states really to prevent abortions at any stage of the pregnancy. The most the states can do is make it inconvenient to get the abortions.* ***To a large extent, such action will be a waste of time and a diversion of effort from the Constitutional amendment"*** *[emphasis added].*[333]

Professor Rice's observations were prescient. In the 1970s and 80s, no meaningful legislation survived judicial scrutiny, other than the withholding of government funding of abortion. Pro-life advocates tried and got close to passing a constitutional amendment but soon, they

---

[333] Ibid., Rice

abandoned that monumental task for the strategy of chipping away at *Roe*.

In 1992, with the rescue movement in full swing and eight Republican appointees on the bench, the Supreme Court adopted the policy that regulation of abortion would be permitted, but the air for abolition was completely sucked out of the room. During the next 25 years, the new undue burden standard would convince a majority of the pro-life movement to give up on abolition and instead, commit to regulating it on the terms set forth by the Supreme Court. The magnitude of this Faustian bargain[334] would be displayed in all its terrible consequences during the first minute of oral arguments in *Gonzales v. Carhart*, the 2007 case that upheld the federal Partial Birth Abortion Ban Act of 2003.

In *Gonzales v. Carhart*, before even a single question was leveled at him, renown litigator and then Solicitor General , Paul Clement, voluntarily argued that Congress' partial-birth abortion ban was constitutional because "no woman would be prevented from terminating her pregnancy."[335] The Catch 22 was complete. Pro-life laws could be constitutional, said the court, if legislators agreed to allow abortion to go on. Sadly, much of the pro-life movement and most of the leadership in the Church agreed.

---

[334] Faust, a German astronomer and necromancer, was said to have sold his soul to the Devil.

[335] Clement, P. (2007). Opening argument in *Gonzales v. Carhart*. [Audio and transcript]. Retrieved from https://www.oyez.org/cases/2006/05-380

False Assumption: Abortion Regulations Reduce Abortion

A recurring pro-life argument made during the *Casey* years was that abortion regulations reduced abortion and therefore, were the moral option for those opposed to it. It was "moral" because, in light of the impossibility of abolishing abortion, these regulations were responsible for a consistent reduction in the incidence of abortion.[336] Some of us have long disputed these claims because, while surgical abortions have decreased, chemical abortions and the use of abortifacient devices have increased and more than made up the difference.[337] The mounting evidence of ever-increasing chemical abortions is proving that these abortions, not pro-life regulations, are more likely the cause of the reduction in reported surgical abortions.[338, 339]

Yet, regardless of the moral or strategic implications of *Casey*-era regulations, *Hellerstedt* essentially held that, going forward, all significant

---

[336] Michael New has been the most vocal advocate of the claim that "pro-life" abortion regulations have been successful in reducing abortions. See: New, M. (2011). Analyzing the effect of anti-abortion U.S. state legislation in the post-Casey era. Retrieved from http://spa.sagepub.com/ content/11/1/28.abstract

[337] France, with its liberal abortion law, is actually seeing a decrease in surgical abortions largely due to the popular alternative of chemical abortion.

[338] In 2015, a survey by the Associated Press showed that abortion rates were decreasing throughout the country, and in fact, the largest decreases were in places where "reproductive" rights experts claimed had experienced increased funding for healthcare, which we can understand as contraceptives. This explanation was again confirmed by Reuter's preliminary analysis of CDC and Guttmacher Institute data late in 2016, which showed that chemical abortions now account for over 50% of all abortions committed in the United States. See: Associated Press. (2015). Abortion rates declining in nearly all states. Retrieved from http://pandce.proboards.com/thread /452607/abortion-rates-declining-nearly-states [original AP story deleted].

[339] O'Bannon, R., PhD. (2016). Number of chemical abortions growing in US, outpacing surgical abortions in many states. Retrieved from http://www.nationalrighttolifenews.org/news/2016/11/number-of-chemical-abortions-growing-in-u-s-outpacing-surgical-abortions-in-many-states/

regulations will be held unconstitutional if the court, not legislatures, determines them to be "unnecessary" and motivated by or resulting in reduced access to abortion. In other words, under the new *Hellerstedt* standard, all *effective* abortion-reducing regulations will be facially unconstitutional.

THE UNDUE BURDEN TEST IN *HELLERSTEDT*

There are three crucial changes to the undue burden standard introduced in *Hellerstedt*. The first change is that courts must now consider the burdens that the challenged law impose on abortion "access" along with the benefits that the court attributes to the law.[340] In other words, an anti-abortion regulation will be considered undue not only if it "places a substantial obstacle in the path of a woman seeking an abortion,"[341] but also if the court determines that the law does not provide sufficient benefits.

Here it is important to note the obvious. The court does not consider the survival of more preborn children as a legitimate benefit. The preborn child is as inexistent to the current court as it is to the abortion industry itself. Ironically, it was precisely this lack of concern for the life of the preborn child in the Blackmun trimester framework that led Justice O'Connor to develop the undue process standard in the first place. For

---

[340] Justice Thomas, in his dissent, explained this new requirement, recalling that the court in "*Mazurek* v. *Armstrong*, 520 U. S. 968 (1997) (*per curiam*), had no difficulty upholding a Montana law authorizing only physicians to perform abortions—even though no legislative findings supported the law, and the challengers claimed that 'all health evidence contradict[ed] the claim that there is any health basis for the law.'" *Id.*, at 973 (internal quotation marks omitted). *Mazurek* also deemed objections to the law's lack of benefits "squarely foreclosed by *Casey* itself."

[341] Ibid., *Planned Parenthood v. Casey*

years before *Casey*, Justice O'Connor critiqued the trimester framework of *Roe*. As previously mentioned, she insisted that "interest in protecting potential human life exists throughout the pregnancy."[342] Justice Kennedy concurred, adding in *Gonzales* that "[w]here it has a rational basis to act, and it does not impose an undue burden, the State may use its regulatory power... in furtherance of its legitimate interests in regulating the medical profession in order to promote respect for life, including life of the unborn."[343] After *Hellerstedt*, this belief no longer holds true.

In Justice Ginsburg's concurring opinion in *Hellerstedt,* we can get a glimpse of the future under the new undue burden standard—a future where a procedure with the express purpose of violently ending the life of a preborn child is compared to a "tonsillectomy, colonoscopy, or an in-office dental surgery."[344] For abortion advocates, the conclusion could not be clearer, the preborn child is a non-entity and any law that is motivated by or results in a benefit to the preborn child is unnecessary.

The second change in the undue burden test brought upon by *Hellerstedt* is an end to the judiciary's respect for the legislature's findings on contested medical issues and a return to *Roe*'s paternalistic exercise of raw judicial power.

Before *Hellerstedt*, the court stated that "[c]onsiderations of marginal safety, including the balance of risks, are within the legislative competence when the regulation is rational and in pursuit of legitimate

---

[342] Ibid., *Planned Parenthood v. Ashcroft,* O'Connor at 461
[343] Ibid., *Gonzales v. Carhart*
[344] Ibid.,*Hellerstedt,* Ginsburg at 1

ends."[345] Now, the court finds that "the statement that legislatures, and not courts, must resolve questions of medical uncertainty" is incorrect and should be replaced by the court's own opinion based "upon evidence and argument presented in judicial proceedings."[346] Highlighting the court's return to Blackmun's post-*Roe* strict scrutiny standard, Justice Breyer dismissed Texas' justification that higher health standards were necessary to prevent another Kermit Gosnell[347] by flippantly stating that, while "Gosnell's behavior was terribly wrong ... there is no reason to believe that an extra layer of regulation would have affected that behavior. Determined wrongdoers, already ignoring existing statutes and safety measures, are unlikely to be convinced to adopt safe practices by a new overlay of regulations."[348]

Wisconsin's solicitor general, Misha Tseytlin, and others quickly pointed out the double standard being applied to abortion, noting, "It takes little imagination to see how this same logic would just as well apply to invalidate regulations affecting other businesses. After all, many businesses—sometimes rightly, sometimes wrongly—argue that laws impose needless burdens on their operations without any commensurate public benefit. Yet, under modern Supreme Court doctrine, these businesses do not typically get the benefit of the "overlay of regulations"

---

[345] *Stenberg v. Carhart*. (2000). 530 US 914 No. 99-830, Kennedy dissenting at 971.

[346] Ibid., *Hellerstedt,* Breyer at 20

[347] Gosnell is a former abortionist serving a life sentence for murdering infants born alive after failed abortions at his severely substandard "house of horrors" facility in Philadelphia.

[348] Ibid., *Hellerstedt*, Breyer at 27

inquiry that the Court offered in this case."[349] Imagine a ruling by the liberal wing of the Supreme Court that strikes down gun control laws by arguing that there are enough gun regulations and "determined wrongdoers" are already ignoring them. Clearly, the liberal justices will bend any standard to fit their desired end to make the putative right to abortion untouchable.

Lastly, the new *Hellerstedt* undue burden test requires laws to have more than a rational basis justification, even when they do not substantially impede access to abortion. Here again, we circle back to the question of whether defending the right to life of the preborn child is a legitimate interest. Before *Hellerstedt*, if a law did not create a substantial obstacle to abortion, the state only needed to show that its regulation was rationally related to its legitimate goal of promoting the respect for life of the preborn. Now, that argument is gone, as the Supreme Court has effectively ruled the preborn child out of existence.

THE TRAGIC EFFECT OF HELLERSTEDT'S UNDUE BURDEN STANDARD

To understand the dimension of these three fundamental changes in abortion jurisprudence, it is important to return to the stated goals of the laws that *Hellerstedt* invalidated. The two Texas laws required abortion providers to obtain admitting privileges at nearby hospitals and applied ambulatory surgical standards to licensed abortion facilities. The text of the law, which also included several other unchallenged sections like a 20-week pain capable ban, contained numerous references to the

---

[349] Tseytlin, M. (2016). "Overlay of regulations" and the abortion industry. Retrieved from http://www.scotusblog.com/2016/06/symposium-overlay-of-regulations-and-the-abortion-industry/

preborn child, including one that attributes the care of the preborn as the explicit motivation for the law.[350]

In Section 5 of H.B. 2 (one of the sections that amended the Texas Health Code to require abortion facilities to comport with Texas' ambulatory surgical standards), the legislature required providers to record "the probable post-fertilization age of the unborn child based on the best medical judgment of the attending physician at the time of the procedure."[351] The legislature had explicitly changed the existing language in this section from "period of gestation" to "age of the unborn child," indicating a clear desire to highlight the presence of the state's interest in protecting the preborn child apart from the mother. And yet, the majority opinion written by Justice Breyer in *Hellerstedt* was willfully blind to the state's interest. He wrote, "Unlike in *Gonzales*, the relevant statute here does not set forth any legislative findings. Rather, one is left to infer that the legislature sought to further a constitutionally acceptable objective (namely, protecting women's health)."[352] This is simply not true. As noted, H.B. 2 was full of references to the desire to protect the preborn child apart from the mother. In fact, the word "unborn" is mentioned 27 times in H.B. 2's 20 pages of text, but it is never mentioned in the majority's 40-page opinion.

Cornell Law professor, Michael Dorf, who applauded the court for calling out H.B. 2 as a pretextual sneak attack on abortion under the

---

[350] "The state has a compelling state interest in protecting the lives of unborn children ..." See: Texas Legislature. (2014). H.B. 2. Retrieved from http://www.legis.state.tx.us/tlodocs/832/billtext/pdf/HB00002F.pdf

[351] Ibid.

[352] Ibid., *Hellerstedt*

guise of women's health,[353] unwittingly pointed out the fundamental problem with the constitutional right to abortion. For what else, other than pretextual arguments, exist to justify the intentional killing of one innocent person by another? If one recognizes the child as a human being—as a person—then no burden imposed on abortion providers should be undue. If on the other hand, the child is not a human being or a person, then any burden on the woman's right to bodily integrity would be undue.

OUR PRO-LIFE DILEMMA

Roe and *Casey* set up a Catch 22, and pro-life attorneys have not been able to break its deadly grip. Justice Scalia summarized these standards best in his famous *Casey* dissent.

> *"Thus, despite flowery rhetoric about the State's 'substantial' and 'profound' interest in 'potential human life,' and criticism of Roe for undervaluing that interest, the joint opinion (Casey) permits the State to pursue that interest only so long as it is not too successful ... Reason finds no refuge in this jurisprudence of confusion."*[354]

Attorneys should be on notice that science, logic, and the letter of the law do not matter when it comes to abortion. After *Hellerstedt,* they should also be aware that legislative findings that disagree with a district court judge's opinion can be jettisoned and substituted for the trial

---

[353] "Lawyers should be on notice that justices cannot be tricked into ruling against their druthers, at least if the law leaves any wiggle room at all." See: Dorf, M. (2016). The wages of guerrilla warfare against abortion. Retrieved from http://www.scotusblog.com/2016/06/symposium-the-wages-of-guerrilla-warfare-against-abortion/

[354] Ibid., *Planned Parenthood v. Casey*, Scalia at 992

court's own opinions. All abortion law is mere power politics in the hands of a tyrannical judiciary, which distorts and corrupts any and all legal obstacles to support its goal of abortion on demand.

This general abortion distortion in the law was the focus of the dissent by Justice Alito, which dealt primarily with the bastardization of legal principles such as *res judicata*,[355] the limitations on third-party standing,[356] and severability.[357]

In Conclusion

The opinions of legal experts and activists leave us with no clear sense of where the pro-life movement stands after *Hellerstedt.* Abortion advocates like Jessica Pieklo of Rewire's "Law and the Courts" generally argue that *Hellerstedt* reaffirms abortion as a fundamental right against the whims of legislatures.[358] On the other side, pro-life lawyers like Denise Burke of Americans United for Life argue that *Hellerstedt*

---

[355] *Res judicata* is often described as the legal principle that prevents litigants from biting the same apple twice. In other words, where a binding decision has been reached in a case, the same litigants may not re-litigate the case. In *Hellerstedt*, Whole Woman's Health tried the same case and lost, but nonetheless, the court decided to give them a second try.

[356] Traditionally, only those parties that are personally affected may pursue a claim in court. Yet in *Hellerstedt*, as in all abortion cases since *Singelton v. Wulff*. (1976). 428 US 106, the party affected is the woman attempting to obtain an abortion, but the abortion facilities and providers are allowed to bring the case, even though they clearly have no personal, constitutionally protected privacy right.

[357] The concept of severability allows judges to limit the impact of their decisions by striking only those sections that are unconstitutional and preserving the rest of the law. In *Hellerstedt*, the court refused to limit its ruling to the sections of the law argued, but instead struck the entire law.

[358] Pieklo, J. (2016). Abortion rights come out of the shadow. Retrieved from http://www.scotusblog.com/2016/06/symposium-abortion-rights-come-out-of-the-shadow/

"disavows precedent by refusing to protect women from abortion industry abuses."[359]

The truth is that both of these conclusions are correct, and yet both are insufficient and nearsighted. As Justice Thomas argued in his poignant dissent, *Hellerstedt* delivers "neither predictability nor the promise of a judiciary bound by the rule of law."[360] Almost two decades ago, Justice Scalia arrived at a very similar conclusion in his dissent to the first partial birth abortion case, *Stenberg v. Carhart*. Referencing his own dissent in *Casey*, he explained, "I wrote that the undue burden test ... created a standard that was as doubtful in application as it is unprincipled in origin... hopelessly unworkable in practice...ultimately standardless. Today's decision is the proof."[361]

It is clear that, while *Hellerstedt* did disavow the immediate precedent in *Gonzales v. Carhart* (in which the court deferred to Congress' policy preferences in the regulation of abortion), the court essentially adhered to its longstanding practice of redefining the legal standard to comport to the policy preference of a majority or a plurality of justices. What is this policy preference? As Breyer asserted, it is the role of the courts, not the legislature, to resolve questions of medical uncertainty that are related to a constitutionally protected liberty.[362] This liberty is, of course, the putative right to deprive a preborn child of life.

---

[359] Burke, D., Esq., (2016). Supreme Court disavows precedent, refusing to protect women from abortion industry abuses. Retrieved from http://www.scotusblog.com/2016/06/symposium-supreme-court-disavows-precedent-refusing-to-protect-women-from-abortion-industry-abuses/

[360] Ibid., *Hellerstedt*, Thomas dissenting at 2

[361] Ibid., *Stenberg*, Scalia dissenting at 955

[362] Ibid., *Hellerstedt* at 20

Justice Stevens espoused this exact view 30 years ago in *Thornburgh* when he explained that "certain values are more important than the will of a transient majority."[363]

So what is the state of abortion law after *Hellerstedt*? Simply put, the judiciary's lawlessness is now more egregious than it has ever been. The law is whatever the pro-abortion judges feel it needs to be in order to guarantee an outcome favorable to abortion. *Hellerstedt* has taken us back to 1986, when laws as innocuous as informed consent, reporting requirements, and post-viability standards of care were deemed unconstitutional.

[Gualberto Garcia Jones is a legal expert on human rights issues for various domestic and international organizations and campaigns. He has drafted dozens of legislative proposals and advocated in defense of universal human rights at the state and federal level. He has written and submitted legal briefs before numerous courts, including the United States Supreme Court and the Constitutional Court of Colombia. Gualberto was born in Spain and emigrated to the United States. He graduated from the University of Wisconsin with a double major in history and political science and received his law degree from The George Washington University Law School. He is admitted to practice law in the Commonwealth of Virginia.]

---

[363] Ibid., *Thornburgh*. Interestingly, Justice Stevens' footnote for this claim explains that the rights beyond the reach of the legislature are first the "right to life," then "liberty, and property, to free speech, a free press, freedom of worship and assembly, and other fundamental rights..." Footnote 12 citing *West Virginia Board of Education v. Barnette*. (1943). 319 U.S. 624, 638.

CHAPTER 13

Personhood: The Legal Heart Of The Pro-Life Movement

By Gualberto Garcia Jones, Executive Director, International Human Rights Group; Vice President and National Policy Director, Personhood Alliance

Justice Blackmun, and later Justice Stevens, were some of the most outspoken proponents of the *abortion-as-a-fundamental-constitutional-right* judicial philosophy. Justice Stevens, one of the most progressive of the many liberal Republican Supreme Court appointees, wrote a concurring opinion in *Thornburgh v. ACOG*[364] that criticized Justice White, one of the original *Roe v. Wade*[365] dissenters. In his opinion, Justice Stevens unwittingly exposed the tortured logic of abortion.

---

[364] *Thornburgh v. American College of Obstetricians and Gynecologists* (1986). 476 US 747, No. 84-498.
[365] *Roe v. Wade*. (1973). 410 US 113, No. 70-18.

THE TORTURED LOGIC OF ABORTION

Not only did Justice Stevens expose abortion's tortured logic, but he also evidenced the inherent problems in the mainstream pro-life movement's attempts to regulate abortion. The full quote is long, but it is worth including in total:

> *"Justice White is also surely wrong in suggesting that the governmental interest in protecting fetal life is equally compelling during the entire period from the moment of conception until the moment of birth. Again, I recognize that a powerful theological argument can be made for that position, but I believe our jurisdiction is limited to the evaluation of secular State interests. I should think it obvious that the State's interest in the protection of an embryo—even if that interest is defined as "protecting those who will be citizens,"—increases progressively and dramatically as the organism's capacity to feel pain, to experience pleasure, to survive, and to react to its surroundings increases day by day. The development of a fetus —and pregnancy itself—are not static conditions, and the assertion that the government's interest is static simply ignores this reality.*
>
> *Nor is it an answer to argue that life itself is not a static condition, and that "there is no non-arbitrary line separating a fetus from a child, or indeed, an adult human being for, unless the religious view that a fetus is a "person" is adopted —a view Justice White refuses to embrace, there is a fundamental and well-recognized difference between a fetus and a human being;* ***indeed, if there is not such a difference, the permissibility of terminating the life of a fetus could scarcely be left to the will of the state legislatures.****[emphasis added] And if distinctions may be drawn between a fetus and a human being in terms of the state interest in their protection —even though the fetus represents one of "those who will be citizens"—it seems to me quite odd to argue that distinctions may not also be drawn between the state interest in protecting the freshly fertilized egg and the state interest in protecting the 9-month-gestated, fully sentient fetus on the eve of birth.*

> *Recognition of this distinction is supported not only by logic, but also by history and by our shared experiences."*[366]

Of course, there is a perfectly reasonable, non-religious view that recognizes the interest in protecting all innocent human beings' right to life by virtue of their mere humanity. Humanity is a classification based not upon a particular theology or mental capacity, but upon basic genetics and biology. The deeper question is: Why are human beings exceptional in the first place? Why not recognize juridical personhood in dolphins, apes, or rivers, as India, Spain, and New Zealand have done?[367, 368]

Up to this point, even courts in liberal states like New York have rejected legal personhood for chimps,[369] but explanations for this rejection are mostly Utilitarian[370] and would, if applied to newborns, strip them of personhood as well.

New York Court of Appeals Judge Karen Peters included a footnote in her opinion in the "Tommy the Chimp" case that attempted to compare chimpanzees to lower-functioning human beings:

---

[366] Ibid., *Thornburgh*, Stevens at 2188

[367] DeGrazia, D. (1997). Great apes, dolphins, and the concept of personhood. *Southern Journal of Philosophy, 35*: 301-320. Retrieved from http://onlinelibrary.wiley.com/doi/10.1111/j.2041-6962.1997.tb00839.x/full

[368] Margil, M. (2017). India court declares personhood for Ganga and Yumana rivers. Retrieved from http://celdf.org/2017/03/pr-india-court-declares-personhood-ganga-yumana-rivers/

[369] *The People of the State of New York ex rel. The Nonhuman Rights Project, Inc. on Behalf of Tommy, v. Patrick C. Lavery*. (2014). State of New York Supreme Court, Appellate Division, Third Judicial Department.

[370] Utilitarianism is a 19th-century philosophy of moral relativism whose intention was to replace God's absolute moral code reflected in the Ten Commandments.

> *"Needless to say, unlike human beings, chimpanzees cannot bear any legal duties, submit to societal responsibilities, or be held legally accountable for their actions...*
>
> *To be sure, some humans are less able to bear legal duties or responsibilities than others. These differences do not alter our analysis, as it is undeniable that, collectively, human beings possess the unique ability to bear legal responsibility."*[371]

The word "undeniable" resonates with the self-evident truths of the Declaration of Independence[372] and points to a more fundamental, unwritten law that complements and is presupposed by our man-made law. But what is evident when applied to chimps is not so when applied to the preborn. Even when the humanity of the preborn is recognized, this, in and of itself, is no guarantee of their right to life. In a case decided in New York's highest court in 1972, the year before *Roe v. Wade,* the court upheld the state legislature's liberalization of abortion. Admitting that, although the preborn child was unquestionably a human being, whether or not he was a person was a legislative question, not a judicial one.[373] This was essentially the unfortunate position of Justice Scalia and other legal positivists, that the child in the womb, while a human being,

---

[371] Ibid., *The People of the State of New York ex rel. The Nonhuman Rights Project, Inc. on Behalf of Tommy, v. Patrick C. Lavery*. Karen Peters opinion. Retrieved from http://www.courts.state.ny.us/Reporter/3dseries /2014/2014_08531.htm

[372] Declaration of Independence. (1776). An Act of the Second Continental Congress. (July 4, 1776).

[373] "It is not effectively contradicted, if it is contradicted at all, that biological disciplines accept that upon conception a fetus has an independent genetic "package" with potential to become a full-fledged human being and that it has an autonomy of development and character although it is for the period of gestation dependent upon the mother. It is human, if only because it may not be characterized as not human, and it is unquestionably alive." See: *Byrn v. New York City Health and Hospitals Corporation*. (1972). 286 N.E.2d at 888 at 887.

may be a non-person. This contradicts a multitude of cases in tort, criminal, property, and inheritance law that hold the preborn child to be a person with protected rights. Charles Rice, in his magnificent comparison of *Roe* to *Dred Scott,*[374] published shortly after *Roe* was decided, forcefully rejected the idea that the preborn or any other human being could ever be legislatively declared a non-person:

> *"In its denial of his right to live, abortion is unjust toward the child in the womb because it deprives him of equality before the law. Nor do we have to go back very far in history to see the baneful effects that can follow the denial of legal equality to a particular class of human beings."*[375]

The Nuremberg Laws, issued by the Nazi regime in the fall of 1935, deprived Jews of their citizenship and political rights. Ultimately, of course, they were deprived of their lives as well, pursuant to a euthanasia program[376] designed to achieve "the destruction of life devoid of value."[377] The inequality inflicted on the Jews by the Nazis meant that they were, as a class, specially regarded as subject to extermination, while other human beings were not.

In 1972, perhaps it would have been unsavory for the Supreme Court to follow the example of New York's highest court by simultaneously

---

[374] *Dred Scott v. Sandford*. (1857). 60 U.S. 393 at 407.

[375] Rice, C. (1973) The Dred Scott case of the twentieth century. *Houston Law Review*. Retrieved from http://scholarship.law.nd.edu/law_faculty_scholarship/780/

[376] Jewish Virtual Library. (2017). The Nazi euthanasia (T-4) program: Background & overview. Retrieved from http://www.jewishvirtuallibrary.org/background-and-overview-of-the-nazi-euthanasia-t-4-program

[377] Meiner, F. (1920). *The release of the destruction of life devoid of value: Its measure and its form.* Leipzig.

holding that the preborn child was a human being but not a person.[378] After all, Nuremberg was still fresh on the nation's mind. For whatever reason, Justice Blackmun ignored the preborn child's humanity as a biological construct and instead, attributed it to unknowable philosophy and religion. As such, he decided that the preborn child was neither a human being nor a person.

Justice Stevens' critique of Justice White in *Thornburgh* employs the same logic as that expressed by Justice Blackmun in *Roe*'s infamous Footnote 54, which cited the lack of equal protection for preborn children in numerous state statutes that allowed for exceptions to the criminalization of abortion.[379] Genocidal consequences aside, Justice Stevens and Justice Blackmun make a strong argument: If the preborn child were a human being and a person with the right to life, then how could the law relegate some preborn children—those conceived in rape and those whose mothers are ill during pregnancy —to second-class status?

The notion of universal prenatal personhood also clashes with pro-life law in the era of *Planned Parenthood v. Casey*,[380] which essentially returned regulation of abortion to the states. If all human beings are persons, how is it that pro-life legislation can include rape and incest exceptions that permit the death of some children? How can pro-life

---

[378] Ibid., *Byrn v. New York City Health and Hospitals Corporation*

[379] "When Texas urges that a fetus is entitled to Fourteenth Amendment protection as a person, it faces a dilemma. Neither in Texas nor in any other State are all abortions prohibited. Despite broad proscription, an exception always exists." Footnote 54 of *Roe v Wade*. Retrieved from https://supreme.justia.com/cases/federal/us/410/113/case.html#F54

[380] *Planned Parenthood of Southeastern Pennsylvania et al v. Casey*. (1992). 505 US 833, No. 91-744.

politicians advocate for a "return to the states" approach on abortion? If the child in the womb is a human being, as no one can credibly deny, and we agree that all human beings should be recognized as persons by the law, then how can we accept a constitutional interpretation that allows Californians to kill preborn children without any restrictions[381], but prevents Texans from killing them beyond 20 weeks gestation, with some exceptions?[382] The clear answer is that pro-lifers cannot and must not consistently maintain their current legislative strategy and hope for any moral consistency.

Abortion, like slavery, is truly a fundamental human rights issue. Dehumanizing the preborn child or attempting to protect it through half measures is never going to end abortion. Some, like Justice Stevens, try to maintain that it is the job of the court to keep issues like abortion out of the hands of citizens. However, they do so not to safeguard the right to life, but to erase it from the Constitution and with it, the humanity of the child.

On the other hand, many like the late Justice Scalia advocate for the democratic process to address the problem of abortion. This is also unsatisfactory. Why would we permit the right to life to be subjected to the whims of the democratic process? History teaches us that the denial of personhood to a class of human beings is at odds with fundamental justice. Neither enlightened justices nor the masses at the polling booth can define the preborn child's personhood. Abortion, like slavery, is an

---

[381] Findlaw. (2017). California abortion laws. Retrieved from http://statelaws.findlaw.com/california-law/california-abortion-laws.html

[382] Findlaw. (2017). Texas abortion laws. Retrieved from http://statelaws.findlaw.com/texas-law/texas-abortion-laws.html

attack upon the inalienable and the inherent—and therefore, it transcends all man-made law and all man-made solutions.

Lincoln, in his speech against the Kansas Nebraska Act, alighted upon this truth, although he did not consistently apply it:

> *"The doctrine of self-government is right—absolutely and eternally right—but it has no just application, as here attempted. Or perhaps I should rather say that whether it has such just application depends upon whether a Negro is not or is a man. If he is not a man, why in that case, he who is a man may, as a matter of self-government, do just as he pleases with him. But if the Negro is a man, is it not to that extent, a total destruction of self-government, to say that he too shall not govern himself? When the white man governs himself, and also governs another man, that is more than self-government—that is despotism. If the Negro is a man, why then my ancient faith teaches me that "all men are created equal;" and that there can be no moral right in connection with one man's making a slave of another."*[383]

At the end of its tragic struggle with slavery, America discovered that there could be no compromise with the deprivation of the fundamental right to liberty. There was no possible legislative solution for Congress to adopt, and the principles of federalism and state rights, while valid, were not so absolute as to justify the enslavement of an entire race. Likewise, legislative and judicial compromises, or state-by-state solutions for abortion, will simply not vindicate the inalienable right to life. There is no other possible end to America's abortion tragedy than a federal amendment to the Constitution.

---

[383] Lincoln, A. (1854, October 16). Peoria speech. Peoria, IL. Text retrieved from https://www.nps.gov/liho/learn/historyculture/peoria speech.htm

Why the Solution Is Constitutional

The pro-life movement proposed federal constitutional amendments immediately following *Roe v. Wade*, and for the next 10 years, these amendments remained under serious consideration. According to the National Committee for a Human Life Amendment, more than 330 Human Life Amendment proposals have been introduced in Congress.[384] Yet, only the Hatch-Eagleton Federalism Human Life Amendment, proposed in 1983, ever received a Senate vote. The amendment stated that "the right to abortion is not secured by [the] Constitution." [385] But it said nothing of the duty to protect the preborn and essentially, left the question of preborn personhood to each individual state. The amendment failed 49-50. Of course, in order send a constitutional amendment to the states for ratification, two thirds of both houses must vote in favor of it. In 1983, the political will to amend the Constitution waned after one Senate vote. Over the years, legislators have proposed many other approaches, including:

- Limits on the appellate jurisdiction of the federal courts
- Congressional exercise of its 14th Amendment power to enforce by appropriate legislation (Life at Conception Act)
- States' 10th amendment exercise of police powers to expand state constitutional rights beyond those extended by the federal government (state Personhood amendments)

---

[384] National Committee for a Human Life Amendment. (2017). Human life amendment. Retrieved from https://www.humanlifeactioncenter.org/issues/human-life-amendment

[385] National Committee for a Human Life Amendment. (2004). Human life amendments: Major texts: p. 2. Retrieved from https://www.humanlifeactioncenter.org/sites/default/files/HLAmajortexts.pdf

- State and local resistance to federal judicial tyranny

All of these proposals, while certainly justified in the case of ending abortion, do not ultimately resolve the problem. For those proposals relying on congressional action, such as the Life at Conception Act, the Supreme Court would be waiting with precedent and further rulings to prevent Congress from usurping its self-ascribed role as the infallible, unreviewable definer of rights. For those approaches relying on state resistance to federal tyranny, again, the courts would have a strong legal argument to prevent enforcement of any such state laws.

Two Options

Essentially, America has two options: The Supreme Court's overturning of *Roe v. Wade* and the people's adoption of a constitutional amendment that requires the equal protection of the preborn. Of these two options, the first seems like the easiest to achieve; only change a few judges and the judiciary's death grip loosens. Yet, experience teaches us that this has been remarkably difficult to achieve. When *Casey* was decided in 1992, the pro-life Republican party had appointed eight out of the nine justices, and yet the right to abortion was affirmed. Of all Supreme Court abortion decisions since and including *Roe v. Wade*, 75% of the votes cast in favor of abortion have been by Republican-appointed judges.[386] Clearly, the prevailing cultural and academic norms, which are overwhelmingly supportive of abortion, make finding pro-life judges very

---

[386] This percentage is calculated by counting and comparing the votes from Republican- and Democrat-nominated justices on abortion decisions from 1973 to present. The number of Republican-appointed justices on the court in the 1970s and 80s makes this percentage high.

difficult. Getting them past the Senate confirmation process is equally difficult.

Even if the time comes when enough judges are willing to discard *Roe* and its progeny, it is highly unlikely that they will do so by recognizing the personhood and equal rights of preborn children. More likely than not, *Roe* will be overturned and returned to the democratic process, to be decided upon state-by-state or by the U.S. Congress. While this would certainly be a step in the right direction, it would do little to protect the millions of preborn children in pro-abortion areas like the populous East and West coasts.

Why a Personhood Amendment Is the Only Solution

An amendment to the U.S. Constitution is the only feasible solution to stop the egregious violations of the fundamental right to life. The preborn child must be recognized as a person, deserving equal protection under the law from his or her biological beginning.

Pro-lifers hold, almost universally, that a constitutional amendment is the ultimate goal of the pro-life movement. But since the early 1980s, the movement has made no concerted, formal efforts to make this a reality. This is a strategic mistake. Not only is there unanimity in the pro-life movement regarding the necessity of a Human Life Amendment, there is also broad agreement as to the content of such an amendment. Debates over incremental steps (i.e., allowing abortion in certain cases) could actually be put aside for purposes of the amendment, because the amendment would be the gold standard, not a mere political maneuver meant to navigate through the status quo. Arguments about limitations imposed by the Supreme Court's interpretations would be null, because an amendment supersedes the court's judicial tyranny. Most importantly, a fundamentally solid Human Life Amendment, such as the one introduced in 1973 by Representative Lawrence Hogan,[387] would serve as a definitive indicator of politicians' pro-life convictions and commitment.

Pope John Paul II, in paragraph 73 of his definitive encyclical, *Evangelium Vitae*, explains the problem of conscience for politicians who support legislation that aims to reduce abortion, versus legislation that opposes it head on. This paragraph has been misinterpreted widely and used to justify cooperation with unjust laws. Pope John Paul II wrote very precisely about this situation:

> *" A particular problem of conscience can arise in cases where a legislative vote would be decisive for the passage of a more restrictive law, aimed at limiting the number of authorized abortions, in place of a more permissive law already passed or ready to be voted on. Such cases are not infrequent. It is a fact that while in some parts of the world there continue to be campaigns to introduce laws favouring abortion, often supported by powerful international organizations, in other nations-particularly those which have already experienced the bitter fruits of such permissive legislation-there are growing signs of a rethinking in this matter. In a case like the one just mentioned, when it is not possible to overturn or completely abrogate a pro-abortion law, an elected official, whose absolute personal opposition to procured abortion was well known, could licitly support proposals aimed at limiting the harm done by such a law and at lessening its negative consequences at the level of general*

[387] U.S. House of Representatives. (1973). H.R. Res. 261. 93rd Congress, 1st Session. "1. Neither the United States nor any State shall deprive any human being, from the moment of conception, of life without due process of law; nor deny to any human being, from the moment of conception, within its jurisdiction, the equal protection of the laws. 2. Neither the United States nor any State shall deprive any human being of life on account of illness, age, or incapacity. 3. Congress and the several States shall have power to enforce this article by appropriate legislation."

> *opinion and public morality. This does not in fact represent an illicit cooperation with an unjust law, but rather a legitimate and proper attempt to limit its evil aspects."*[388]

Pope John Paul II intended this paragraph to apply only to politicians facing a specific vote on a particular piece of legislation. The paragraph does not excuse pro-life advocates, pastors, priests, and bishops to propose and support unjust laws, such as those that permit the killing of children conceived in rape. Most importantly, however, the paragraph requires politicians who support gradual, reductive efforts to make their "absolute personal opposition to procured abortion well-known"[389] in order to avoid illicitly cooperating with an unjust law. Unfortunately, politicians have conveniently left this part out and instead, adopted a compromised gradualist standard. This standard is politically advantageous at election time, but it creates great confusion as to the inherent dignity of preborn children.

A Human Life Amendment is a practical way for politicians, who, for various reasons support all types of incremental measures, to make their "absolute opposition to procured abortion well-known."
A Human Life Amendment also does a great service to the pro-life constituency. Pro-life voters could finally identify which politicians share their end goal of abolishing abortion and uphold their core belief that the right to life is truly unalienable.

---

[388] Pope John Paul II. (1995, March 25). *Evangelium Vitae,* par 73. Vatican.
[389] Ibid.

A constitutional amendment is a very difficult endeavor, but America has successfully achieved this feat 27 times, even as recently as 1992.[390] Surely, we will achieve it again. Support for another option—an Article V convention of states—is emerging, but this option is unprecedented and untested. Nevertheless, we should attempt all constitutional and legal means.

Every day that we delay pushes back our victory. Each delay affords the Enemy of life more time to use the culture of death to destroy countless lives, and in the process, destroy the rule of law and our great nation. The right to life for preborn children should have never been removed from constitutional protection, but experience teaches us that there cannot be any ambiguity in laws that attempt to restore the inalienable rights of the weakest among us.

[Gualberto Garcia Jones is a legal expert on human rights issues for various domestic and international organizations and campaigns. He has drafted dozens of legislative proposals and advocated in defense of universal human rights at the state and federal level. He has written and submitted legal briefs before numerous courts, including the United States Supreme Court and the Constitutional Court of Colombia. Gualberto was born in Spain and emigrated to the United States. He graduated from the University of Wisconsin with a double major in history and political science and received his law degree from The George Washington University Law School. He is admitted to practice law in the Commonwealth of Virginia.]

---

[390] University of Minnesota Human Rights Library. (2017). All amendments to the United States Constitution. Retrieved from http://hrlibrary.umn.edu/education/all_amendments_usconst.htm

CHAPTER 14

The Myth of Judicial Supremacy and the Nullification of Tyranny

By Christopher Kurka, Executive Director, Alaska Right to Life

"And you will know the truth, and the truth will set you free."[391]

In C.S. Lewis's *The Last Battle,*[392] (the final book in the *Chronicles of Narnia* series), there is a scene that perfectly illustrates the enslaving nature and power that a lie has over those who believe it. At the conclusion of Narnia's last battle, Eustace, Jill, King Tirian, and the rest of the surviving Narnians are thrown into a stable by the invading Calormene army. Unbeknownst to all involved, the doorway into the stable is in fact a portal into Aslan's great country. Almost immediately upon entering the stable, the weary and bedraggled soldiers know they are in an extraordinary place. Aslan's country is magnificent in every

[391] John 8:32
[392] Lewis, C.S. (1956). *The last battle*. [1st ed.]. New York: Scholastic. ISBN: 0064405036.

way, from the breathtaking scenery to the smells and tastes of its bountiful food. It is a refreshing, exhilarating, and invigorating place. Yet, while some of the Narnians rejoice in their newfound home, the Dwarfs are held captive in a prison of their minds. They scoff at the Narnians' excitement. They spit Aslan's delicacies out of their mouths, believing that they are in a stable munching straw like the imaginary animals around them. When Aslan, in all his glorious presence, comes near, the Dwarfs refuse to recognize him for who he is. They explain that the trembling earth is but a machine used by "the gang at the other end of the stable."

Amidst a feast of delicious food and fine wine, the Dwarfs continually scoff, held captive by the surroundings they believe they are in. The reality they could experience is more than they can comprehend, so they choose to remain in the prison of their own minds. "The Dwarfs are for the Dwarfs!" they stubbornly declare, as they despise the very truth that would set them free.

The Deceit That Chains Us Down

In John 8:32, Jesus says, "and you will know the truth, and the truth will set you free." This begs the question: If the truth sets us free, then what happens when we believe a lie? Just like the self-absorbed Dwarfs, we are held captive. Satan holds us captive and enslaves us simply by convincing us to believe his lies. This is his primary means of keeping Christians ineffective at following the will of God and advancing His kingdom on Earth. This is a profound truth that applies to all aspects of our Christian walk, but this chapter focuses on a particularly insidious deceit that keeps the pro-life movement captive, misdirected, ineffective, and demoralized.

Roe v. Wade: The Law of the Land

The lie goes like this: In order to end legal abortion, we must elect a Republican president and a Republican majority in the US Senate. Then, over time, we can appoint "pro-life" justices to the Supreme Court of the United States (SCOTUS), who will someday overturn *Roe v. Wade*—the infamous decision that legalized abortion in 1973.[393] Let us divide this lie into two beliefs that underlie it.

First is the premise that Republican judicial appointments will be pro-life and thus, will vote to overturn *Roe.* Yet, time and time again, the pro-life community pours out blood, sweat, and tears to get Republicans elected, only to be disappointed. While a Democrat regime is far less likely to appoint pro-life justices, there is no guarantee that a Republican regime will. The fact is: Six of nine justices on the court that decided *Roe* (7-2) were Republican appointees and since *Roe* , nine of the 13 new justices on the court are Republican appointees.[394]

Second is the premise that SCOTUS is the final arbiter of the Constitution and therefore, we must obey its will. This is one of the most pernicious lies about our republican form of government. If we take this belief to its logical conclusion, SCOTUS has total control and power. Congress and the President—indeed, all laws and decisions—must meet SCOTUS's approval. There is nothing beyond its reach. We see this often in the reactions of pro-life organizations' legal counsel. Even when faced with the most outrageous SCOTUS decisions, counsels say we must fall in

---

[393] *Roe v. Wade*. (1973). 410 US 113, No. 70-18.

[394] US Supreme Court. (2017). Members of the Supreme Court of the United States by president. Retrieved from https://www.supremecourt.gov/about/members.aspx

line like good Americans, advocating for the rule of law. This is much like the Narnian Dwarfs, except it is "the Lawyers are for the Lawyers!"

In the initial phase of the modern pro-life movement, there were efforts to pass a Human Life Amendment to the Constitution.[395] The movement has largely abandoned this strategy, due to ongoing disagreements over whether to include exceptions. It would be prudent to amend the Constitution to protect the preborn, but not because we need an amendment to overrule SCOTUS. A constitutional amendment would provide preborn children equal protection under the law in all states and would be extremely difficult to reverse. However, under our current jurisprudence, even a constitutional amendment would be under threat from a SCOTUS opinion. If SCOTUS is the sole and final interpreter of the Constitution, then what would stop the court from reinterpreting any amendment to fit its political agenda?

Here in Alaska this is not just theory. In 1998, Alaskans approved an amendment to the state constitution that recognized marriage between one man and one woman.[396] However, in 2005, the Alaska Supreme Court ruled that the public employee benefits provided for married couples must be provided for same-sex couples because they were equal

---

[395] National Committee for a Human Life Amendment. (2016). Human life amendment. Retrieved from https://www.humanlifeactioncenter.org/issues/human-life-amendment

[396] Alaska Election Commission. (1998). Ballot measure 2: Constitutional amendment limiting marriage. Retrieved from http://www.elections.alaska.gov/doc/oep/1998/98bal2.htm

to married couples.[397] This decision essentially thwarted the marriage amendment, and several subsequent decisions broadened the effect.[398]

When discussing the problem of our over-powerful judiciary, I often hear that the framers of our Constitution greatly erred when they created the parameters for the judiciary. But what does this say about our view of the founding fathers and their "brilliant system of checks and balances" as so many call it? Certainly, the founders were sinful human beings and prone, like any, to make mistakes. But do we honestly believe that they gave a few unelected attorneys *carte blanch* power over our country? I think not. Where, then, did this dangerous idea of judicial supremacy emerge?

Marbury v. Madison: The Reach for Power

It started with the *Marbury v. Madison*[399] decision in 1803, in which SCOTUS declared themselves the right to judicial review. This declaration meant that SCOTUS had power to review any action or inaction the President or Congress took, deem it in violation of the Constitution, and render it null and void. Let us pause for a moment to consider the incredible arrogance of such a declaration. This is akin to the banker in a Monopoly® game declaring, "Hey guys, new rule. Since I am running the bank, I get to use the bank's cash to help me win." We certainly do not tolerate such attempts at self-appointed power in Monopoly. Why do we

---

[397] *Alaska CLU v. State of Alaska*. (2005). S-10459. See: https://www.aclu.org/node/36355

[398] Ford, Z. (2014). How the Alaska Supreme Court is circumventing the state's ban on same-sex marriage. Retrieved from https://thinkprogress.org/how-the-alaska-supreme-court-is-circumventing-the-states-ban-on-same-sex-marriage-1ac04f52074

[399] *Marbury v. Madison*. (1803). 5 US (1 Cir.) 137.

tolerate it in the halls of government? Thomas Jefferson's response to the *Marbury* decision was prophetic and instructive:

> *"You seem to consider the judges as the ultimate arbiters of all constitutional questions; a very dangerous doctrine indeed, and one which would place us under the despotism of an oligarchy. Our judges are as honest as other men, and not more so. They have, with others, the same passions for party, for power, and the privilege of their corps... Their power [is] the more dangerous as they are in office for life, and not responsible, as the other functionaries are, to the elective control. The Constitution has erected no such single tribunal, knowing that to whatever hands confided, with the corruptions of time and party, its members would become despots. It has more wisely made all the departments co-equal and co-sovereign within themselves."*[400]

This brings us to the heart of the matter. The reason the judiciary has usurped so much power is because the executive and legislative branches have acquiesced to the demands of a runaway court. It is often easier for politicians to patronize pro-life voters than to do what is necessary and risk the wrath of the abortion lobby. But how far will they take their blind obedience to court opinion?

Suppose SCOTUS ruled that women are non-persons and can be bought, sold, and treated as property? What would the remedy be for such an injustice? Congress could impeach the offending justices, but that would not undo the ruling. Impeachment, appointment of new justices, and Senate confirmation of those justices would take time. The ruling would stand while the process was underway. In the meantime,

---

[400] Jefferson, T. (1820, September 28). The writings of Thomas Jefferson: Letter to William Jarvis. Retrieved from http://thefederalistpapers.org/founders/jefferson/thomas-jefferson-judges-as-the-ultimate-arbiters-of-all-constitutional-questions-would-place-us-under-the-despotism-of-an-oligarchy

would state governors, sheriffs, and police officers enforce it? Of course not. Yet our modern American jurisprudence dictates that the executive branch is duty bound to enforce such a miscarriage of justice, simply because it is the opinion of SCOTUS. Such an outrageous decision is not mere theory. SCOTUS has a record of insidious opinions.

The Power to Deny Rights

SCOTUS's infamous *Dred Scott v. Sandford*[401] decision in 1857 denied Americans of African descent their rights, creating a second class of human beings in the eyes of the law. The decision has never been overturned by the court. But *Dred Scott* was just the beginning. Many other notorious SCOTUS decisions denied constitutionally protected rights to certain people.

Buck v. Bell (1927)

In the court's eugenic *Buck v. Bell*[402] decision, it sanctioned the forced sterilization of institutionalized people who were deemed "imbeciles," in order to protect the social welfare of the State. *Buck v. Bell* tested Virginia's Racial Integrity Act of 1924, a sterilization law built on a model developed by Harry Laughlin, a leader in the American Eugenics Movement.[403]

Dr. Albert Sidney Priddy initiated the case when he petitioned to forcibly sterilize Carrie Buck, an 18-year-old patient at the Virginia State Colony of Epileptics and Feeble Minded. Dr. Priddy claimed Carrie had a

---

[401] *Dred Scott v. Sandford*. (1857). 60 US 393.
[402] Buck v. Bell. (1927). 274 US 200.
[403] Eugenics Archive. (2017). Sterilization laws. Retrieved from http://eugenicsarchive.org/html/eugenics/static/themes/3.html

mental age of nine and therefore, posed a genetic threat to society. According to him, Buck's 52-year-old mother had a mental age of eight and a record of prostitution, having had three children without good knowledge of their parentage. Carrie, one of these children, had been adopted. Carrie was promiscuous, according to Dr. Priddy, evidenced by her giving birth to an illegitimate child. Carrie's family committed her to Dr. Priddy's institution because she was allegedly "epileptic, feeble-minded, and morally delinquent."[404] In reality, Carrie's child had been conceived as a result of rape by her adopted mother's nephew, and her family had sent her to the institution to cover up the crime.[405]

Echoing with Justice Holmes' declaration that "three generations of imbeciles are enough,"[406] the court's decision opened the flood gates for other states to enact their own eugenic laws. Many of these laws were used against the Black population, particularly in the South in the 1950s, where forced sterilizations were initiated to control the population of welfare recipients, who were predominantly Black.[407] Virginia's Racial Integrity Act also became the model for Adolf Hitler's Law for the

---

[404] Thompson, P. (2005). Silent dissent: A Catholic justice dissents in Buck v. Bell. *Catholic Lawyer, 43*(1). Retrieved from http://www.academia.edu/ 3526025/Silent_Protest_A_Catholic_Justice_Dissents_in_Buck._v._Bell

[405] University of Virginia. (2007). Carrie Buck revisited and Virginia's apology for eugenics. Retrieved from http://exhibits.hsl.virginia.edu/eugenics /5-epilogue/

[406] Ibid., *Buck v. Bell*, Holmes at 207

[407] Schoen, J. (2011). "Reassessing eugenic sterilization: The case of North Carolina." pp. 141-60 in *A century of eugenics in America: From the Indiana experiment to the human genome era*. [Ed. Lombardo, P.] Bloomington: Indiana University Press.

Prevention of Hereditarily Diseased Offspring.[408] During the Nuremberg trials, Nazi doctors explicitly cited Justice Holmes' opinion in *Buck v. Bell* as a defense for forced sterilizations.[409]

> *"It is better for all the world if, instead of waiting to execute degenerate offspring for crime or to let them starve for their imbecility, society can prevent those who are manifestly unfit from continuing their kind."*[410]

It is important to note that, like *Dred Scott*, the *Buck v. Bell* decision was never overturned by the court.

Korematsu v. United States (1944)

The internment of Japanese Americans during World War II is another black mark on American history. In *Korematsu v. United States*,[411] SCOTUS permitted the federal government to strip the rights of Fred Korematsu, a natural-born American citizen, simply because of his Japanese ancestry. This decision was in direct violation of due process in the 5th Amendment. The *Korematsu* decision was also never overturned. Like the *Buck v. Bell* and *Dred Scott* decisions, *Korematsu* is standing case law. But these cases are ignored and not enforced because they are some of the most embarrassing, malevolent decisions in the court's repertoire of egregious injustices.

---

[408] Law for the Prevention of Offspring with Hereditary Diseases (July 14, 1933). In US Chief Counsel for the Prosecution of Axis Criminality, *Nazi Conspiracy and Aggression*. Vol. 5, Washington, DC: United States Government Printing Office, 1946, 3. Document 3067-PS, pp. 880-83.

[409] Bruinius, H. (2007). *Better for all the world: The secret history of forced sterilization and America's quest for racial purity*. New York: Vintage Books. ISBN: 978-0-375-71305-7.

[410] Ibid., *Buck v. Bell*, Holmes at 207

[411] *Korematsu v. United States*. (1944). 323 US 214.

Of course, the most egregious SCOTUS decision in modern history by virtue of direct consequence is *Roe v. Wade.* This decision has ushered in the genocide of nearly 60 million preborn Americans. Yet the political class tells us that, "*Roe v. Wade* is the law of the land."[412] But history begs the question: Why should we treat *Roe* any different than *Dred Scott*, *Buck*, or *Korematsu*? If other deplorable SCOTUS decisions can be ignored, why not something as horrific as *Roe*?

Separation of Powers and a Check on Judicial Tyranny

Most of us are familiar with American system of checks and balances put in place to prevent any one branch of government from taking control. The President cannot seize complete power because Congress has the law-making authority and holds the purse strings. Congress cannot assume total authority because the President controls the administration and has enforcement power. But what of the judicial branch? What are the checks on the power of an out-of-control Supreme Court? Let us examine some of them.

First, let us look at court jurisdiction. The second clause in Article III, Section II of the Constitution reads:

> *In all Cases affecting Ambassadors, other public Ministers and Consuls, and those in which a State shall be Party, the supreme Court shall have original Jurisdiction. In all the other Cases before mentioned, the supreme Court shall have appellate Jurisdiction,*

---

[412] Johnson, B. (2015). John Kasich: *Roe v. Wade* is the law of the land. [Video]. Retrieved from https://www.lifesitenews.com/news/john-kasich-roe-v.-wade-is-the-law-of-the-land-video

> *both as to Law and Fact,* ***with such Exceptions, and under such Regulations as the Congress shall make"*** *[emphasis added].*[413]

In plain language, this means Congress can tell SCOTUS what kind of cases they can and cannot hear. If Republicans in Congress were serious, they could vote to remove abortion from the jurisdiction of the courts tomorrow, essentially nullifying *Roe*. Congress could pass a bill granting legal protection to the preborn with a clause that removes the bill from the jurisdiction of the federal courts. Of course, they would have to be serious about ending the killing of the preborn first. Congress has already exercised its power in this way. To prevent environmental lawsuits from blocking the Trans-Alaska Pipeline Project, Congress limited court jurisdiction in the Trans-Alaska Pipeline Authorization Act of 1973.[414]

Let us look at what Alexander Hamilton penned in Federalist Paper 78 regarding the separation of powers:

> *Whoever attentively considers the different departments of power must perceive, that, in a government in which they are separated from each other, the judiciary, from the nature of its functions, will always be the least dangerous to the political rights of the Constitution; because it will be least in a capacity to annoy or injure them. The Executive not only dispenses the honors, but holds the sword of the community. The legislature not only commands the purse, but prescribes the rules by which the duties and rights of every citizen are to be regulated.* ***The judiciary, on the contrary, has no influence over either the sword or the purse;*** *no direction either of the strength or of the wealth of the society; and can take no active resolution whatever. It may truly be said to have neither force nor will, but merely*

---

[413] Cornell University Law School. (2017). U.S. Constitution: Article III. Retrieved from https://www.law.cornell.edu/constitution/articleiii

[414] H.R. 9130: Trans-Alaskan Pipeline Authorization Act. (1973). An Act of the 93rd Congress (1973-1974).

> *judgment;* ***and must ultimately depend upon the aid of the executive arm even for the efficacy of its judgments"*** *[emphasis added].*[415]

In Federalist Paper 81, Hamilton gives us guidance regarding actions the government can take when the courts overstep their limited authority:

> *It may in the last place be observed that the* ***supposed danger of judiciary encroachments on the legislative authority,*** *which has been upon many occasions reiterated,* ***is in reality a phantom****. Particular misconstructions and contraventions of the will of the legislature may now and then happen; but they can never be so extensive as to amount to an inconvenience, or in any sensible degree to affect the order of the political system. This may be inferred with certainty, from the general nature of the judicial power, from the objects to which it relates, from the manner in which it is exercised, from its comparative weakness,* ***and from its total incapacity to support its usurpations by force.*** *And the inference is greatly fortified by the consideration of the important constitutional check* ***which the power of instituting impeachments in one part of the legislative body, and of determining upon them in the other, would give to that body upon the members of the judicial department****. This is alone a complete security. There never can be danger that the judges, by a series of deliberate usurpations on the authority of the legislature, would hazard the united resentment of the body entrusted with it, while this body was possessed of the means of punishing their presumption, by degrading them from their stations. While this ought to remove all apprehensions on the subject, it affords, at the same time, a cogent argument for*

---

[415] Publius. [Hamilton, A.]. (1788, June 14). The Federalist No. 78. *Independent Journal*. Retrieved from http://www.constitution.org/fed/federa78.htm

> *constituting the Senate a court for the trial of impeachments" [emphasis added].*[416]

Hamilton twice references the most obvious check on a judiciary that usurps the law-making authority of Congress: The President can simply not enforce the court's opinions. In fact, nothing in the Constitution requires a president, governor, or state or federal agency to enforce a SCOTUS opinion.

The President's oath of office is to "...preserve, protect and defend the Constitution of the United States"[417] not "...protect and defend the Constitution *as interpreted by the Supreme Court.*" If the President believes an action of SCOTUS or Congress violates the Constitution, he has a duty to not enforce it. Indeed, every officer or agent of federal, state, or local government—from the President all the way down to the local police officer—has a duty to defend the Constitution and protect the rights of the people in this way. When politicians refuse to stand in the way of evil and act in defense of the innocent within the power, scope, and duty of their office, they are, in fact (knowingly or not), colluding with the evil actions of the errant branch of government.

Nullification And Interposition: A Remedy to Tyranny

Here is where the principles of nullification and interposition become a remedy. The case for nullification of federal overreach by state

---

[416] Publius. [Hamilton, A.]. (1788, June 25, 28). The Federalist No. 81. *Independent Journal*. Retrieved http://www.constitution.org/fed/ federa81.htm

[417] U.S. Constitution. Article II, Section I, Clause 8.

governments is more thoroughly and scholarly laid out elsewhere,[418] but here, I will simply give a brief description and a few prime examples.

In this context, *nullification* occurs when a state declares the edicts of the federal government (be they law or court opinion) to be null and void by virtue of their violation of the Constitution. *Interposition* happens when an officer or agent of government places him or herself between an aggressor and their intended victim in order to stop an evil act from occurring. This can occur in the context of nullification, where state or local law enforcement would interpose between the people and federal agents attempting to enforce the unconstitutional edict in question. Interposition can also occur in the context of the Christian doctrine of the lesser magistrate or the related doctrine of subsidiarity (discussed later in this chapter). Let us look at some examples of nullification.

Virginia and Kentucky Resolutions

The most famous, often-cited examples of state nullification in our nation's history are the Virginia[419] and Kentucky[420] resolutions of 1798. In 1798, President John Adams signed into law the Alien Act and the Sedition Act.[421] The Sedition Act essentially made it a federal crime to criticize the President or federal government. In response, the Virginia and Kentucky legislatures passed resolutions declaring the acts

---

[418] Woods, T. E., Jr. (2010). *Nullification: How to resist federal tyranny in the 21st century*. Washington, DC: Regnery Publishing. ISBN: 1596981490.

[419] Constitution Society. (2017). Virginia Resolution of 1798. Retrieved from http://www.constitution.org/cons/virg1798.htm

[420] Constitution Society. (2017). Kentucky Resolutions of 1798. Retrieved from http://www.constitution.org/cons/kent1798.htm

[421] University of Oklahoma College of Law. (2017). The Sedition Act of 1798. Retrieved from http://www.law.ou.edu/ushistory/sedact.shtml

"unconstitutional"[422] and "altogether void, and of no force."[423] President Woodrow Wilson signed a second Sedition Act into law in 1918.[424, 425] SCOTUS upheld the Sedition Act in *Abrams v. United States*,[426] but Congress repealed the act in 1920.

Personal Liberty Laws

In response to the Fugitive Slave Acts of 1793 and 1850, numerous state legislatures in the North passed personal liberty laws. These laws served to thwart slave owners and federal agents in their attempts to recapture slaves that had escaped into northern states.[427]

Firearms Freedom Act

With federal firearms regulations encroaching on the 2nd Amendment, particularly during the Obama administration, 11 states passed a Firearms Freedom Act,[428] nullifying federal regulations. Between 2008 and 2014, more than three-quarters of U.S. states proposed nullification of federal firearms laws.[429]

---

[422] Ibid., Virginia Resolution of 1798

[423] Ibid., Kentucky Resolutions of 1798

[424] Sedition Act. (1918). Pub.L. 65–150, 40 Stat. 553.

[425] *New York Times* archive. (1918, May 7). Sedition bill sent to Wilson by House. Retrieved from https://query.nytimes.com/mem/archive-free/pdf?res=9C04EFD61F3FE433A2575BC0A9639C946996D6CF

[426] *Abrams v. United States*. (1919). 250 US 616.

[427] *Cyclopædia of Political Science, Political Economy, and the Political History of the United States.* (1899). [Ed. J.J. Lalor]. Personal liberty laws. III.50.1 - III.50.7. Retrieved from http://www.econlib.org/library/YPDBooks /Lalor/llCy820.html

[428] Kant, G. (2013). New law protects Second Amendment from feds. Retrieved from http://www.wnd.com/2013/04/new-law-protects-2nd-amendment-from-feds/

[429] McDaniel, J., Korth, R., & Boehm, J. (2014). In states, a legislative rush to nullify federal gun laws. Retrieved from https://www.washingtonpost

The State Sovereignty Movement

According to a National Conference of State Legislatures analysis, overreaching federal mandates are igniting a surge in state-level nullification efforts. For example, states have proposed and enacted measures to refuse to implement the Real ID Act and grant citizens opt-out rights for the Affordable Care Act.[430] The uprising of this 10th Amendment-based movement is due largely to the Internet, which has given conservatives a voice to push back against the federal government and return important issues to the states. But nullification is not just a conservative strategy.

THE LEFT'S EMBRACE OF NULLIFICATION

The Left has demonstrated some of the most effective nullification efforts in their push for sanctuary cities, which, according to the Center for Immigration Studies, now number in the hundreds.[431] Progressives have also nullified federal marijuana laws in 28 states[432] through legislative measures or direct-ballot initiatives that directly violate the federal ban on medicinal and recreational marijuana use. And yet, no one seems to care. The discussion of proposed legislation always focuses on

---

.com/blogs/govbeat/wp/2014/08/29/in-states-a-legislative-rush-to-nullify-federal-gun-laws/?utm_term=.f2754244e669

[430] Weiss, S. (2010). Sovereignty measures and other steps may indicate an upsurge in anti-federal sentiment in legislatures. Retrieved from http://www.ncsl.org/research/about-state-legislatures/facing-off-with-the-feds.aspx

[431] Dinan, S. (2015). Number of sanctuary cities grows to 340; thousands of illegal immigrants released to commit new crimes. Retrieved from http://www.washingtontimes.com/news/2015/oct/8/number-of-sanctuary-cities-grows-to-340-thousands-/

[432] Steinmetz, K. (2016). These states just legalized marijuana. Retrieved from http://time.com/4559278/marijuana-election-results-2016/

the efficacy of the proposed changes in state regulation, not on the violation of federal law.

Rule of Law

Some argue that we are a nation of laws, and as such, the rule of law must be preserved. In this argument, nullification equates to lawless anarchy, and the Civil War has already answered the question of states' rights. I submit to you that any law that sanctions the execution of 60 million innocent Americans is no law at all! How can anarchy be a concern when the abortion holocaust that we preside over is the greatest genocide that humanity has ever perpetrated upon itself in the history of the world? Like the politicians and law enforcement of today, the Nazi war criminals at the Nuremburg trials claimed that they were "only following orders."[433] We did not tolerate this plea then, and we certainly should not tolerate it now.

The Doctrines of the Lesser Magistrate and Subsidiarity

The truth is that, even if *Roe* was "the law of the land" and nullification was not a legitimate option, our state and local civil governments still have a duty to interpose on behalf of the preborn. This is because we *all* answer to a higher authority. Scripture makes it clear that we are to obey the lawful authority placed over us,[434] but when there is conflict with God's commands, "We ought to obey God rather than men."[435] This declaration, as well as the duty to protect the

---

[433] King, H.T., Jr. (2002). The legacy of Nuremberg. *Case Western Journal of International Law, 34.* p. 335.e.
[434] Romans 13:1-7
[435] Acts 5:29

innocent,[436] are the foundation of the Christian doctrine of *the lesser magistrate*. Although this doctrine is thoroughly defined and assessed elsewhere,[437, 438] it can be simply defined as follows: When a higher government authority makes an unjust and/or immoral law or decree that violates God's law, the lower ranking government authority has a right and duty to refuse to comply with the superior authority. The lesser authority even has the right and obligation to actively resist the superior authority and to interpose on behalf of the higher authorities' intended victims. The doctrine often goes hand-in-hand with nullification and interposition. In many cases, this doctrine is easier to initiate at the local level, through a pro-life county sheriff or mayor.

One could also appeal to the doctrine of *subsidiarity* in defiance of a tyrant and in interposition for the oppressed. Pope Pius XI outlined subsidiarity in his encyclical, *Quadragesimo Anno*:

> *"[I]t is an injustice and at the same time a grave civil evil and disturbance of right order, to transfer to the larger and higher collectivity functions which can be performed and provided for by lesser and subordinate bodies. Inasmuch as every social activity should, by its very nature, prove a help to members of the body social, it should never destroy or absorb them."*[439]

---

[436] Proverbs 24:11-12 and 31:8-9

[437] Junius Brutus. (1689). A defence of liberty against tyrants. [Translation of The Vindiciae Contra Tyrannos]. (1923). Retrieved from http://www.constitution.org/vct/vind.htm

[438] Pastors of Megdeburg. (1550). The Magdeburg Confession: 13th of April 1550 AD. [English translation]. (2012). CreateSpace Independent Publishing Platform. ISBN-10: 1470087537.

[439] Pope Pius XI. (1931, May 15). *Quadragesimo Anno*: Encyclical of Pope Pius XI on reconstruction of the social order. [Vatican].

Subsidiarity is related to, but distinct from, the doctrine of the lesser magistrate, in that subsidiarity goes further. It holds that certain types of actions wrought by a higher political order upon a lower order may possibly be unjust (and thus, subject to disobedience by the lesser magistrate). But it also presumes that any interference with the internal life of a lower order must necessarily be unjust, unless certain exceptions are met (for example, support in the case of need or common good).

In Conclusion

Scripture tells us we must be wary of the lies meant to hold us captive:

> *"See to it that no one takes you captive by philosophy and empty deceit, according to human tradition, according to the elemental spirits of the world, and not according to Christ."*[440]
>
> *"Take no part in the unfruitful works of darkness, but instead expose them."*[441]

It is in this spirit that I propose the following legal strategy to achieve equal protection for the preborn:

1. Ignore the "lawyers that are for the lawyers." Work with ethical attorneys that do not prostrate themselves in reverence before the Supreme Court.
2. Enact meaningful Personhood legislation at the state level using the confrontational model provided in another chapter in this book: "Political Failure and the Path to Victory."

---

[440] Colossians 2:8
[441] Ephesians 5:11

3. Get governors who, along with the backing of their legislatures, will enforce the Personhood legislation in defiance of the federal government.
4. Work toward a federal constitutional amendment to protect the preborn in all states and prevent future pendulum swings that would likely decriminalize abortion.

[Christopher Kurka has spent his life in Alaska, pouring his energies into political efforts in the state since a young teenager. He joined the board of Alaska Right to Life in 2006, serving as Vice President and Treasurer before becoming Executive Director in 2013. Christopher served on the board of the National Right to Life Committee for 4 years before leaving to pursue more principled means of ending abortion. He now sits on the board of Personhood Alliance and helps facilitate 1-day classes for the Foundation for Applied Conservative Leadership. Christopher's passion is to establish justice for the preborn and see God's people raised up to call the pro-life movement to a new standard. Christopher lives in Palmer, Alaska with his wife, Haylee, and their two sons, Justice and Samuel.]

CHAPTER 15

THE WISCONSIN PERSONHOOD AMENDMENT

By Matt Sande, Director of Legislation, Pro-Life Wisconsin

After 44 years of abortion-on-demand in America, the pro-life movement is losing patience with an incremental legislative approach that simply manages the killing of our preborn brothers and sisters. For this reason, work to restore legal personhood to the preborn child is gaining momentum across the country. From South Carolina to California, state-by-state efforts to codify prenatal personhood are generating a new enthusiasm in the pro-life movement. Since its founding in 1992, Pro-Life Wisconsin[442] has worked steadily to enshrine total protection for every preborn child into Wisconsin law. We now have an opportunity to make our efforts permanent in a proposed Wisconsin Personhood Amendment.[443]

---

[442] https://www.prolifewi.org/

[443] Wisconsin General Assembly. (2013). Assembly Joint Resolution 49.

Ending Abortion, Not Restricting It

The Wisconsin Personhood Amendment, authored by State Representative André Jacque, would extend the inalienable right to life already found in the Wisconsin Constitution to all preborn humans from their biological beginning. The amendment seeks to end abortion in Wisconsin, not to regulate or restrict it. It seeks to end all violence toward preborn children in Wisconsin—be it surgical, chemical, or experimental—at all stages of development. It considers the preborn human being a person; a citizen upon whom full legal rights confer. Simply put, it treats the preborn child like you and me.

The Wisconsin Constitution contained a glaring error at its outset. In specifying the beneficiaries of human rights, it referenced only those people who are "born." The proposed Wisconsin Personhood Amendment simply substitutes the following inclusive personhood definition:

> *Article 1. Declaration of Rights. Equality; inherent rights. SECTION 1. All people are ~~born~~ equally free and independent, and have certain inherent rights; among these are life, liberty and the pursuit of happiness; to secure these rights, governments are instituted, deriving their just powers from the consent of the governed. As applied to the right to life, the terms "people" and "person" shall apply to every human being at any stage of development.*[444]

A Constitutional Amendment, Not a Statute

A constitutional amendment, rather than a statutory change, is necessary in the state of Wisconsin. Should *Roe v. Wade*[445] be overturned

---

[444] Ibid.
[445] *Roe v. Wade*. (1973). 410 US 113, No. 70-18.

and the abortion issue remanded to the states, an activist Wisconsin Supreme Court could use "born" to interpret an independent right to abortion in the constitution itself. In so doing, the court could nullify any current or future pro-life laws.

The changing makeup of the Wisconsin legislature could also put current and future pro-life laws in jeopardy. Every two years, our state election process determines the majority party in Madison. Legal protection of the preborn, and their inherent right to life, should not and must not be contingent upon which party controls the state legislature. A constitutional amendment helps to address this threat, in that, by law, it requires passage in two successive legislatures, followed by a simple majority vote of the people.

Pro-Life Wisconsin's proposed Personhood Amendment is not intended or worded as a challenge to *Roe,* or as an attempt to define personhood under the 14th Amendment of the United States Constitution. Rather, the amendment seeks only to bring into the Wisconsin Constitution equal protection for all human life, as endorsed by Wisconsin citizens. We recognize that the amendment's protections cannot be fully effective as long as *Roe* remains, but we believe a proper definition of personhood must in place should Wisconsin be freed from the effects of that unjust decision.

A Call to Stand

Americans, born and preborn, deserve total, permanent, and equal protection of their right to life. Now is the time to demand that the personhood of all humans be enshrined in our state constitution. We must oppose incremental legislative proposals that expressly deny protections for certain preborn children, through exceptions for rape, incest, and fetal anomaly, for example. In like manner, we must also oppose improperly constructed definitions for life or health of the mother exceptions, because they, too, reinforce the unjust foundations of *Roe*.

It is time to be bold. Every week, abortion destroys 105 preborn children in Wisconsin. It is time to be principled. Making compromises, allowing exceptions, caving to political pressures, and waiting for "the right time" can only lead to failure. President Ronald Reagan, in his 1988 National Sanctity of Human Life Day proclamation, said it best:

> *"Our nation cannot continue down the path of abortion, so radically at odds with our history, our heritage, and our concepts of justice. This sacred legacy, and the well-being and the future of our country, demand that protection of the innocents must be guaranteed and that the personhood of the unborn be declared and defended throughout our land."*[446]

[Matt Sande joined Pro-Life Wisconsin as the organization's Director of Legislation in 2003. Public policy and politics are his passion. A 1991 political science graduate from the University of Notre Dame and a former legislative aide in both the Wisconsin State Assembly and State Senate, Matt has directly participated in the political process for over 20 years. He resides in the city of Jefferson with his wife Rebecca and six children.]

---

[446] Reagan, R. (1988, January 14). Proclamation 5671: National Sanctity of Human Life Day, 1988. Retrieved from https://reaganlibrary.archives.gov/archives/speeches/1988/011488d.htm

CHAPTER 16

Personhood Does Not Criminalize Miscarriages, IVF, or Contraception

By Dr. J. Patrick Johnston, D.O., Director, Association of Pro-Life Physicians; President, Personhood Ohio

Having long defended the right to life, I am accustomed to the smoke and mirrors put forth by abortion advocates. The case for the right to life focuses like a laser on the biological beginning of life, for there the cause is won or lost. But rather than deal with definitive embryological science, abortion advocates regularly detract from the moral and scientific clarity on this subject to excite bias and confuse the uninformed.

The Straw Man Argument

Abortion advocates often resort to scare tactics, as they have in Georgia, Iowa, Mississippi, Montana, North Dakota, Oklahoma, and other states, by accusing the proposed personhood legislation or amendment of having the potential to criminalize miscarriages, ban *in vitro* fertilization, and outlaw contraceptives. These accusations need to be addressed.

Personhood Law Defined

Before we evaluate what personhood legislation is not, let us briefly establish what it is. A personhood amendment or piece of legislation simply declares that, for the purpose of law, life begins at conception, or fertilization. It is interesting to note that Dr. Landrum Shettles, known as the father of *in vitro* fertilization, concurs with this fact:

> *"Conception confers life and makes that life one of a kind."*[447]

Even the father of modern genetics, Dr. Jerome Lejeune, added his voice to the resounding chorus that confirms life begins at conception, or fertilization:

> *"To accept the fact that after fertilization has taken place a new human has come into being is no longer a matter of taste or opinion... it is plain experimental evidence."*[448]

Personhood legislation brings law into compliance with the facts of biological development[449] and into alignment with the divine commandment, "You shall not murder."[450] The constitutional separation

---

[447] Shettles, L., MD, & Rorvik, D. (1983). *Rites of life: The scientific evidence for life before birth.* Grand Rapids, MI: Zondervan Publishing House, p.36.

[448] U.S. Senate. (1981). Report, Subcommittee on Separation of Powers to Senate Judiciary Committee S-158, 97th Congress, 1st session. See: Alcorn, R. (2017). Scientists attest to life beginning at conception. Retrieved from http://naapc.org/why-life-begins-at-conception/

[449] Terzo, S. (2015). 41 quotes from medical textbooks prove human life begins at conception. Retrieved from http://tinyurl.com/o9ahgm7

[450] Exodus 20:13

of powers, per the 9th and 10th Amendments,[451] enables state legislatures to criminalize the killing of all preborn children. This is state legislatures' lawful jurisdiction for criminal justice, defying judicial tyranny if they must.

Personhood Law Does Not Criminalize Miscarriage

Before *Roe v. Wade*,[452] when abortion was criminalized in most states, was a woman who had a miscarriage ever prosecuted for the death of her child? Of course not. Personhood legislation certainly does not criminalize the unintentional loss of human life. When a child is stillborn, when an infant inadvertently dies during surgery, or when a baby dies of sudden infant death syndrome (SIDS), are parents or physicians ever convicted in court for murder? Never. Murder, by definition, implies intent to kill. A miscarriage is an unfortunate, unintentional death of another human being. Even if a couple repeatedly conceived and miscarried every child, they would not be prosecuted because there was no intent to kill.

Personhood Law Does Not Ban In Vitro Fertilization

In IVF, the intent is to bring human life into existence, not to destroy human life. IVF practitioners would not be affected by personhood legislation as long as IVF procedures do not knowingly endanger or intentionally kill a human being. However, if an IVF practitioner intentionally killed a human being conceived through IVF—as is often

---

[451] University of Minnesota Human Rights Library. (2017). All amendments to the United States Constitution. Retrieved from http://hrlibrary.umn.edu/education/all_amendments_usconst.htm

[452] *Roe v. Wade*. (1973). 410 US 113, No. 70-18.

recommended to selectively reduce multiple implanted embryos or when embryos are intentionally destroyed—prosecution would be appropriate. These are living human beings created in the image of God, and killing them is always wrong.

Couples trying to conceive through IVF would not be affected by personhood legislation unless they consented to the intentional endangerment or destruction of their embryonic children. Unfortunately, IVF practitioners have almost universally adopted the immoral practice of intentionally destroying human embryos, but this destruction is not necessary for IVF to be effective at helping parents conceive.

Personhood Law Does Not Outlaw Contraception

Lastly, personhood legislation does not criminalize contraception. Contraception, by definition, prevents conception. "Contra" is a prefix meaning "against."[453] Thus, contraception means "against conception." Preventing conception never involves abortion. If a contraceptive caused the death of an embryo, it would not in that case be a contraceptive, but an *abortifacient* (an abortion-inducing drug).

Some have argued that hormonal contraceptives act by causing abortions at least some of the time by preventing the implantation of the embryo into the *endometrium* (the inner lining of the uterus). The FDA-approved product inserts of hormonal contraceptives assert that one of the modes of action is to prevent implantation, which would thus

---

[453] Miller-Keane. (2003). Contra. [entry]. *Miller-Keane Encyclopedia and Dictionary of Medicine, Nursing, and Allied Health*, [7th Ed.] Saunders-Elsevier, Inc.

facilitate the expulsion and demise of the newly created human being.[454] However, an often-cited finding in the *American Journal of Obstetrics and Gynecology* echoes the present consensus on this issue:

> *"Hormonal methods, particularly low-dose progestin-only products and emergency contraception pills have effects on the endometrium that, theoretically, could affect implantation. However, no scientific evidence indicates that prevention of implantation actually results from the use of these methods."*[455]

Theoretically is the key term here. At present, preventing implantation is still a suspected, yet unproven mode of action of hormonal contraceptives. In spite of the FDA's assertion that hormonal contraceptives act in part by preventing implantation, there is a lack of definitive evidence that they do so. It is true that hormonal contraceptives thin the endometrium increasingly over many *anovulatory* (non-ovulating) cycles, and it is true that a thinner endometrium decreases the chances of implantation in IVF in anovulating women, but ovulation changes everything. The natural function of the corpus luteum, which is activated by ovulation, is to prepare the thinner endometrium for implantation. In a breakthrough ovulation, it is possible that the physiological effect of the corpus luteum is adequate to prepare the endometrium for implantation in the 6 to 12 days it takes the newly conceived embryo to traverse the fallopian tube

---

[454] Conscience Laws Project. (2017). FDA-approved methods of birth control: Mechanisms of action. Retrieved from http://www.consciencelaws .org/background/procedures/birth014-002.aspx#

[455] Rivera, R., MD, Yacobson, I., MD, & Grimes, D., MD. (1999). The mechanism of action of hormonal contraceptives and intrauterine contraceptive devices. *American Journal of Obstetrics and Gynecology, 181*: 1263-9. Retrieved from http://www.ajog.org/article/S0002-9378(99)70120-1/fulltext

to the uterus. This possibility is evidenced by the existence of those who were conceived despite their mothers' hormonal contraceptive use (including this author!).

If a state enacted a personhood law, hormonal contraceptive use may need to be suspended for a careful investigation to demonstrate their safely for children conceived in breakthrough ovulations, but they would not necessarily be banned. Doubtless, the medical community and governing authorities are culpable for not requiring such safety studies before approving these substances for contraceptive use. If hormonal contraceptives were demonstrated to be a threat to human embryos, these drugs would be considered abortifacient and certainly not appropriate for contraceptive use.

In Summary

A law or amendment declaring the indisputable, biological fact that the onset of human life occurs at fertilization is appropriate and long overdue—all of the smoke and mirrors of abortion advocates notwithstanding. Personhood would definitely establish a new paradigm through which contraceptive and IVF technology would require evaluation and possibly, modification. In the face of scientific uncertainty, the precautionary principle should always lead us to adopt the necessary provisions to safeguard the wellbeing of innocent human beings by erring on the side of life. Just as the moral imperative of ending slavery created serious questions about the care of freed slaves in the largely racist South, forbidding the destruction of human embryos from abortifacients and IVF would likewise be a moral imperative that engenders inconvenience. However, any inconvenience that society endured for protecting the slaves, and would endure for protecting the preborn, pales in comparison to the grave evil of shedding innocent blood. As Thomas Jefferson so aptly stated:

> *"The care of human life and happiness, and not their destruction, is the first and only object of good government."*[456]

[Dr. Patrick Johnston is a family practice physician and the father of ten home-educated children. He has authored ten novels, including *The Reliant*, which he has produced as a full feature film starring Kevin Sorbo, Brian Bosworth, and Eric Roberts. He also directs ProLifePhysicians.org and Personhood Ohio, but marrying the love of his life, Elizabeth, aka "The Activist Mommy," is his claim to fame.]

---

[456] Jefferson, T. (1871). Letter to the Republican citizens of Washington County, Maryland. *The Writings of Thomas Jefferson*. [Ed. Washington, H.A.], vol. 8, p. 165.

SECTION V

Personhood and Politics

CHAPTER 17

Personhood Provides Equal Protection Without Discrimination

By Rebecca Kiessling, Esq., Founder and President of Save the 1; Co-founder, Hope After Rape Conception

All children deserve to be equally protected. However, in many jurisdictions, the rape-conceived are not only denied equal protection in the womb, but are also discriminated against in such a way that politicians even ensure tax dollars pay for us to be killed. It is simply inhumane to punish an innocent child for someone else's crime. I know this injustice personally, as I was conceived in rape. I did not deserve the death penalty for the crime of my biological father. My own mother tried to end my life twice in 1969, through illegal abortion. When we finally met in 1988, she was pro-choice. But today, we are thankful we were both protected from the horror of abortion while she was still pregnant with me.

Rape exceptions, and other exceptions in pro-life law, send a message to my people group that our lives are worth less than others.

We feel both the sting of discrimination and the apathy directed toward us. Mothers who are victims of rape grieve how their children are ruthlessly targeted, devalued, and exploited for political gain. Some women are even accused of lying about being raped because they gave their children life.

While we appreciate and wholly acknowledge sincere concern for rape victims, we also know that calls for abortion in cases of rape come from a corrupted version of compassion and actually do harm to the rape victims themselves. Rape victims who abort their children are four times more likely to die within the year after their abortion, as opposed to those victims who give birth.[457] This is because, after an abortion, rape victims have a higher rate of death from murder, suicide, and drug overdose, among other related causes. [458] Harm also comes from the environment in which the victim lives.

Rapists, child molesters, and sex traffickers rely on abortion because it destroys the evidence of their crimes and enables them to continue perpetrating. Oftentimes, a young girl's mother is exploiting her, or leaving her unprotected in the home, and is the one seeking the abortion. It is always the baby who exposes the rape or delivers a girl out of an abusive situation. It is the baby who protects her and helps to bring

---

[457] Reardon, M. S., Dr. (2000). *Victims and victors: Speaking out about their pregnancies, abortions, and children resulting from sexual assault*. St. Paul, MN: Acorn Publishing.

[458] Ibid.

her healing.[459] To truly care about rape victims is to protect them from their perpetrators *and* abortion, not their baby.

Lethal Discrimination in the Law

The sad truth is that some candidates and organizations are "more pro-life" than others. The compromises they feel they must make for incremental gain are, at their core, lethal discrimination enshrined in the law. For this reason, it is important to know where candidates and organizations stand. This is not a political game. I literally owe my life to the law being there to protect me. My heroes are pro-life legislators who recognize that mine was a life worth saving, even in the case of rape. My mother did not choose life for me. She chose abortion but ultimately backed out because it was illegal. Whether our mothers want to abort us or not, the rape-conceived are in need of heroes – those who are willing to protect us without exception and without compromise.

Protected by the Law

I am from Michigan where there has never been a rape exception in a single law. It is not because Michigan is a red state—we are actually purple. It is because Right to Life of Michigan (RLM) is a no-exceptions, no-compromise organization. RLM made the determination in the early 1970s that they would never forsake the child conceived in rape. This means a candidate does not get their PAC endorsement in the primaries if he or she makes a rape exception. RLM also does not endorse any legislation in Michigan that contains a rape exception. As a result,

---

[459] Kiessling, R., Esq. (2017). Pregnant by rape stories. Retrieved from http://www.rebeccakiessling.com/other-conceived-in-rape-stories/pregnant-by-rape-stories/

Michigan has passed some of the most principled laws in the nation—clean laws, with no exceptions. Legislators even overrode the governor's veto of an abortion insurance bill a couple of years ago with a statewide petition drive and a majority vote in the House and Senate.[460] This was due to RLM's stellar pro-life leadership.

For many years, RLM was the only affiliate of National Right to Life Committee (NRLC) who refused to compromise on the rape exception. In the early 1970s, there was a schism within the pro-life movement over whether to forsake the child conceived in rape. Nellie Gray, founder of the March for Life, helped to lead the principled stance. Each year at the march, organizers read the Life Principles,[461] a statement of values that outlined Nellie's no-compromise declarations.[462] Judie Brown, President of American Life League, also knows this schism all too well. She, too, has fought for equal protection for every human life, without exception.[463] Sadly, the majority voice on the national level has been that of compromise. The movement at large and innocent children conceived in rape have suffered as a result.

Pragmatism and Pro-life Victory: You Can Have Both

At the state level, RLM was able to successfully persuade other state groups across the nation to embrace the no exceptions, no compromise

---

[460] Oosting, J. (2013). Michigan legislature approves controversial abortion insurance bill. Retrieved from http://www.mlive.com/politics/index.ssf/2013/12/michigan_legislature_approves_1.html

[461] March for Life. (2017). Life principles. Retrieved from http://marchforlife.org/life-principles/

[462] March for Life. (2013). Nellie Gray: Pro-life hero. Retrieved from http://marchforlife.org/nellie-gray-pro-life-hero/

[463] American Life League. (2017). Abortion exceptions. Retrieved from http://www.all.org/learn/abortion/exceptions/

model, including Georgia Right to Life (GRTL). Daniel Becker, former President of GRTL, details Georgia's dramatic transformation in his book, *Personhood: A Pragmatic Guide to Pro-Life Victory in the 21st Century and the Return to First Principles in Politics.*[464] Americans United for Life had ranked Georgia the worst pro-life state in the nation—even worse than California or New York, because it had no enforceable pro-life laws on the books.[465] Only 3% of legislators in Georgia were 100% pro-life. When GRTL decided to move to the no exceptions, no compromise model, half of their board left. Both Democrats and Republicans told them they were finished in Georgia and rendered irrelevant. Within 10 years, Georgia's pro-life ranking went from 50th to 8th,[466] including an "All Star" rating.[467] Georgia's laws have no rape exceptions! Every statewide elected official, from the Governor and the Lt. Governor to the Secretary of State and Attorney General, was 100% pro-life.[468] In fact, the officials signed an affidavit with GRTL vowing not to compromise on their no-exceptions stance. This is *only* because of GRTL's leadership and their refusal to abandon their principles.

---

[464] Available at http://www.tkspublications.com

[465] Becker, D. (2011). *Personhood: A pragmatic guide to pro-life victory in the 21st century*. Alpharetta, GA. p 156, endnote 16. In the year 2000, Georgia had no enforceable pro-life laws. "We did have a partial-birth abortion ban that was neutered and rendered useless [unenforceable] by the Georgia Supreme Court."

[466] Burke, D., et al. (2010). *Defending life 2010: Proven strategies for a pro-life America*. Washington, DC: Americans United for Life, 509.

[467] Americans United for Life. (2013). AUL's 2013 Life List: All stars. Retrieved from http://www.aul.org/auls-2013-life-list-all-stars/

[468] Georgia is the only state in the nation in which all of its top executive officers (elected on a statewide ballot) are pro-life without exceptions.

INTO THE FIRE

Meanwhile, in the U.S. Congress, almost no work is being done to put equal protection into action. The NRLC and other national organizations view their strategy of compromise as effective and thus, do not pressure lawmakers to stand on principle. The burning building analogy is often used to defend this strategy, which suggests that when a building is on fire, the firemen will try to rescue as many people in the building as they can, while working toward saving all of them. Their slogan is, "Save the 99, in exchange for the one." This leaves the 1% behind, whether the 1% is conceived in rape or has fetal abnormalities. This analogy fails, however, because the compromisers are not working to save all. The reality is that they shut the water off, send the fire trucks home, and then watch the building burn with the one left inside. They never go back to save the 1%.

The Hyde Amendment's rape exception has been in place for almost three decades, but instead of working to challenge it, organizations have allowed the rape exception to become the standard. Now, the Hyde Amendment is regularly used to justify legislative language because a bill "merely incorporates the terms of Hyde." They have already determined that the child conceived in rape is an expendable casualty and not worth the effort to defend.

JESUS ON THE EXCEPTIONS

Whenever I encounter efforts to "save the 99 in exchange for the one," I think of the Parable of the Lost Sheep.[469] Jesus was all about

---

[469] Matthew 18:12-14; Luke 15:3-7

saving the one! He begins with this admonition: "See that you do not despise any of these little ones." Despise? What a strange thing to say. Who would despise a little one? Unfortunately, many. Conservative commentator Sean Hannity labeled us an "evil seed" while interviewing Lila Rose in 2013.[470] Bishop Paul Morton , Jr., called us a "demon seed, not what God created" at a 2014 pastors conference with 2,000 in attendance.[471] We are called "a horrible reminder of the rape," "demon spawn," and "monster's child," and are accused of "tainting the gene pool." Yes, we are despised—certainly more than any other people group today.

Jesus continues: "For I tell you that their angels in Heaven always look upon the face of my Father in Heaven." He explains how the Good Shepherd leaves the 99 to save the one and ends by saying, "In the same way, your Father in Heaven is not willing that any of these little ones should perish." Neither should we be willing! Who are "the least of these" of whom Jesus spoke?[472] Are not children conceived in rape the least of the least in today's society? Perhaps many pro-life leaders are willing to let these little ones perish because we are so despised and therefore, it is somehow easier on them. This is contrary to the heart of God.

---

[470] Hannity, S. (2013, April 13). Lila Rose: Undercover in America's late-term abortion industry. [Audio recording]. Retrieved from https://soundcloud.com/seanhannityshow/lila-rose-undercover-in

[471] Childress, C., Jr., Rev. (2014). Bishop Paul Norton calls children conceived in rape, demons... Retrieved from http://www.blacknews.com/ news/bishop-paul-morton-calls-children-conceived-in-rape-demons/#.WOU7x8s2xMs

[472] Matthew 25:40

Back Into the Fire

Let us look at the burning building analogy again from the perspective of the legislator. Here, we have people (political candidates) lining up for job interviews (campaigns) to become firefighters (legislators). In their interviews, these prospective firefighters tell the fire chiefs (the leaders in the pro-life movement), "Just so you know, I discriminate. Yeah, if I go into a burning building and there are children in the midst of the fire in the back of the building, I am not going to save them. They are going to be painfully disfigured and thus, will be a horrible reminder of the fire. I am just not going to do that to their parents, so I am going to let them die. And if you try to force me to go in and save them, I just won't go in and save any." What kind of fire chief would hire such a person? And what kind of fire chief would not only hire him, but give him recognition for leaving the children in the back of the building to die? Unfortunately, this is what far too many pro-life leaders do when they endorse candidates who embrace exceptions and even reward them with "100% pro-life" approval ratings. The burning building predicament is entirely preventable because there are good firefighters who do not discriminate. However, there is another reality to consider.

Not only do many fire chiefs hire and reward the discriminatory firefighters, they also attack the other fire chiefs who refuse to do the same. In Georgia, for example, the actions of Georgia Life Alliance threaten to undermine the work of GRTL by destabilizing their hard-won policy of non-discrimination. In 2016, Georgia Life Alliance gave U.S. Congressman Doug Collins (Georgia, 9th district) a 100% approval rating and honored him with the Federal Legislator of the Year award,[473] even though he allows for rape exceptions. Let me be clear: With actions such as these, Georgia Life Alliance will bring the state of Georgia back to the days of last place.

National-level organizations like NRLC do this often as well. For example, in 2013, then-House Majority Leader Eric Cantor enjoyed a 100% approval rating by the NRLC, even though he introduced the rape exception in the Pain Capable Unborn Child Protection Act.[474] It is critical for people to understand that 100% approval ratings from pro-life organizations do not necessarily mean candidates are actually 100% pro-life. It merely means the politician voted the way NRLC wanted them to.

The Sting of Discrimination

Not only do preborn children conceived in rape feel pain, but the 450+ members of my organization, Save The 1, who were conceived in rape or who are mothers from rape, feel it, too. I assure you, the pain inflicted when we are targeted and devalued is life-long.

Far too many for far too long have treated my people group as a scapegoat and pawn—the bargaining chip of the pro-life movement. Over and over, we are punished, not only for the sins of our biological fathers, but also for the sins of mediocre politicians. Consider the outrage if we replaced the rape-conceived with any other people group, for

---

[473] Georgia Life Alliance. (2016). GLA life at the party gala re-cap. Retrieved from http://georgialifealliance.com/gla-life-at-the-party-gala-re-cap/

[474] LifeSiteNews. (2013). GOP leadership adds rape, incest exceptions to 20-week abortion ban; House votes tomorrow. Retrieved from https://www.lifesitenews.com/news/gop-leadership-adds-rape-incest-exceptions-to-20-week-abortion-ban-house-vo

example, "except in cases of being Jewish," or African-American, or Muslim. What message would that send to every member of that community? It would speak clearly to them that their lives are not as valuable; that they are not as worthy of protection as everyone else. Make no mistake. No other people group is as systematically targeted and discriminated against in today's society as the child conceived in rape.

Some have challenged my strong stance on this issue, saying: “This is not about you, Rebecca. You take this strategy too personally.” Or sometimes I hear: “It’s nothing against you personally.” But I *am* a person, so how can it not be personal? Nothing is more personal than an attack on someone’s right not to be killed. However, I am alive. I am safe. It would be selfish not to protect others like me from being killed. So this begs the question: If “pro-life” laws do not protect people like me from being killed, who exactly are they protecting? The tragic answer is politicians.

A Culture of Life

A good nation is one that establishes a culture of life in which all people are loved and accepted. Exceptions are a symptom of a culture of death and discrimination. Personhood defeats the culture of death at its foundation, because there are no exceptions. Either you are a person deserving of equal protection under the law, or not. Section 1 of the 14th Amendment affirms:

> *“No state shall make or enforce any law which shall abridge the privileges or immunities of citizens of the United States; nor shall*

> *any state deprive any person of life, liberty, or property, without due process of law; nor deny to any person within its jurisdiction the equal protection of the laws.*[475]

Rape exceptions violate equal protection. One cannot claim to support constitutional government while also denying its equal protection requirements for all of its people. This is why I urge pro-lifers to support Personhood Amendments at the state and national level. I also encourage the legal community to challenge legislation like the Hyde Amendment on the grounds that it violates the equal protection clause of the 14th Amendment.

Personhood is a superior strategy—not only morally, but practically. A politician's 100% approval rating really should mean what it suggests. It should be the litmus test for how passionate a candidate is about protecting all human life, regardless of how a person was conceived. Politicians can truly be our champions. They can bring the pro-life movement out of political stagnation and help bring reason back into pro-life policy. So let us punish rapists, not babies, and let us protect babies, not politicians.

[Rebecca Kiessling is a wife, a mother of 5, an attorney, and an international pro-life speaker. She is the Founder and President of the global pro-life organization Save The 1, which addresses all of the so-called "hard cases" in the abortion debate. Rebecca is also the co-founder of Hope After Rape Conception and an Executive Committee Board Member of and national spokeswoman for Personhood Alliance.]

---

[475] Cornell University Law School. (2017). 14th Amendment. Retrieved from https://www.law.cornell.edu/constitution/amendmentxiv

CHAPTER 18

Political Failure and the Path to Victory

By Christopher Kurka, Executive Director, Alaska Right to Life

"When you sit down to eat with a ruler, observe carefully what is before you, and put a knife to your throat if you are given to appetite. Do not desire his delicacies, for they are deceptive food." [476]

As the years pass and we approach a half century of preborn genocide in the United States, the pro-life movement ought to step back and assess our progress. Are we winning? How far have we come? Is our strategy working, and what about our tactics? Are we closer to our goal? How far are we from achieving total personhood protections for the preborn, elderly, and infirm?

Undoubtedly, on the cultural and spiritual side of the war, we are winning. A majority of the Millennial generation opposes abortion.[477] 40 Days for Life is seeing record numbers participate in their prayer

---

[476] Proverbs 23:1-3

[477] Wetzstein, C. (2015). Millennials bucking trends on abortion approval. Retrieved from http://www.washingtontimes.com/news/2015/jan/25/millennials-bucking-trends-on-abortion-approval/

vigils,[478] and while pregnancy resource centers multiply,[479] the number of abortion facilities continues to drastically decline.[480]

But what about the political front? Congress passed the Partial Birth Abortion Ban Act (the PBA ban) in 2003,[481] and state legislatures have passed hundreds of abortion restrictions. Nevertheless, can we honestly say that, as a country, we are meaningfully closer to equal protections for the preborn? Incremental compromise is repeatedly addressed elsewhere in this book. Here, I will assess in detail the political strategy and tactics of the pro-life movement.

THE BATTLE FOR ZERO GROUND: STRATEGY NULLIFIES POLICY

Let us look first at the PBA ban. Leading organizations in the pro-life movement spent nearly 15 years fighting to get the PBA ban enacted into law. In that time, they certainly advanced a strategic goal—to expose the horror of abortion to the general public and increase the number of pro-life supporters and activists. But what was the policy value gain?

Unfortunately, the PBA ban did not move us an inch closer to equal protection for the preborn. In *Gonzales v. Carhart,*[482] the Supreme Court

---

[478] Maslak, M. (2015). Record-breaking 40 Days for Life campaign sees monumental results. Retrieved from http://www.catholicnewsagency.com/news/record-breaking-40-days-for-life-campaign-sees-monumental-results-42367/

[479] Dias, E. (2010). The abortion battleground: Crisis pregnancy centers. Retrieved from http://content.time.com/time/nation/article/0,8599,2008846,00.html

[480] Deprez, E. (2016). Abortion clinics are closing at a record pace. Retrieved from https://www.bloomberg.com/news/articles/2016-02-24/abortion-clinics-are-closing-at-a-record-pace#media-4

[481] The Partial-Birth Abortion Ban Act. (2003). Pub.L. 108–105, 117 Stat. 1201, enacted November 5, 2003, 18 U.S.C. § 1531, PBA Ban.

[482] *Gonzales v. Carhart*. (2007). 550 US 124, No. 05-380.

upheld the PBA ban, but not because it recognized the preborn child's right to life. Instead, the court determined that banning this particular procedure did not impose an undue burden on a woman seeking an abortion—a standard set by *Planned Parenthood v. Casey*[483] in 1992. What about the fight to pass the PBA ban? Did it at least get us politically closer to a Personhood Amendment at the federal level? Not only is the answer no, but the opposite is true. Pro-abortion Democrat Senator Mary Landrieu's reelection in 2003 is credited to her vote for the PBA ban, because she was able to campaign on her "pro-life" vote, thus garnering pro-lifers' support.[484]

At most, the only benefit we can point to in the end is that the fight to pass the PBA ban grew the size of pro-life movement. But was this growth worth a zero policy gain? Could we have fought this intense battle on a more meaningful piece of legislation? Consider also that this single, long-term benefit is itself questionable. While the number of Americans opposed to late-term abortions has increased through exposure of partial-birth abortion, the number of Americans who favor restricting abortion to the first trimester, as opposed to ending it, is now approaching 80%.[485] Yet, this was the pro-life movement's greatest political effort since its inception. From a policy standpoint, we are still far from our goal—the equal protection for all human beings, through

---

[483] *Planned Parenthood of Southeastern Pennsylvania et al v. Casey*. (1992). 505 US 833, No. 91-744.

[484] US Senator Mary Landrieu has been a solid vote for the pro-abortion agenda in Congress.

[485] Benson, G. (2017). Large majorities oppose abortion restrictions. Retrieved from https://townhall.com/tipsheet/guybenson/2017/01/23/ marist-abortion-poll-n2275329

the restoration of legal personhood. After nearly a half century, we should be further along.

Unintended Consequences: Cleaning The Face Of Genocide

The PBA ban brings up a strategic consideration. To God, abortion on the day of conception is just as offensive as the day before birth. Yet, to our human sensibilities, an early chemical abortion pales in comparison to the barbarism of late-term abortion procedures like partial-birth, saline distillation, and dismemberment. If we systematically prohibit all the "ugly" abortions, will not banning first trimester abortions become more difficult? We can longer point to the gruesomeness of the uncommon late-term abortion and successfully associate it with the very common first trimester abortion.[486] Even heartbeat bills can make it more difficult to ban early chemical abortions. Consider the bills that have an exception for rape and incest. Will it not be nearly impossible to go back to protect those equally valuable children conceived in rape?[487]

This is not to say that incremental pro-life legislation is always strategically bad. However, we must analyze the long-term impact on our end goal, especially when there is such limited (or zero) policy gain. In the case of the PBA ban, and other late-term abortion restrictions, very few preborn children are protected in the long run.

---

[486] Two-thirds of abortions occur in the first 8 weeks of pregnancy. 89% occur in the first 12 weeks. See: Guttmacher Institute. (2017). Induced abortion in the United States. Retrieved from https://www.guttmacher.org/ fact-sheet/induced-abortion-united-states

[487] According to pro-life attorney Rebecca Kiessling, Esq., there is no known recorded case of a state or federal law having these deadly prejudices removed—*ex post facto*.

Reassessing our Gains

With the enormous size of the grassroots pro-life movement, how is it that we are not any closer to securing personhood protections for the preborn than we were in 1973? On the contrary, Progressives have gained much. The LBGTQ movement has crushed its opposition, through legislation, the courts, and even through the culture. Yet, adults who identify as LBGTQ make up only 3.4% of the U.S. population.[488] The power of unions in politics is another example. Even though only 10.6% of U.S workers are union members,[489] unions have significant influence over both political parties, particularly the Democrat party. Why are they winning? What is it that they are doing that we are not?

Many pro-life activists have become disillusioned with the movement's political strategy and have left the political arena altogether. They vote out of duty, or not at all, believing the political process is a waste of time. However, to end the genocide of abortion, personhood protections for the preborn must be enacted politically. Every year in this country, approximately 1 million preborn children are killed.[490] We owe it to them to learn how to win.

---

[488] Gates, G. J., & Newport, F. (2012). Special report: 3.4% of U.S. adults identify as LGBT. Retrieved from http://www.gallup.com/poll/158066 /special-report-adults-identify-lgbt.aspx

[489] U.S. Department of Labor. (2017). Union members summary. Retrieved from https://www.bls.gov/news.release/union2.nr0.htm

[490] This Guttmacher Institute-reported number only includes surgical abortions. See: Jones, R.K., & Jerman, J, (2014). Abortion incidence and service availability in the United States, 2014. *Perspectives on Sexual and Reproductive Health, 2017, 49*(1). Cited in https://www.guttmacher.org/fact-sheet/induced-abortion-united-states.

Our Political Conundrum

Most of us are here in obedience to our Lord and the burden He has placed on our hearts for His preborn image-bearers—the modern-day innocents that are being sacrificed. We are not trained in the art of political warfare, and we have misconceptions about how politics really works. As a first step, we must learn the true nature of politics. Simply put:

> *"Politics is the adjudication of power. It is the process by which we determine who rules whom."*[491]

Many in the pro-life movement feel we should not "waste time" on politics and instead, they believe that we need to focus on educating the public on the evil of abortion. Once the majority learns the truth about the preborn person, then we will win. A related idea is that the media must be educated, and with the media onboard, we can win. The fact is, newspapers, television, and social media do not cast votes or control elections. If this were true, Donald Trump would not have been elected president. Education is very important and has a specific purpose (more on this later), but education is not a workable strategy or path to effective legal protection for the preborn, for a very simple reason: *Public policy does not represent public opinion.* Let that sink in. Instinctively, we should know this is true. Consider the following examples:

- *Right to work:* 71% of Americans oppose forced unionism and favor right-to-work laws; yet such laws exist in only 24 states.[492]

---

[491] Rothfeld, M. (2017). The real nature of politics and politicians: America's system works, but not the way you think. Retrieved from https://www.nationalgunrights.org/about-nagr/strategy

- *Gun control:* 55% of Americans believe "the laws covering the sale of firearms should be made more strict,"[493] yet all of President Obama's efforts to do so failed.

Confrontational Politics: A New Paradigm in Pro-life Action

To see who actually decides elections and understand why public policy does not reflect public opinion, let us consider this generalized breakdown of voting in any given general election:[494]

Population	Population % Needed for Victory
100%, all people	50%, plus 1 voter
70% are eligible to vote (excludes non-citizens, felons, and minors)	35%, plus 1 voter
40% are registered to vote (approximately 60% of eligible)	20%, plus 1 voter
20% vote on election day (50% of registered voters)	10%, plus 1 voter
7% almost always vote Republican	
7% almost always vote Democrat	
6% are swing votes	3%, plus 1 voter

Our organizing goal in the pro-life movement needs to focus on the 3% plus one voter, because "this is where politicians live and die,"[495] particularly in contested elections. If we look at state primaries and local elections, in which turnout is often substantially less than 50% of

[492] Gallup. (2014). Americans approve of unions but support right to work laws. Retrieved from http://www.gallup.com/poll/175556/americans-approve-unions-support-right-work.aspx

[493] Gallup. (2017). Topics in depth: Guns. Retrieved from http://www.gallup.com/poll/1645/Guns.aspx

[494] Ibid., Rothfield

[495] Ibid., Rothfeld

registered voters (I have seen less than 15%), the margin is far less than the 3% plus one.

> "The average politician lives in constant fear of alienating any substantial portion of this three percent plus one voter he needs in a hotly contested race to win. What is the best way not to alienate these voters? Do nothing to make them mad, which almost always means ... do nothing.
>
> *This is why, even when new politicians are elected, little seems to change. Inertia, or the status quo, is the most powerful force in politics. However, by mobilizing and directing voters [who are] rallying around a specific issue, you can change the political environment for a politician or even a group of politicians. One relatively small group can make it costlier for the politician not to act, than it is for him or her to act as you want [them] to."*[496]

In other words, we need to be loyal to the preborn and not a politician or party brand. Pro-life film producer Jason Scott Jones puts it bluntly:

> *"We must help our friends, punish our enemies, and avenge ourselves on traitors. And 'friends' cannot be defined as 'anyone who threw us a rhetorical bone.' We shouldn't be 'disappointed' when people we supported wilt under pressure and turn against us. We should be enraged, and ready to impose retribution. We should work to destroy such a politician's career, and send him back to practicing small-town law under an assumed name with an unlisted phone number."*[497]

One of the main reasons the pro-life movement loses politically is that politicians fear Planned Parenthood's political wrath more than they fear us. Leadership Institute Founder, Morton C. Blackwell, notes:

---

[496] Ibid.

[497] Jones, J. S. (2015). The pro-life art of war. Retrieved from https://www.lifesitenews.com/opinion/the-pro-life-art-of-war

> *"The winner in a political contest over time is determined by the number and the effectiveness of the activists and leaders on the respective sides... [This] explains why the side that's right doesn't necessarily win."*[498]

Notice that he did not say that victory is determined by getting the majority of the populace on our side, but by the number of activists and their effectiveness. This is why the homosexual and labor union lobbies so often get their legislative agenda through.

> *"They have groups of voters who can, and will, vote on their issue alone. And they often have workers and sometimes money to use against any politician who crosses them."*[499]

This is where the properly understood purpose of education comes in: To recruit, inform, and mobilize more activists; to build an army for politicians to fear—an army dedicated to the effort of securing personhood protections for the preborn.

WHAT WOULD JESUS DO?

Here, the objection inevitably comes up: "Christians should be peaceful and should not act this way." Certainly, we ought not to sin when exhibiting righteous indignation, and we should only ever speak the truth and conduct ourselves in a Christ-like manner. But sadly, being Christ-like is often misconstrued as being nice. What did Jesus say about this?

> *"If the world hates you, know that it has hated me before it hated you. If you were of the world, the world would love you as its*

[498] Blackwell, M. C. (2017). The real nature of politics. Retrieved from https://www.leadershipinstitute.org/writings/?ID=32

[499] Ibid., Rothfeld

own; but because you are not of the world, but I chose you out of the world, therefore the world hates you. Remember the word that I said to you: 'A servant is not greater than his master.' If they persecuted me, they will also persecute you. If they kept my word, they will also keep yours."[500]

"Do not think that I have come to bring peace to the earth. I have not come to bring peace, but a sword."[501]

And what did Jesus do when he saw that the religious leaders had allowed the temple to be overtaken by commerce, leaving no room for the Gentiles and outcasts to come and draw near to the Lord?

"And making a whip of cords, he drove them all out of the temple, with the sheep and oxen. And he poured out the coins of the money-changers and overturned their tables."[502]

Likewise, Jesus publicly called out the religious leaders many times:

"Woe to you, scribes and Pharisees, hypocrites! For you are like whitewashed tombs, which outwardly appear beautiful, but within are full of dead people's bones and all uncleanness. So you also outwardly appear righteous to others, but within you are full of hypocrisy and lawlessness."[503]

"You brood of vipers! How can you speak good, when you are evil? For out of the abundance of the heart the mouth speaks."[504]

"You serpents, you brood of vipers, how are you to escape being sentenced to hell?"[505]

---

[500] John 15:18-20
[501] Matthew 10:34
[502] John 2:15
[503] Matthew 23:27-28
[504] Matthew 12:34
[505] Matthew 23:33

As did John the Baptist:

> *"But when he saw many of the Pharisees and Sadducees coming to his baptism, he said to them, 'You brood of vipers! Who warned you to flee from the wrath to come?'"*[506]

If we look at Jesus in the context of the leadership structure of his time and thus, the Pharisees as the establishment, it is clear that Jesus was one of the most controversial, confrontational, and hated reformers in history.

So, who is ready to be Christ-like?

HOW POLITICIANS REACT TO PRESSURE

Politicians react in particular ways when activists apply organized pressure. Political consultant and grassroots organizer Mike Rothfeld explains this well:

> *"The first thing the politician will do is try to make you go away without giving you anything of substance. If he gives you anything of substance, then those organized on the other side will be mad. So most politicians will try to make you quit by intimidation, explanation, or buying you off.*
>
> *Many politicians—especially those used to being treated like royalty rather than public servants—may try to threaten and intimidate. Statements such as, 'If you ever try something like this again, I'll vote against [your issue] for sure,' or 'I'll tell the newspaper you're a trouble-maker' are not uncommon. A rudely spoken, 'I don't know who you think you are, but that's not how*

---

[506] Matthew 3:7

> *we do things here, and no one will work with you again' followed by a slammed-down phone receiver is another favorite."*[507]

Here is the typical order of reactions:

1. Ignore you
2. Tell you to "try to sound reasonable"
3. Whine
4. Threaten
5. Have others threaten you
6. Attempt to buy you
7. Tell you they may vote your way

Common political excuses for *not* acting include:

- "I am too busy with the budget, take it to Representative..."
- "I am with you, but you don't understand how it works down here."
- "I have got to appear reasonable."
- "The governor will not sign it."
- "The courts will kill it."
- "The political reality is..."
- "You will get something worse."
- "You are the only one talking about this."
- "You have not done your homework, let me explain."

If you have spent any amount of time pushing pro-life legislation, these political canards undoubtedly sound familiar to you.

---

[507] Ibid., Rothfeld

The Seduction of Power and Access

> *"When you sit down to eat with a ruler, observe carefully what is before you, and put a knife to your throat if you are given to appetite. Do not desire his delicacies, for they are deceptive food."* [508]

Politics has seductive traps. Again, Mike Rothfeld explains:

> *"The chance to rub elbows with elected officials, being looked up to by people in your community as someone in the know, invitations to and recognition at special events, being quoted in the media, helping to write 'acceptable' compromise language, an appointment to some committee or task force, or even a paid job in the politician's office or campaign—all this could be yours if you become a grassroots leader... Before long, instead of delivering to the politician the grassroots' message to pass or defeat specific legislation, you become the politician's representative, telling grass-roots activists what they must settle for.*
>
> *Right now, today, decide whether you want access or power. Access is calling a politician and having him take your call. He listens to what you want, and may or may not do it... Power is the ability to tell a politician what you want, and either get it or deliver substantial pain."*[509]

I believe this is where much of the leadership of the pro-life movement has unwittingly gone astray. Lured by the deceptive seduction of access, they have become the representatives of the politicians, "telling the grassroots level what [we] must settle for."[510] A good

[508] Proverbs 23:1-3
[509] Ibid., Rothfeld
[510] Ibid., Rothfeld

example is the Pain Capable Unborn Child Protection Act of 2013,[511] a federal ban on abortion after 20 weeks of gestation. Republican congressional leadership wanted a rape and incest exception added to the bill to increase the number of Republican congressmen who would be willing to vote for it, even though additional votes were not needed for its passage. In other words, the goal was to enable more Republicans to be able to go back to their districts and campaign on how "pro-life" they were, even though they refused to extend protections to preborn children conceived in rape. Aside from obvious ethical concerns, the strategic failure of such a move should be readily apparent. Working to keep politicians in office that are hostile to our end goal—equal protection for all preborn children—will prevent us from *ever* reaching that goal.

The Biggest Lie in Politics

One of the largest pitfalls that has plagued the pro-life movement is its perception of itself as a subsidiary of the Republican party. This leads us to the biggest lie in politics: *Good people are obligated to support the lesser of two evils.* Until the pro-life movement stops believing this lie, we will never be able to hold the GOP accountable. How can we? The GOP leadership knows they can take us for granted. No matter what Republican politicians do or do not do, pro-life leadership in Washington, DC, will tell the pro-life faithful to vote for the "lesser of two evils"—

---

[511] H.R. 1797. (2013). Pain-Capable Unborn Child Protection Act. 113th Congress (2013-2014). See text: https://www.congress.gov/bill/113th-congress/house-bill/1797

Republican. Instead of being that 3% plus 1, loyal-to-our-cause group of activists, we have become loyal to a political party.

Christians must not view political parties as something we ought to be loyal to, but rather, as tools to be used when and *if* it furthers alignment with God's will and advancement of His Kingdom here on Earth. For the time being, the GOP is the most practical tool for us to use and is where we should be focused in primary elections. However, when the GOP fails to give us a pro-life candidate that we can support, a third-party candidate can actually become a useful tool. Let us look at an example.

The late pro-abortion Republican U.S. Senator Ted Stevens was nearly impossible to beat. He was like a demigod in Alaska politics. Stevens had been in the Senate for four decades, nearly since the founding of Alaska's statehood. In 2008, he handily won the primary and was challenged by popular pro-abortion Democrat Mark Begich. However, former Alaska Right to Life president, Bob Bird, campaigned hard as a third-party candidate. After all the election returns were counted, Begich won with a plurality (by a mere 3,953 votes),[512] with Stevens in second, and Bird in third. At the time, Alaska Right to Life supported Bird out of principle, without realizing the strategic importance of the move. When his term was up, Begich was beaten by a Republican who campaigned on being pro-life.

This example shows where a committed 3% plus 1 can be so powerful. Under this paradigm, in order to get and hold power,

---

[512] Ted Stevens was convicted of a federal crime 2 weeks before the election, which likely impacted results as well.

Republican party leaders must give us what we want or lose. Progressives (especially unions) have used this tactic far more effectively. It only takes an election or two for the lesson to stick. All the noise we make during the legislative season with phone calls, emails, and petitions is meaningless if we are not willing to bring the pain during election season. As President Reagan once said, "Our job is not to make Congress see the light, but to feel the heat."[513] In politics, there are only two options for the pro-life movement: We can either be loved and manipulated or feared and respected.

A Paradigm Shift

The old access-based policy of endorsing whatever candidate is the "lesser of two evils" fails time and time again. We must demand and expect 100% commitment to protecting the lives of the preborn. In this regard, consider these five levels of political sincerity:

1. Votes yes on controversial, principled bills
2. Co-sponsors bills
3. Signs a written promise
4. Provides a public, verbal promise
5. Only gives a private, verbal promise
   (This is useless and probably dangerous.)

Over 15 years ago, Georgia Right to Life embarked on a new principled political strategy, in which it would only endorse legislation and candidates that were 100% pro-life—that is, without exceptions. Before Georgia Right to Life would endorse candidates, it required them

---

[513] De Toledano, R. (1975, 1 July). Getting the heat to Congress. Quoting Ronald Reagan in *Aiken Standard,* p. 4, col. 3.

to sign an affirmation in support of personhood protections for the preborn.[514] This strategy had far-reaching consequences. Long-time "pro-life" politicians had their endorsements revoked. Georgia Right to Life made powerful Republican enemies. But the strategy was a massive success.

In 2000, at the beginning of this grand experiment, the state of Georgia ranked last in the nation in enforceable laws that protected the preborn.[515] Within a few years after the strategy was implemented, Americans United for Life (AUL) ranked Georgia as the 8th most protective state in the nation as part of its annual Life List.[516] In 2013, AUL gave Georgia the All-Star State award.[517] By 2014, Georgia was the *only* state in the nation in which all statewide elected officials were pro-life without exceptions.[518] Today, Georgia is one of two states[519] that have no rape and incest exceptions in any of their pro-life laws. Over the last few years, Alaska Right to Life and several other state-level pro-life groups

---

[514] See Appendix 1

[515] Becker, D. (2011). *Personhood: A pragmatic guide to pro-life victory in the 21st century*. Alpharetta, GA: TKS Publications. [p 156, endnote 16]. In the year 2000, Georgia had no enforceable pro-life laws. "We did have a partial-birth abortion ban that was neutered and rendered useless [unenforceable] by the Georgia Supreme Court."

[516] Burke, D., et al. (2010). *Defending life 2010: Proven strategies for a pro-life America*. Washington, DC: Americans United for Life, 509.

[517] Americans United for Life. (2013). AUL's 2013 Life List: All stars. Retrieved from http://www.aul.org/auls-2013-life-list-all-stars/

[518] Stith, N. (2014). Nine statewide "no exceptions" candidates elected in Georgia. Retrieved from https://www.personhood.org/index.php/political/personhood-in-politics/9-statewide-no-exceptions-candidates-elected-in-georgia

[519] Michigan also does not have any exceptions in its pro-life laws.

have adopted the same strategy and came together to form Personhood Alliance.[520]

As we think about the future of the pro-life movement in the 21st century, consider this pledge that Alaska Right to Life makes to our constituents at our annual fundraising banquet:

> *"We will never be a representative of the politicians, telling you what you must settle for. But we will represent you to the politicians, telling them what they must do!"*

To explore confrontational politics further, read the book, Confrontational Politics, by Senator H.L. Richardson.[521] To really become effective at confrontational politics attend a one day class from The Foundation For Applied Conservative Leadership.[522]

[Christopher Kurka has spent his life in Alaska, pouring his energies into political efforts in the state since a young teenager. He joined the board of Alaska Right to Life in 2006, serving as Vice President and Treasurer before becoming Executive Director in 2013. Christopher served on the board of the National Right to Life Committee for 4 years before leaving to pursue more principled means of ending abortion. He now sits on the board of Personhood Alliance and helps facilitate 1-day classes for the Foundation for Applied Conservative Leadership. Christopher's passion is to establish justice for the preborn and see God's people raised up to call the pro-life movement to a new standard. Christopher lives in Palmer, Alaska with his wife, Haylee, and their two sons, Justice and Samuel.]

---

[520] See Appendix 2 for information for how your group can join Personhood Alliance to transform pro-life politics and re-establish the sanctity of life in law.

[521] Richardson, H. L. (2009). *Confrontational politics*. Ottowa, IL: Jameson Books, Inc. IBSN: 0915463768.

[522] https://facl-training.org

CHAPTER 19

Personhood Now! If Not Now—When?

By Daniel Becker, President, Personhood Alliance

"Many seek the face of a ruler, but it is from the Lord that a man gets justice."[523]

"Not from the stars do I my judgment pluck . . .
. . . not to tell of good or evil luck . . .
Nor can I fortune to brief minutes tell,
Or say with princes if it shall go well."

William Shakespeare, *Sonnet 14*

For over a generation, the pro-life movement in the United States has awaited a propitious alignment in the political stars and built an entire strategy around it. This strategy demands a President who will appoint pro-life Supreme Court Justices, a U.S. Senate majority that will approve those Justices, a U.S. House and Senate that will pass legislation "protecting the babies," and a President who will sign these long-awaited

[523] Proverbs 29:26

bills, which will stand up to Supreme Court challenge. For over 40 years, we have anxiously waited. We may now live in that much-anticipated day of celestial political alignment.

Many hope that President Donald Trump's election, Republican majorities in both houses of Congress, and a future conservative Supreme Court will bring about sustainable federal legislation and the overturning of *Roe v. Wade*.[524] Realistically, this would return the power to legislate or prohibit abortion to the states, which have an overwhelming majority of Republican governors and state legislatures. Is this a realistic expectation? One would think so. After all, this has been a strategic objective for roughly 35 years. However, this strategy has several flaws that could subvert immediate and substantial changes in our laws to protect the preborn.

The strategy places too much faith in a political party and the political process. Both are subject to pressures that work against us. Too often, politicians take the path of least resistance, prioritize fiscal issues over life issues, and use, then ignore, the pro-life base. But more importantly, this strategy forces the pro-life movement to abandon its role as a standard-bearer. As a consequence, the movement's prime objective becomes electing Republican majorities in order to create the desired alignment—that is, choosing the role of king-maker. We only need to look at our history to see what has already resulted.

By advancing politicians to achieve a partisan majority, the pro-life movement deferred its objectives. Pursuing a lesser goal of electing a majority undercut the movement's principled position of standing for all

---

[524] *Roe v. Wade*. (1973). 410 US 113, No. 70-18.

preborn lives. We have seen this when Republicans, who were endorsed and elected as "pro-life," become resistant or even hostile to life issues when a principled stand for innocent life is required.

Not all of the pro-life movement has agreed with this strategy over the years. Some have adhered to a different perspective and plan of action. Faith, we are told, is only as good as its object. For decades, as a political action director and lobbyist, I dealt with self-described pro-life politicians and lawmakers. My experience proved to me that trusting their fidelity to the cause does not yield meaningful laws that protect the most vulnerable. How often have solidly pro-life politicians wilted under the pressures of legislative leaders who added deadly exceptions to pro-life bills? Instead, firm consequences are required to secure genuine progress.

Polluted Wells?

Unfortunately, in recent years, mainstream pro-life leadership itself has demanded a flawed, depreciated standard. When leaders promote or accept deadly exceptions for rape, incest, or fetal anomaly, they contradict the movement's foundational premise that every innocent human being is precious and deserving of protection.

An example of this contradiction is the Family Policy Alliance's Statesmen Academy, a Christian program that "educat[es] politicians in the practice of effective politics to carry on the fight for godly values."[525] This training program is a partnership between Clarke Forsythe, President of Americans United for Life, and Tom Minnery, former Senior

---

[525] Family Policy Alliance. (2017). Statesmen academy. Retrieved from http://familypolicyalliance.com/statesmen-academy/

Vice President of Public Policy for Focus on the Family. When I met with Tom Minnery,[526] he confirmed that the Statesmen Academy program includes teaching political prudence. When asked specifically if that meant teaching lawmakers to vote, when necessary, for these deadly exceptions he said, "Yes". Unfortunately, the Statesmen Academy's "unwavering principles"[527] only extend to some preborn children. This is no small matter. Proverbs 25:26 states, "Like a muddied spring or a polluted fountain is a righteous man who gives way before the wicked." God exhorted the nation of Israel to root out sources of pollution:

> *"Beware lest there be among you a root bearing poisonous and bitter fruit, one who, when he hears the words of this sworn covenant, blesses himself in his heart, saying, 'I shall be safe, though I walk in the stubbornness of my heart.'"*[528]

The Personhood movement has long-stood against this tide of compromise, and in this very book, is calling for a rejection of "poisonous and bitter fruit" and a return to first principles. We are often accused of "insisting on perfection," "being 100%ers," "being willing to let millions of babies die," and even "siding with Planned Parenthood." Yet, the accusers' websites, emails, donor letters, and social media posts never acknowledge the departure from their stated missions. They continue to proclaim they are fighting to protect and defend "the right to life of every innocent human being from the beginning of life to natural death." [529]

---

[526] This meeting was held at the Georgia Right to Life office in March, 2017.
[527] Ibid., Family Policy Alliance
[528] Deuteronomy 29:18-19
[529] National Right to Life Committee. (2017). Mission. Retrieved from http://www.nrlc.org/about/mission/

The alternative approach is to uphold a biblical sanctity-of-life standard in principle *and* strategy, in endorsement and communication, and in legislation and fundraising. If all of the pro-life movement embraced standard-bearing instead of king-making, the power of the grassroots would be unleashed. Politicians need pro-life voters. We deliver the margin of victory in many races. If we demanded a principled approach, the half-hearted moderates would have to change, or they would lose their pro-life constituencies. Later in this chapter, I provide examples of two states where this principled approach produced tremendous results.

Exceptions Undercut the Ground We Stand Upon

Either all innocent human beings are worthy of protection, or they are not. Abortions based on manner of conception are as much a violation of the sanctity of life as those based on inconvenience, familial situation, school and career plans, or financial challenges. A child who is conceived in rape or who is disabled is just as human, just as capable of pain, and just as innocent as any other preborn child. Why are they not worthy of the same protections? Or, have they simply become bargaining chips for political gain?

A more difficult question arises: Is "pro-life" an accurate designation for those who embrace exceptions? Consider that God's moral law clearly commands "nor shall children be put to death because of their fathers [sin]."[530] In what other context do we legalize killing the innocent child for the crimes of the father? None. We call it murder. In what other

[530] Deuteronomy 24:16

context do we legalize killing the innocent child just because he or she is disabled? None. We call it murder. Within this logical framework, then, is it not accurate to say that those who embrace exceptions also embrace "murder of innocents by statute?" This is a difficult message to hear. But consider that the entire premise of the pro-life message is destroyed by exceptions.

All preborn children are worthy of life, not just some. Every innocent human being deserves protection, from life's beginning until natural death. The Personhood movement embraces the preciousness and worthiness of every human being because each bears God's own image, regardless of manner of conception, disability, degree of dependency, or any other feature of existence. Let us look at another way that biblical personhood becomes compromised by politics.

A Deadly Message Bill

A message bill is a bill that is not expected to become law, either because there is insufficient support to pass it in one or both chambers of Congress or because, if passed, it will be vetoed by the President. Message bills are strategic in nature, in that they educate and shape the public dialogue and debate. At the very least, a message bill energizes, informs, and equips our base and our own lawmakers as to the consequences of violating the sanctity of life. A message bill always includes some measure of instruction that is intended to flag future legislative objectives. Therefore, it is imperative that we do not send a mixed message that lays the groundwork for future defeat. In this way, the Pain-Capable Unborn Child Protection Act of 2015 (H.R. 36)[531] failed on several counts. Its saga is illustrative of king-maker pragmatism sabotaging our role as standard-bearers.

Indeed, the message of the pain-capable approach is instructive. It teaches that preborn children of 20 weeks gestation feel pain. This focuses the discussion on the defenseless child and engenders a visceral reaction to the barbarity of abortion. It highlights the humanity of the child and her need for protection. However, it fails to extend those protections for children younger than 20 weeks gestation. Personhood Alliance prefers a message bill such as the Sanctity of Life Act, which establishes our end goal even though it may seem unattainable at present. Nevertheless, let us explore the history of the pain-capable effort and why it failed.

How the Message Became a Mess

Three successive Pain-Capable Unborn Child Protection Acts were introduced in 2012, 2013, and 2015. In each case, the promoters knew the Senate would filibuster the bill and stop it there. If it were somehow to pass the Senate, President Obama promised to veto it.[532] The bill had no chance of becoming law and did not provide any way to save any children, but the educational and political potentials were excellent.

---

[531] H.R. 36. (2015). Pain-Capable Unborn Child Protection Act. 114th Congress (2014-2015). See text: https://www.congress.gov/bill/114th-congress/house-bill/36

[532] Obama Threatens to Veto Abortion Bill, http://thehill.com/policy/healthcare/230075-obama-threatens-to-veto-abortion-bill

Pro-life stalwart, Representative Trent Franks of Arizona, introduced the first bill, H.R. 3803,[533] with no exceptions in January, 2012. The bill applied only to the District of Columbia. It passed the House but failed to get the two-thirds majority required under Senate rules.

In 2013, Representative Franks introduced the bill again as H.R. 1797.[534] On a Friday, the Judiciary Committee expanded its scope to apply nationwide and voted down proposed amendments that included rape, incest, and health of the mother exceptions. The bill passed the full committee to be taken up by the House. In the days that followed, Congressional leaders held meetings with congressmen and representatives of national pro-life organizations. As is often the case, many "pro-life moderates" refused to vote for a bill that did not include deadly exceptions for rape and incest. When the bill came to the House from the Monday Rules Committee meeting, it included those deadly exceptions. That Tuesday (June 18, 2013), it passed the House, but as expected, the Senate refused to take it up.

In the fall of 2014, national pro-life organizations and their pro-life counterparts in Congress held meetings to discuss the pro-life strategy for the next Congress. On January 6, 2015, Representative Franks introduced H.R. 36, the third Pain-Capable Unborn Child Protection Act. This time, appallingly, it included rape and incest exceptions *at its introduction*. The "murder of innocents by statute" was embedded in the

---

[533] H.R. 3803. (2012). District of Columbia Pain-Capable Unborn Child Protection Act. 112th Congress (2011-2012). See text: https://www.congress.gov/bill/112th-congress/house-bill/3803/text

[534] H.R. 1979. (2013). Pain-Capable Unborn Child Protection Act. 113th Congress (2013-2014). See text: https://www.congress.gov/bill/113th-congress/house-bill/1797

new bill, which the national pro-life organizations supported and promoted. It passed the House, but as predicted, it was withdrawn in the Senate after several failed attempts to invoke cloture.

Like other message bills, it had no chance to pass[535] and no expectation that it would truly save lives, but in this case, the equal protection standard was voluntarily breached without a fight. The message was a mess from the beginning—only some preborn children should be protected from pain and death. More on this in a moment.

There is another key feature of message politics that must be understood. The top priority of many message bills is to protect incumbents in the next election, and the bills are often scheduled accordingly. Incumbent legislators vote on a message bill not to try to ensure it becomes law, but to "earn" a 100% approval rating on their pro-life scorecards. They return to their home districts trumpeting their pro-life credentials, often with national endorsements. Repeatedly, our true pro-life statesmen warn us that pro-life leadership provides opportunities for moderate Republicans to appear pro-life to their conservative bases without actually enacting legislation that would effectively restrict abortion and save preborn lives. These leaders and the Republican party get all the benefits and none of the risks of being truly pro-life.

---

[535]Zanona, M. (2015). Reporting language in abortion bill arouses concern. Retrieved from http://www.rollcall.com/news/reporting_language_in_abortion_bill_arouses_concern-239450-1.html

A Flawed Message from Compromised Messengers

The aforementioned strategic meeting in the fall of 2014 included major national pro-life leaders and several well-known U.S. representatives. During this meeting, House leadership announced plans for a vote on H.R. 36 on January 22, 2015, which coincided with the annual March for Life in Washington, DC. If H.R. 36 passed the House, the victory would be announced to the hundreds of thousands at the national march. This fanfare would garner media attention and reignite the base. But this did not happen. Instead, civil war erupted among pro-life advocates.

The normal procedure for introducing a pro-life bill is to construct a "clean" bill and then battle over the language in committee. Amendments and other legislative procedures introduce compromise language, usually authored during closed-door debates between pro-life leaders and caucus members. Arguments of acceptance then emerge: "This is the best we could get," or "this grants us the greatest good for the greatest number." This greatest-good approach was first introduced by 19th-century Utilitarian philosopher Jeremy Bentham,[536] who, in seeking a replacement for the 10 Commandments as the universal moral code, also said:

> *"The greatest happiness of the greatest number is the foundation of morals and legislation."*[537]

---

[536] Burns, J.H. (2005). Happiness and utility: Jeremy Bentham's equation. *Utilitas, 17*(1). Retrieved from https://www.utilitarianism.com/jeremy-bentham/greatest-happiness.pdf

[537] Ibid.

For the first time in nearly four decades of pro-life political advocacy, leaders offered a message bill that included rape and incest exceptions as part of their *public policy position*, as opposed to their *subsequent strategic compromise*. Both strategies are equally flawed, but this was the first time in my experience that pro-life leadership approved inclusion of exceptions on the front-end. There was no clean bill. As noted earlier, H.R. 36's author, Representative Trent Franks, had offered an almost identical bill in the 2013 session, but as standard pro-life protocol dictated, it did not include exceptions.[538] Those were negotiated later. He violated this protocol in his 2015 bill by introducing it with the exceptions.[539]

The pro-life movement has long-debated whether exceptions are needed as a matter of strategy in order to pass pro-life legislation. But that debate has always been accompanied by a rationalization: Exceptions are not a desired *policy* goal, but a *strategy* of compromise as a means to save some. When challenged, the movement has been quick to declare that exceptions are indeed violations of our movement's policy, even if political pragmatism is "required to save the 99." But this was beginning to change, and many in the movement rightly called it out. Efforts were no longer made to cover the hypocrisy of "pro-life" bills that allowed the termination of some innocent preborn children.

This paradigm shift was also emerging in other areas of the movement. A few years earlier, Troy Newman, Executive Director of Operation Rescue, had proposed this strategy to a meeting of national

---

[538] Ibid., H.R. 1979
[539] Ibid., H.R. 36

pro-life leaders.[540] He rejected the biblical approach in favor of "the greatest good for the greatest number." Criticizing Mother Teresa's premise that God calls us to be faithful, not successful,[541] he wrote:

> *"After 40 years of unabated child-killing in America, we can no longer settle for being 'right' while the failure of our efforts results in the slaughter of innocent lives. Our mission is not to be morally superior; our mission is to be successful in saving every baby and ending all abortion."*[542]

He advocated acceptance of the supposed political reality that exceptions are necessary in pro-life strategy. In other words, the end justifies the means.[543] It did not matter what God, Mother Teresa, or principled pro-life activists said. He advocated that our guiding star should be pragmatism. Like Jeremy Bentham did in the 19th century, Newman dismissed biblically based moral objections as obstructionist and called for the isolation of dissenting groups.[544] Soon, this practice of rejection was invoked by the National Right to Life Committee.[545] This Utilitarian strategy of "the greatest good for the greatest number" became a poison pill that prolonged suffering and death, rather than a sound prescription for the pro-life movement's health.

---

[540] Newman, T., & Sullenger, C. (2013). Refocusing the pro-life movement for victory: A strategy proposal from Pro-Life Nation. Retrieved from http://tinyurl.com/jyq4cmj

[541] Arnold, C. (2013). A lesson from Mother Teresa. Retrieved from http://thepapist.org/a-lesson-from-mother-teresa/

[542] Ibid., Newman & Sullenger, p. 28

[543] "The end justifies the means" is also a core tenet of Utilitarianism.

[544] Ibid., Newman & Sullenger, p. 30

[545] Craddock, Josh (2015), NRLC removes Georgia Right to Life's affiliation for being too pro-life. Retrieved from http://www.liveaction.org/news/nrlc-removes-georgia-right-to-lifes-affiliation-for-being-too-pro-life/

FALLEN STARS

Prior to the January, 2015 vote on the pain-capable bill and in my capacity as President of Georgia Right to Life, I had visited and spoken personally with most of our pro-life Georgia delegation. I persuaded them to go to U.S. House Speaker Paul Ryan and demand removal of the exceptions. Thankfully, some did. I had every reason to believe that they would act in accordance with their sworn word and vote against this practice, as they had proven in past battles in Georgia. I was wrong.

Most of these men had been champions of life issues throughout their service as state and federal legislators. We regarded them as the nucleus of a new cadre of principled statesmen who would change the pro-life dynamic at the U.S. Capitol precisely because of their understanding of personhood. Included in this respected group were two pastors, a former Georgia Right to Life chapter leader, and former state Personhood Amendment sponsors in the Georgia legislature. Each of them compromised their deeply held beliefs. To understand why, we must first look at the standards set by the Georgia Right to Life (GRTL) PAC.

Through the efforts of the GRTL PAC, Georgia became one of only two states in the nation with no rape and incest exceptions in any of its pro-life laws.[546] State congressional leaders admit that they have been "trained not to allow rape and incest exceptions." [547] Georgia is the only state in the nation in which all of its top executive officers (elected on a statewide ballot) are pro-life without exceptions.

---

[546] Michigan also has no rape and incest exceptions in any of its pro-life laws.

[547] Stated by Georgia Senate Leader Bill Cowsert in 2013

Personhood

Nine of the 10 Republicans in the Georgia congressional delegation had applied for and received the endorsement of the GRTL PAC, which has one of the toughest pro-life endorsement standards in the nation. Before the PAC considers a candidate, he or she must first sign a Personhood Affirmation to assert 100% agreement with the PAC's positions on all pro-life issues, not just abortion. Each of the nine pro-personhood U.S. House members in our 14-member delegation, with the exception of Representative Tom Price,[548] was elected upon their signing of the Personhood Affirmation, which upholds protection for those conceived in rape and incest:

> *"As a candidate for public office I agree to uphold these (Personhood) principles and position...*
> *I affirm my support for a Human Life Amendment to the Georgia Constitution and other actions that would support these principles. This would assure that regardless of race, age, degree of disability,* ***manner of conception*** *. . . the civil rights of the preborn...are violated when we allow...abortion (in the rare case that the mother's life is indeed endangered by a continuation of the pregnancy, sound medical practice would dictate that every effort be made to save both lives)" [emphasis added].*[549]

GRTL PAC made it very clear that the consequence of perjury would result in removal of its PAC endorsement:

> *"The GRTL PAC will regard a vote for legislation containing language in violation to that described above as a vote in direct opposition to the Affirmation you signed. This action will result in immediate removal of your GRTL PAC endorsement and will be reported in subsequent communications from Georgia Right to*

---

[548] Rep. Tom Price (GA 6), currently President Trump's HHS Secretary, was the only Georgia Republican who did not sign the Personhood Affirmation.

[549] Georgia Right to Life PAC Personhood Affirmation. See Appendix 1 for full text.

> *Life to the grassroots activists in our state" [Underlined emphasis in the original].*[550]

Mystery Solved

Even though these were all long-time friends and allies, all nine House members lost their GRTL PAC endorsement. The mystery was: What caused these men we trusted and knew so well to suddenly abandon their convictions? The answer was telling. Leaders in the national pro-life movement pressured these Congressmen to violate their consciences. They caused them to stumble, and they fell.[551] Before the vote, in visit after visit, these men shared their stories with me. All had one thing in common: Pro-life leaders told them that if they voted their consciences, they would score them with the pro-aborts—and they did.[552] One Georgia Congressman, with tears in his eyes, shared his Bible verse for that day:

> *"Fathers shall not be put to death because of their children, nor shall children be put to death because of their fathers..."*[553]

His voice choking with emotion, he said he agreed with us, but could not afford to offend these powerful pro-life/pro-family groups. But what about offending Almighty God? Repeatedly, I was told, "Until your own pro-life establishment leaders get their act together, we are going to have to violate our consciences in this area. This is not our fault!" Dr.

---

[550] Ibid.

[551] Mark 9:42 "Whoever causes one of these little ones who believe in me to sin, it would be better for him if a great millstone were hung around his neck and he were thrown into the sea."

[552] Representatives Jody Hice in 2015 for voting Present instead of Yea, and Rob Woodall and Paul Broun in 2013 for voting Nay

[553] Deuteronomy 24:16

Martin Luther King, Jr., decried the flawed character of his day when he said:

> *"The ultimate measure of a man is not where he stands in moments of comfort and convenience, but where he stands at times of challenge and controversy. The true neighbor will risk his position, his prestige, and even his life for the welfare of others."*[554]

Flawed Endorsements Undermine the Cause

One of Georgia's outstanding pro-life advocates in Congress through 2014 was Representative Paul Broun. For many years, he sponsored the Sanctity of Human Life Act,[555] the landmark bill that embodied the pro-life movement's stated goal. A Christian medical doctor by profession, Broun was uniquely qualified to represent the personhood of all human beings when he ran for an open U.S. Senate seat in 2014. However, Susan B. Anthony List chose not to endorse him in favor of Georgia Secretary of State Karen Handle, who supported exceptions[556] and had no pro-life track record in her previous elected offices. On the contrary, she had voted as Chairman of the Fulton County Board of Commissioners to fund Planned Parenthood facilities in Georgia.[557] After Handle lost the U.S. Senate race, she joined Susan G. Komen for the Cure as Senior Vice

---

[554] Letter from Birmingham Jail, April 16, 1963

[555] H.R. 212. (2011). Sanctity of Human Life Act. 112th Congress (2011-2012). See text: https://www.congress.gov/bill/112th-congress/house-bill/212/text

[556] Particularly, the justification of selective reduction of embryos produced in the IVF process

[557] Fulton County Board of Commissioners. (2005). Meeting minutes (March 16, 2005). [Page 12, item 2: Planned Parenthood extended family planning contract]. [Page 13 Motion proposed, unanimous vote to award the contract]. Retrieved from http://www.politicalvine.com/karenhandel/Page12BOC-PlannedParenthoodVote.pdf

President of Public Policy, but resigned amidst the controversy over the organization's funding of Planned Parenthood.[558]

Susan B. Anthony List also enthusiastically endorsed Representative Renee Ellmers of North Carolina:

> *"A new women's movement which affirms its original pro-life roots is making its way to the House of Representatives, and Ellmers is one of its brightest new stars."*[559]

Ellmers advocated for exceptions based on a preborn child's manner of conception. This is certainly not an affirmation of the "original pro-life roots" of the women's movement.[560] Later, Susan B. Anthony List joined other groups who denounced Ellmers as a "pro-life traitor" [561] when she opposed the 2015 pain-capable bill because it was too stringent in its rape exception. In an ironic twist, Susan B. Anthony List President, Marjorie Dannenfelser, vilified and targeted one of their "brightest new stars".

> *"Susan B. Anthony List exists to support and amplify pro-life women's voices. Rep. Renee Ellmers was our ally until she led the charge to derail the Pain-Capable Unborn Child Protection Act.*

---

[558] Kliff, S., & Aizenman, N. C. (2012). Komen vice president Handle resigns. Retrieved from https://www.washingtonpost.com/blogs/ezra-klein/post/komen-vice-president-karen-handel-resigns/2012/02/07/gIQAYP0WwQ_blog.html?utm_term=.750928033398

[559] Susan B. Anthony List (2014). SBA List endorses Renee Ellmers for Congress in North Carolina's 2nd district. Retrieved from http://www.christiannewswire.com/news/1467414385.html

[560] The pioneering feminists of the first wave were overwhelmingly pro-life. See: Feminists for Life. (2017). Her story worth repeating. Retrieved from http://www.feministsforlife.org/herstory/

[561] Ertelt, S. (2016). Pro-life groups defeat 'pro-life traitor" Renee Ellmers, who almost sabotaged abortion ban. Retrieved from http://www.lifenews.com/2016/06/08/pro-life-groups-defeat-pro-life-traitor-renee-ellmers-who-almost-sabotaged-abortion-ban/

> *That's why we had to flex the political muscle of the pro-life movement," said Marjorie Dannenfelser, SBA List president and a North Carolina native. "She has her own failed leadership to blame for this loss."*[562]

National Right to Life President , Carol Tobias, said this about Ellmers:

> *"Nothing has the potential to do more damage to pro-life efforts than people who run as pro-life candidates back home in their pro-life districts and then stab the babies in the back when they come to DC and work against pro-life efforts... Thankfully, we've been given the chance to send Rep. Ellmers packing."*[563]

Computer programmers have reduced this type of flawed reasoning to a single phrase—"garbage in, garbage out." Endorsing someone whose moral compass allows for the killing of some results in the justified killing of the innocents. Insanity has been defined, "As doing the same thing over and over and expecting a different outcome." Something is deeply wrong when a movement calls evil good and good evil. "We have met the enemy and he is us."[564]

AN ALTERNATE PATH: PRINCIPLED INCREMENTALISM

The experiences of Right to Life of Michigan (RLM) and Georgia Right to Life (GRTL) destroy the fallacy that biblical standards prevent political and legislative success. Georgia has seen widespread no-compromise political and legislative victory.[565] We have accomplished this without

---

[562] Ibid.

[563] Ibid.

[564] Kelly, W. (1971). Pogo comic strip.

[565] Georgia does have an exception in one of its many pro-life laws. Five State Senators insisted that an exception for fetal anomaly be added to the Georgia Pain-Capable Bill in closing hours of the 2013 legislative session. The GRTL PAC withdrew its endorsement of the bill and publicly opposed the five

surrendering the basic biblical tenets of the sanctity of life. Perhaps this proves the maxim:

> *"You do not have, because you do not ask."*[566]

GRTL successfully created a culture of life in Georgia by upholding a scriptural standard that God has chosen to empower to His glory. We have passed several bills that chip away at abortion-on-demand, without exceptions, including a women's-right-to-know counseling law, a 24-hour waiting period, parental notification, and preventing abortion coverage in state employee health insurance plans.

We have enacted other laws that affirm the preciousness of every life as well, including an embryo adoption law that facilitates adoption of embryos as children to whom the state owes "rights and privileges," rather than as owned property to be transferred by contract. We also passed a law that outlines the procedure for terminating the parental rights of rapists, which protects women from their assailants as they raise their children conceived in rape. We enacted a law to create a cord blood bank, which recognizes the efficacy of cord blood cells in treatment of disease, rather than embryonic stem cells, which requires the destruction of human beings. The 2017 annual report *Defending Life*, published by Americans United For Life, listed Georgia as the 8th most protective state in the nation, proving that a principled approach can be achieved without compromise in a large metropolitan culture. The other state which has

---

senators who compromised the bill. As of the time of writing, four of those senators no longer serve as lawmakers.

[566] James 4:2

required a no-exceptions policy—Michigan—is right behind us as the 9th most protective state.[567]

Impetus for Change: The Forming of Personhood Alliance

The clear violation of the personhood of the preborn in the H.R. 36 message bill precipitated another overt break in the pro-life ranks. This break was the impetus for the Personhood arm of the movement to create a new national effort called Personhood Alliance. The new group raised its voice to object to the adulteration of the message, the strategy, and the emerging shift in policy of the major pro-life organizations.[568] In an unprecedented move, LifeSiteNews.com allowed both sides to air their concerns in a very public debate.[569, 570] Many alleged this violated the so-called 11th commandment—speaking ill of fellow pro-lifers. Previously, this spurious decree had been a useful tool for the pro-life establishment to silence principled opposition.

---

[567] Americans United for Life. (2017). Defending life report 2017. Retrieved from http://www.aul.org/wp-content/uploads/2017/03/DefendingLife2017.pdf

[568] Kiessling, R. (2016). You want us to compromise our pro-life values MORE?!! Retrieved from http://www.grtl.org/?q=you-want-compromise-pro-life-values-more

[569] Jones, G. G. (2015). Four reasons why I can't support the 20-week abortion ban and you shouldn't either. Retrieved from https://www.lifesitenews.com/opinion/four-reasons-why-i-cant-support-the-20-week-abortion-ban-and-you-shouldnt-e

[570] Nance, P. (2015). Why the pro-life movement should unite behind the pain-capable 20-week abortion ban. Retrieved from https://www.lifesitenews.com/opinion/why-the-pro-life-movement-should-unite-behind-the-pain-capable-20-week-abor

Molly Smith, President of Cleveland Right to Life[571] and coordinator of Bringing America Back to Life[572] (one of the nation's largest annual pro-life conventions), said:

> *"The exception betrays the whole premise of the sanctity of human life upon which the pro-life movement is built—that ALL human life is precious."*[573]

In her public statement, she urged her Ohio representatives to oppose the pain-capable bill until it was corrected. Organizations like Cincinnati Right to Life and Toledo Right to Life led the effort. Like-minded groups all across the country quickly joined them. Together, they pressed their U.S. House members to rigorously object to the national organizations' 2015 agenda. Dustin Siggins, writing for *Crisis Magazine*, referred to these organizations as "Beltway life groups:"

> *"They clearly missed the boat on the 20-week ban (H.R. 36), despite telling everyone to fall into line because they supposedly knew the situation in D.C. They knew what could pass, and could not, and the rest of us ought to listen to them, we were told.*
>
> *But as is often the case, having D.C. expertise does not always translate to electoral or policy victories, and often compromise is the first step Beltway life groups make, rather than the last. Certainly, the H.R. 36 experience makes it clear that the D.C.-based pro-life organizations can no longer demand grassroots pro-lifers simply send checks and let them do their work."*[574]

---

[571] Previously, in 2013, Cleveland Right to Life and GRTL had their 40-year affiliation with NRLC revoked.

[572] http://bringingamericabacktolife.org/

[573] Ibid., Jones

[574] Siggins, D. (2015). How to strengthen Republican opposition to abortion. Retrieved from http://www.crisismagazine.com/2015/getting-republicans-take-abortion-seriously

Groups like National Right to Life Committee, Susan B. Anthony List, Priests for Life, and Family Research Council were subsequently confronted by their constituents and donors for supporting H.R. 36. Efforts escalated when it became clear that some of these groups punished conscience votes, as noted earlier in this chapter. As U.S. House leadership heard the widespread concerns of the Personhood movement, they realized a train wreck loomed on the horizon. Pro-life public opinion was deeply divided and for the first time, a very vocal alliance of Personhood advocates called for removal of the destructive language.[575]

Republican leadership attempted to shift the controversy from a widespread movement revolt to a dispute over rape reporting, highlighted by Representative Ellmers. Despite the misdirection, the true nature of the conflagration became apparent. The bill's author, Representative Trent Franks, explained why the House abandoned the much-trumpeted vote. Speaking the day after the March for Life on National Public Radio's *Morning Edition,* Franks acknowledged that the cause of the abandonment was personhood, not the rape-reporting controversy:

> *"The last time that this country debated or argued among ourselves an issue of this nature and magnitude, where the personhood of a certain group of people was denied in the courts, we shot ourselves to doll rags on the battlefields of the Civil War.*

---

[575] Personhood Alliance. (2015). Congress to authorize abortion in 'pro-life' bill. Retrieved from https://www.personhood.org/index.php/press/ press-releases/congress-to-authorize-abortion-in-pro-life-bill

> *At least today, we are talking amicably and trying to work it out."*[576]

However, the two opposing sides were not successful in working things out. It appears that the sanctity of every human life, embodied in personhood, will be the battleground on which future generations of pro-life activists engage. It is a battle worth fighting.

In Conclusion

Have the political stars aligned in the heavens? Does it matter? Our job as pro-life advocates and ministry leaders is to uphold a biblical standard and call all mankind to that standard. We are not kingmakers. Winning politically at any cost bankrupts us morally and separates us from God's favor. In *Julius Caesar*, Shakespeare concludes his star-struck advice to Brutus by declaring:

> *"The fault, dear Brutus, is not in our stars, but in ourselves."* [577]

Astrology has never been a trustworthy foundation for life's actions. Instead, we must act faithfully and put our trust in the Lord and His ways.

> *"Put not your trust in princes,*
> *in a son of man, in whom there is no salvation.*
> *Blessed is he whose help is the God of Jacob,*
> *whose hope is in the Lord his God."*[578]

---

[576] Summers, J. (2015, January 23). House approves measure that would bar federal funding for abortion. Morning Edition. [Transcript of radio interview with Rep. Trent Franks. Host, David Greene]. Retrieved from http://www.npr.org/2015/01/23/379282671/house-approves-measure-that-would-bar-federal-funding-for-abortions

[577] William Shakespeare, *Julius Caesar* (1599)

[578] Psalm 146:3-5

> *"Many seek the face of a ruler, but it is from the Lord that a man gets justice."*[579]

Russian author Alexander Solzhenitsyn shared a profound insight during his famous commencement speech at Harvard University in 1978:

> *"There are telltale symptoms by which history gives warning to a threatened or perishing society. Such are, for instance, a decline of the arts or a lack of great statesmen."*[580]

If we are to seek justice for the preborn, then our ways must begin and end in alignment with God's decrees. To do otherwise is to prolong the injustice. God cannot bless that which His commandments forbid. "Changing unjust laws justly" [581] requires godly prudence in dealing with rulers, not ungodly actions. Rulers are God's means[582] but not His end. Only Jesus is the Alpha and Omega, the beginning and the end.[583] This we can put our faith in!

[Daniel Becker is the Founder and President of Personhood Alliance. He is also the former President and PAC Director of Georgia Right to Life and a former board member of National Right to Life. He studied at L'Abri Fellowship under the mentorship of Dr. Francis Schaeffer in 1973. A widower, Daniel enjoys investing in the lives of his 26 "grand-blessings."]

---

[579] Proverbs 29:26

[580] Solzhenitsyn, A. (1978). A world split apart. [Commencement address delivered at Harvard University]. Retrieved from http://www.forerunner.com/forerunner/X0113_Solzhenitsyns_Harvar.html

[581] Harte, C. (2005). *Changing unjust laws justly: Pro-life solidarity with "the last and the least."* Chicago: Catholic University of America Press.

[582] Romans 13

[583] Revelation 22:13

SECTION VI

Testimonies of Life

CHAPTER 20

How the Radical Notion of Personhood Brought Unity

by Tim Overlin, Executive Director, Personhood Iowa

There is an old adage that you are only as strong as your weakest link. But what happens when the links are not even connected to the same chain? This problem is what Personhood Iowa set out to solve in the summer of 2015. At that time, there were about 20 pro-life/pro-family groups in Iowa—all fighting the good fight—but we were in separate camps. We knew that, to challenge major pro-abortion forces, we would have to become a united front. To understand how we came to that realization, let us start with a little background on the pro-life movement in Iowa and within me.

The 2012 Iowa caucus was my introduction to the personhood concept. Personhood USA, a national organization founded on the principles of personhood, sponsored a debate among the Republican presidential candidates at a church just up the street from my house. The organization introduced a personhood pledge[584] to the candidates before the forum, and all but one of them signed it.[585] The language of this pledge was clear:

> *"I believe that in order to properly protect the right to life of the vulnerable among us, every human being at every stage of development must be recognized as a person possessing the right to life in federal and state laws without exception and without compromise. I recognize that in cases where a mother's life is at risk, every effort should be made to save the baby's life as well; leaving the death of an innocent child as an unintended tragedy rather than an intentional killing.*
>
> *I oppose assisted suicide, euthanasia, embryonic stem cell research, and procedures that intentionally destroy developing human beings.*
>
> *I pledge to the American people that I will defend all innocent human life. Abortion and the intentional killing of an innocent human being are always wrong and should be prohibited."*[586]

Personhood USA had partnered with The Family Leader (TFL), the leading family-issue advocacy group in Iowa, during a presidential caucus. It was an amazing occurrence and a national story.

A short time later, TFL hosted a meeting with nearly 30 pro-life groups. The president of Personhood Alliance[587] and the leading voice of the Personhood movement, Daniel Becker, spoke about the no-

---

[584] Personhood USA. (2011). Personhood Republican presidential candidate pledge. http://www.p2012.org/interestg/personhood121411.html Retrieved February 10, 2017.

[585] Mitt Romney did not sign the pledge.

[586] Ibid., Personhood USA

[587] www.personhood.org

exceptions, no-compromise paradigm and handed out his book, *Personhood: A Pragmatic Guide to Pro-Life Victory and a Return to First Principles in Politics,*[588] which has become the seminal book of the movement. At the time, I was completely unaware that these experiences would have such a massive impact on my life.

My part in this fight also began in 2012. On August 1, my world dramatically changed. My father had been battling cancer for about four years and finally went home to be with the Lord. Thankfully, I attended a *Men's Fraternity* class the previous year and had been digging into my faith, learning what biblical manhood was, and thinking about things like leaving a legacy and the "greater reward." After the funeral, I really started thinking about how to honor my dad. Only the good Lord knows what dark path I might have gone down without that foundation and the amazing people around me.

The Lord's Answer: Be the Change

I had been pro-life for as long as I could remember. I could argue with the best of them on social media, but I began to ask myself: What difference was I really making? The Lord answered me loud and clear through my wife, Jas, who reminded me that, to create change, you have to be the change. Message received! Not long after, Jas caught an incredible story on ESPN about Down Syndrome and the sanctity of life. It was segment on an episode of their E:60 program, called *Perfect*.[589] She does not even watch ESPN! It was a beautiful, uplifting pro-life story, and

---

[588] Retrieved at http://www.tkspublications.com/

[589] ESPN. (2012). *Perfect*. [Series episode]. Video clip available from http://www.espn.com/video/clip?id=8450488

I wondered, "Why do we not see more of that?" This was my beginning of being the change.

I encouraged some friends of mine in radio to create a regular segment with positive and uplifting pro-life stories. I liken that experience to being patted on the head. This led to an offer to do my own show on a local Christian radio station, which eventually became *Life Right Now*. I just needed a host, who I found in my friend, Rebekah Maxwell. After some initial meetings about the direction we wanted to go, Rebekah and I were off. Somewhat clueless and probably a bit naive, we set out to do a weekly show that refused to shy away from tough subject matter, but highlighted the ministries on the front lines, the fascinating stories of individuals, and the maddening world of politics in an upbeat and compelling way. The people and ministries I was blessed to connect to and build friendships with formed the foundation that I stand on today. God works in mysterious ways!

Seed Planting

Early in 2015, as I was traveling to speak to a group about Personhood Iowa, I got a phone call from a friend who is also an executive director of a pro-life ministry. Our conversation about a challenging Facebook post led to a broader discussion about accountability, conflict, and Christians' command to resolve disputes according to Matthew 18:15-17. Empowered by that conversation, I spent the next several days contacting those I had met along the way, even back to the *Life Right Now* days, with the same message—if we are going to actually stop the taking of innocent human life through abortion, we *must* work together. Unity only happens when we get to know and trust each other, when we are open and honest with each other, and most importantly, when we truly care about one another and our organizations.

Growth

Beginning in December of 2015, we started what would become monthly meetings, on our way to forming the Greater Iowa Pro-Life Fellowship. We were serious, and we wanted to make this work. So we started with a covenant to each other.[590]

> *WHO WE ARE: A fellowship of life-affirming organizations working together to partner with churches in Iowa*
>
> *MISSION STATEMENT: (what we do now/how we get to the vision) Unifying God's people to empower, educate, and equip Iowans toward a God-honoring culture of Life*
>
> *VISION STATEMENT: (what the future looks like): To see God's Church in Iowa leading Iowans in a culture of Life*
>
> *POINTS OF COMMITMENT to each other:*
> *1. Foster relationships outside of meetings.*
> *2. Ensure meeting content is private.*
> *3. Use the Matthew 18:15-17 principle if potential conflict arises, especially going to the person you have a grievance with first.*
> *4. Optionally, go to peacemaker.net (procedures for resolution) if point #3 stalls.*
> *5. There must be no recording of meetings.*
> *6. There must be no public criticism of any other group.*
> *7. We need to have each other's back – privately and publicly (when possible).*
>
> *Example public statement: "We respect their (the group's) heart for Life and know they are doing their best, according to their*

---

[590] Greater Iowa Pro-life Fellowship. (2016). Covenant among members.

> *guiding principles. They feel called to address the needs of Iowa as they understand them."*
>
> *The ideal here is to understand each ministry's heart to the point of being a "lay liaison" (cheerleader) for each other, when appropriate.*

We began to seek projects to work on together. We discussed forming committees and affiliates that could act as liaisons for all of us at the Church level.[591] We rotated the hosting of our monthly meetings, gathering in a ministry's office or a church nearby so we could get to know each other and our missions better. But amidst all of this amazing unity, there was still a piece missing—still some unconnected links. This disconnection centered around disagreement on political strategy, which state politicians often exploited to avoid getting much done on the issue of life. "You pro-life groups can't even figure out what you want," they would exclaim. "How are we supposed to?"

As we geared up for more stagnation in the 2016 election, however, we were slightly optimistic. Favorable winds were blowing in Iowa political circles—talk of finally taking back the Senate and wresting control out of the iron grip of Senate Majority Leader Mike Gronstal, a Democrat who relentlessly blocked any legislation that even remotely appeared to be pro-life. We prepared for a slim majority in the Senate, in addition to a comfortable one in the House, to be able to possibly, finally send actual pro-life legislation to the pro-life Republican Governor Terry Branstad. But we needed to challenge the status quo, both at the capital and within the Fellowship itself.

---

[591] The Greater Iowa Pro-Life Fellowship is ecumenical, made up of Catholics and several denominations of Protestants and Evangelicals.

On the night before the 2016 election, the pro-life landscape in Iowa began to change. At a little historic café made famous by Clint Eastwood and Meryl Streep during the filming of *The Bridges of Madison County*, a small group of us cautiously met. Most of the ministry leaders in the room were already part of the Fellowship, but there were some hardships to address and important issues to iron out. Thanks to the encouragement of Scott Valencia, the newly hired COO at Iowa Right to Life, we agreed to keep meeting.

A Season of Harvest

Election 2016 sent a shockwave through the nation, and Iowans were elated with our local returns. Not only had we wrestled away control of the Senate from Majority Leader Gronstal, but the unthinkable happened. He was defeated in a major upset, and we gained enough seats to give the Republicans a 29-20 majority![592] Republicans picked up additional seats in the House as well, giving us a 59-41 majority there.[593] This was the first time in almost 20 years that Republicans controlled the Senate, House, and Governor's office in Iowa.

Suffice it to say, election night started salving old hurts. So the group met again to work on a pledge to ensure unity in this new world of opportunity.[594] But personhood and a life-at-conception strategy were a

---

[592] Petroski, W., & Pfannenstiel, B. (2016). GOP wins majorities in Iowa House, Senate; Gronstal defeated. Retrieved from http://www.desmoinesregister.com/story/news/politics/2016/11/09/gop-wins-majorities-iowa-house-senate-gronstal-defeated/93087764/

[593] Ibid.

[594] Vander Hart, S. (2016). Iowa's pro-life leaders start legislative session in unity. Retrieved from https://caffeinatedthoughts.com/2017/01/iowas-pro-life-leaders-start-legislative-session-in-unity/

tough sell in the group. I believe the term "tilting at windmills" may have been sent my way a few times. But we persevered, and we kept meeting and talking. The more we talked and the more educated people became on personhood, the more a consensus began to form. The group eventually agreed that the way forward was unity around two main goals: Reallocating funds away from abortion providers and a Life at Conception Act. People chose to put past grievances and disagreements aside and work together to protect all human life through the "radical" notion of personhood!

Today, legislation to deny taxpayer funding to all clinics that provide abortion is headed rapidly toward the Governor's desk. He has already promised to sign it. We continue to work on the Life at Conception Act. It will be an uphill battle, mostly with Republican politicians who claim to be pro-life, but one thing is certain: Without our group setting and maintaining the standard, we would have never been this close to recognizing the sanctity of all human life as law. We are stronger than our parts. We are the voice for the voiceless, and we now stand united.

[Tim Overlin is the Executive Director of Personhood Iowa where he lobbies, writes, and builds networks across the state to help people engage in pro-life ministry and principled politics. He co-founded the radio program *Life Right Now* and currently lives in Grimes, Iowa, with his wife Jasmeen.]

CHAPTER 21

INTERNATIONAL PERSONHOOD: STORIES OF FAITH AND HOPE

By Dr. Patricia McEwen, President, Life Coalition International; Vice President, Personhood Florida

"God be gracious to us and bless us,
And cause His face to shine upon us— Selah.
That Your way may be known on the earth,
Your salvation among all nations."[595]

The Lord has a plan for eliminating abortion worldwide. I firmly believe He does not desire for any child to die of abortion anywhere in any country. He desires His Church to let His way be known throughout the nations, so that He can bless us.

AMONG THE NATIONS

For years, America has sent out missionaries to many lands, but we have exported our cultural sin as well. In the 1950s, Planned Parenthood

[595] Psalm 67:1-2

Federation of America, and other population control organizations, began to spread the idea that family planning, including abortion, was a eugenic solution to many economic, social, environmental, and familial problems. The founding of International Planned Parenthood Federation (IPPF) brought this propaganda to foreign lands and along with it, a new global campaign for "women's rights to control their own fertility."[596] IPPF introduced tragic stories to shape the narrative, for example, women who had been raped, women who were sick and could not sustain a healthy pregnancy, and women who were too poor to raise children. All of these problems were real, but they were positioned as reasons for the necessity of abortion, not as evils that could be overcome. This strategy was the wedge used to begin legalization of the insidious evil of abortion.

American pro-life organizations began to react to these claims, not by refuting them, but by inserting exceptions into law that matched the pro-abortion rhetoric. Each new law entrenched abortion deeper into our legal system. As the years passed, we labored long and hard to try to stop abortion, but we blindly fell into the Enemy's trap. We embraced the very exceptions that the pro-abortion movement had used to get their foot in the door of these nations. Today, we are shocked to realize how far we have strayed from God's plan to end abortion. We know we cannot do this without the Lord, yet we keep fighting in our own strength and ways.

---

[596] International Planned Parenthood Federation. (2017). About us. Retrieved from http://www.ippf.org/about-us

Life Coalition International

My involvement in pro-life ministry and activism began in the 1980s, during the rise of the rescue movement. I saw within the movement a shift toward a no-exceptions stance that would eventually coalesce into today's Personhood movement. The rescue movement included many individual groups—first, Catholic, and later, Evangelicals. Those of us evangelicals who were "no exceptions" were lumped together with like-minded Catholics like Dr. Jack Wilke and Joe Scheidler. One of the first largely evangelical groups to embrace the no-exceptions stance was Operation Save America, led by Flip Benham. Through Flip, I was introduced to the term *personhood* and to Daniel Becker, then-president of Georgia Right to Life. It has been a wild ride ever since.

During Keith Tucci's leadership of Operation Rescue (which later became Operation Save America), he founded Life Coalition International (LCI).[597] In a few years, Keith handed the reigns of this international spin off to me. Through LCI, I have gained insight into the global pro-life movement. LCI's vision is to identify pro-life efforts that are indigenous to each nation—not made up of US missionaries—and to help them in any way we can. This means we see pro-life South Africa, for example, through lenses tinted by the culture of South Africa, not America.

International Overview

To understand the impact of abortion worldwide, let us briefly examine current abortion law, cultural context, and pro-life efforts in individual nations.

---

[597] http://www.lifecoalition.com/

Let the nations be glad and sing for joy;
For You will judge the peoples with uprightness
And guide the nations on the earth. Selah.[598]

South Africa

The Abortion and Sterilization Act of 1975 first made abortion in South Africa legal for limited conditions. These conditions were health of the mother and rape and incest. In America, we recognize these conditions as exceptions in our efforts to make abortion illegal, but in South Africa, they are reasons for legal abortion. In our own country's attempt to legislate certain limitations on abortion, we actually export and codify the death sentence for many innocent children abroad. This is because U.S. pro-life policy and strategy serves as guidance for other nations.

In 1997, South Africa's ANC party proposed and passed the Choice in Termination of Pregnancy Act. Many groups in Africa, such as Christian Lawyers Association and Doctors for Life International, challenged this law. In 1998, in *Christian Lawyers Association and Others v. Minister of Health,*[599] the court declared that, although there is a right-to-life clause in the South African constitution, the fetus is not a "person" and therefore has no rights. In 2006, in *Doctors for Life International v. Speaker of the National Assembly and Others,*[600] the Choice in Termination of Pregnancy Act was found unconstitutional, but the high

---

[598] Psalm 67:4

[599] *Christian Lawyers Association and Others v. Minister of Health*. (1998). (4) SA 1113 (T) (10 July 1998).

[600] *Doctors for Life International v. Speaker of the National Assembly and Others. (2006).* (CCT12/05) [2006] ZACC 11; 2006 (12) BCLR 1399 (CC); 2006 (6) SA 416 (CC) (17 August 2006).

court allowed time for the government to make changes before the law was struck down.

Christians have been involved in fighting legalized abortion in South Africa for many years, with the help of outside church groups and organizations like LCI, Human Life International, Frontline Fellowship, and Doctors for Life International. The leadership of Doctors For Life International understands personhood but they, and other groups, are fighting a culture where health of the mother and rape and incest conditions have been ingrained as reasons for abortion, instead of exceptions.

Things are moving in South Africa, and there is hope for re-establishing personhood. Many other nations in Africa are fighting the same battle. South Africa has the most advanced infrastructure of all the African nations and thus, they have a powerful influence. "As goes South Africa, so goes Africa!" is a familiar maxim. It is likely that Africa's battle for life will be fought on South African ground.

African Witch Doctors as Abortionists

When abortion became legal in South Africa, many doctors refused to perform abortions. Doctors were brought in from Cuba and other nations to fill the gap. This shortage of abortionists slowed acceptance of the procedure for a while, but the rise in abortions in other Sub-Saharan nations, such as Zambia, Botswana, Zimbabwe, and Mozambique, can be attributed to an emerging battleground—traditional medicine. Traditional medicine is legal in many of these nations, but it is actually the work of witch doctors. Witch doctors are unregulated but accepted in society because many Africans think of them as simply cultural. In reality, they are practitioners of the occult. When working in the bush, I saw many women visit the witch doctor because of an unwanted pregnancy. Often, both the mother and the preborn child died as a result. Statistics regarding the number of abortions or the deaths or injuries resulting from them do not include records of this unregulated cultural industry.

China

In the early 1950s, China legalized abortion for specific conditions that threatened the mother, such as tuberculosis. In the mid 50s, the government extended the conditions to hypertension and epilepsy, among others. From 1979 to 2015, China implemented its infamous One Child Policy, which was imposed through rigid birth permits, forced abortion, and forced sterilization. In 2016, China created a few exceptions to this brutal policy, but its core remains intact.[601]

LCI was very active in fighting this policy. We gained information from Chinese women who were smuggled on to the Golden Venture ship that ran aground off the coast of New Jersey. The refugee women were kept in the hold of the ship with no sanitation facilities and little food or water. Many died in the passage. When the boat was discovered, they, not their smugglers, were held in federal prison in York, Pennsylvania. In working for their asylum, we arranged for them to tell their stories to a congressional committee. The stories were heartbreaking. One of the women, Fai,[602] told of living in a rural village and becoming pregnant with her second child. She had a birth permit, but she did not conceive and give birth within its one-year timeline. Fai, and those like her, moved

---

[601] Women's Rights Without Frontiers. (2017). One-child policy has not been relaxed. Retrieved from http://womensrightswithoutfrontiers.org/index.php?nav=one_child_policy

[602] A pseudonym

from village to village to avoid the Family Planning Police, but she was finally caught. Her husband was beaten, and she was bound, put in a pig cart, and taken for an abortion. Walking home after the abortion, she heard a child cry from the side of the road. Often, a woman in China who delivers a girl abandons her for a chance to get another birth permit and perhaps deliver a boy, which is preferred in Chinese culture. In other words, girls in China are not persons if their parents have one birth permit and want a boy. Fai took the abandoned baby girl home and hid her with different relatives for a couple of years. Eventually, Fai lost heart and paid smugglers for a passage on the boat to America.

We were able to arrange refugee status for the women from Ecuador and Venezuela, and they soon traveled there. The women thrived in their new land and eventually, we were able to bring family members to Ecuador also. Fai broke down in tears when she saw the little girl she had rescued from the side of the road.

The great ending to this sad story is a young man named Joe. I went to meet with Joe in China in 2015. Joe was a missionary there, but had worked with us in the early days of Personhood Florida, when he was a student at Ave Maria University in Naples. Joe was always upbeat and on fire for the Lord, but while we spent time together in China, the spark for personhood started to reignite in him. He talked of starting a pro-life group in China, beginning with an education campaign out of Hong Kong, which, as a former British protectorate, is less regulated. In the fall of 2016, Joe told me about the beautiful, pro-personhood advertisements he was putting on the trains and in other public places. Who would guess that a pro-life movement would spring up among young people in China, one of the most restrictive, pro-abortion areas of the world? Then again,

Joe is not limited by circumstances. He follows the Lord. I hope many more young lions like Joe rise up to fight abortion the Lord's way and trust Him for the results.

Israel

In 1977, abortion was legalized in Israel under certain conditions, with permission from a committee if the mother was under the legal age to marry. These conditions included rape and incest, fetal anomaly, and life and health of the mother. In 2014, the law was changed to allow abortion-on-demand for almost any reason. The law dictates that abortions be performed by gynecologists in hospitals, but some illegal private facilities still exist. Military service is mandatory for young Israelis, and abortions for women serving in the military are legal and paid for by the state (no more than two.) This situation makes pro-life activities in Israel difficult. Despite these challenges, the pro-life group, Be'ad Chaim, perseveres. Sandy Shoshani is the director there, and Pastor Tony Sperandeo and Ted Walker work together to host an international conference every two years. In Tel Aviv, Ishai and Anat are active in street evangelism and helping women who are in need. Many babies have been saved from abortion because of the work of these faithful people.

In 2015, I was invited to come to Israel for the conference and to speak in churches and encourage local pastors and people to attend. Unfortunately, I was diagnosed with cancer and was unable to attend due to treatment. My colleague and leading personhood proponent, Daniel Becker, went in my place. There are now plans to produce a documentary on personhood, and the next conference will focus on personhood as the main subject. This experience reminded me that when you do not see a solution in sight, God takes over and supplies the victory.

Auschwitz

Returning from ministering in Turkey, I decided to take a side trip to see Auschwitz—ground zero for the Holocaust. While touring Auschwitz and the nearby Berkinau camp, we stopped at the place where German doctors would examine the Jews coming off the trains and separate them into two groups: One for forced labor and the other for immediate extermination. I asked our guide how doctors could condemn children to death and then go home to their families. Our guide, a young girl from Oswiecim replied, "because they did not think of Jews as persons." A few years later, I visited Hadamar, Germany with Daniel Becker and saw the facility where the T-4 Action Euthanasia Program was launched to kill disabled children. We are tentative to compare the Holocaust to abortion, but the roots are identical—denying personhood to the "exceptions" and then killing them. How can we claim to be pro-life and deny personhood to certain groups of people?

Belgium

I was invited to a pro-life march in Brussels a few years ago and was excited to go because it was to be well-attended by youth. Brad Mattes, president of Life Issues Institute, and I had spoken to a group of college-age professionals in Brussels a number of years ago, and I was hoping our input had born fruit. The march was very well organized and had a very interesting theme: Panda bears pleading to "save the baby humans." All of the people assigned to crowd control, route guidance, and speaker assistance were dressed in panda suits. It not only made it easy for the speakers to find where we were to assemble, but it added an air of youth and fun to what could have otherwise been a very solemn affair.

In addition to the usual hecklers, there was an increased watchfulness over the crowd. The Archbishop of Brussels was supposed to attend, and there were many threats of attack from the Fems (a group of young women who violently oppose the Catholic Church's stance on contraception and abortion and are usually naked from the waist up). The Archbishop did appear and speak, as he was surrounded by pandas. It was great to see. At lunch after the march, I learned some history on the group of young people who had organized the march. They were enthusiastic about the success of the march and already planning their next event. The Archbishop had the same enthusiasm as the young people, and all of them spoke of the importance of personhood. When the younger generation in the movement stands on personhood, there is much hope for the future.

European Union

While at the march in Brussels, I also spent a lot of time with Michael and Jennifer van der Mast from the Netherlands. They told me of the new pro-personhood, no-exceptions movement among EU members called One of Us. They had gathered thousands of signatures on a petition to the EU that year. They are young, have the blessing of the Vatican, and represent many EU nations.

Netherlands

When I returned to the Netherlands this year for their March for Life, I hoped to interview Michael about One of Us, but I learned he had died. He was a courageous man whose faith affected so many. Alex van

Vuueren, the new co-director of the Netherlands' Schreuuw om Leven (Cry for Life) who now is the lead evangelical at One of Us, said that Michael had been such a strengthener of his faith. Alex and the former Schreuuw om Leven director, Bert Dorenbos, spoke at length with me about the idea of personhood. Their interest and receptivity was greater than I had known before. Alex told me of his interest in attending Cleveland Right to Life's Bringing America Back to Life convention. In March of 2017, Alex came to America to attend the convention and Personhood Alliance's annual board meeting, seeking to establish a connection to the US group.[603]

The nations are becoming more and more receptive to the personhood message—from Turkey, Indonesia, Peru, and Ecuador to Romania, Poland, Germany, and Russia. I am seeing the fruit of personhood grow in the international pro-life movement. Things are changing! May the Lord get the credit, and may I live to see personhood in the nations!

[Dr. Patricia McEwen is President of Life Coalition International and Vice President and co-founder of Personhood Florida. In 2017, Pat received the Personhood Alliance Lifetime Achievement Award for her life-long commitment and dedication to equal protection for all human beings. She continues to serve as the Administrative Director of Operation Save America, a position she has held for 23 years.]

---

[603] Since the meeting, Personhood Alliance president Daniel Becker received a sponsorship from Cry for Life to attend the *2nd European Pro-Life Forum,* organized by the 1st federation of national pro-life movements (EU) in Budapest, Hungary, for the purpose of introducing personhood as the biblical path to pro-life victory in the 21st century.

CHAPTER 22

Choices Have Consequences

By Kitti Hataway, Development Director, Personhood Florida

"I have set before you life and death, blessing and curse. Therefore choose life, that you and your offspring may live, loving the Lord your God , obeying his voice and holding fast to him, for he is your life."[604]

I have observed the evolution of the pro-life movement in the aftermath of *Roe v. Wade* from a personal perspective. You see, regretfully, I made the choice to sacrifice my baby on the altar of convenience just months after the Supreme Court decriminalized abortion. At that time, abortion was not widely championed as a woman's right to choose but rather, the baby was considered merely a blob of tissue.

As a senior in high school, there was never discussion that my baby's fate was being decided, only that a doctor could "easily fix this problem."

[604] Deuteronomy 30:19-20

This perspective is the beginning of the slippery slope—to regard a baby as a problem, rather than a gift given by our Creator that has purpose and destiny. Make no mistake: We never have the right to take the life of another innocent person, no matter how we regard them. The Word of God tells us:

> *"Behold, children are a heritage from the Lord, The fruit of the womb is a reward."*[605]
>
> *"Before I formed you in the womb I knew you, before you were born I set you apart."*[606]

These scriptures and many others show us that God uniquely fashions each of us in His image and has a plan—a calling for our lives on this Earth. The baby in my womb may have been a consequence of my bad choice, my sin, but ALL life is a gift, ordained by the breath of God. So why would we think it acceptable to reject such a gift?

Changes in Rhetoric

Another way words are used to dehumanize life in the womb is to refer to the preborn child by its scientific stage of development—an embryo or fetus, instead of a baby. Back in the early days of *Roe*, there were no ultrasounds available. There was no window into the womb. The general public simply accepted that if our government legalized abortion, then it must be okay. And if we used medical terms to describe pregnancy, then it must be acceptable in the healthcare community. In reality, however, many people deceived themselves because they wanted an escape, but the result of this escape was devastating. Since

---

[605] Psalm 127:3
[606] Jeremiah 1:5

Roe, nearly 60 million babies have been killed,[607] which means that 120 million women and men have also been adversely affected, not to mention grandparents, relatives, and friends.

With advancements in science and technology, and ultrasound in particular, it eventually became impossible to claim that a baby in the womb was not a baby or that it was simply part of the mother's body. Because most women do not pursue abortion once they see their baby on an ultrasound or hear its tiny heartbeat,[608] these advancements forced a change in language. What was once a blob of tissue became a woman's right to choose and later, a woman's access to healthcare.

Today, rhetoric surrounds the question: When does a fetus become a person? This question harkens back to Justice Blackmun's opinion in *Roe*; that if the fetus was ever proven to be a person, the core of the decision would collapse.[609] Other questions are used to detract from the truth about life. For example, at what gestational age does the fetus feel pain? Currently, the pro-life movement focuses much of its political efforts on pain-capable legislation, which often bans abortion after 20 weeks[610] or requires an abortionist to administer anesthetic to the preborn child before killing her. Consider this is similar to asking a terrorist to spare only those of a certain age or anesthetize his victims before beheading them. We would never permit this compromise in the killing of innocents

---

[607] www.numberofabortions.com is a real-time tracking tool that displays the number of children killed by surgical abortions in the U.S. and the world.

[608] Terzo, S. (2013). Ultrasound images save lives, change hearts. Retrieved from http://www.liveaction.org/news/ultrasound-images-save-lives-change-hearts/

[609] *Roe vs. Wade*. (1973). 410 US 113. No. 70-18. Blackmun at 156.

[610] The currently debated scientific point at which a fetus can feel pain

in the Middle East. Why, then, do we permit it in the killing of innocents in America?

Other questions also shape the national conversation: Is the fetus compatible with life? How potentially severe will a disability be? Was the fetus conceived in rape? Our politicians and pro-life leaders are distracted by these questions and have turned away from efforts to protect all humans equally, at every stage. The truth is: Taking the life of another innocent human being is never justified, for any reason.

Forty-four years after the legalization of abortion, a nation that can put men on the moon, perform surgery on babies in the womb, and successfully transplant major organs, is still debating the question of personhood. There are consequences for our refusal to acknowledge the truth.

Spiritual Consequences

A spirit of death has fallen on this nation like a thick, dark cloud, and the ground has swallowed up the innocent blood that cries out for justice. The blessings that once made our nation great have been replaced with a curse, because we no longer value His most precious creation—human life, without exceptions, from biological beginning to natural death.

> *"Therefore, as surely as I live, declares the Sovereign Lord, I will give you over to bloodshed and it will pursue you. Since you did not hate bloodshed, bloodshed will pursue you."*[611]

---

[611] Ezekiel 35:6

> *"For the time has come for judgment to begin at the house of God; and if it begins with us first, what will be the end of those who do not obey the gospel of God?"*[612]

After I made the deadly decision to abort my child, I sobbed all night, asking God to forgive me for what I had done. What had happened to "it's not a baby" and "abortion will solve your problem," which I had convinced myself of just a few hours earlier? They were lies. I had been deceived. My poor choice resulted in a terrible consequence, and it was irreversible.

It is time for the Church to acknowledge our sin and refuse to play political games. Abortion is not a political issue, but a heart issue. God created us as relational beings who desire life and love. Deep in every woman's heart, she knows her baby is a baby, not a blob of tissue. I walked this journey many years before I broke the code of silence and repented. When I did, God granted me forgiveness and healing and set me free from guilt and shame. God allowed me to see my baby in the arms of Jesus and told me his name. His tender love and mercy are there for all to receive.

> *"Because of this, I tell you that her sins which are many, have been forgiven, because she loved much."*[613]

> *"If My people who are called by My name will humble themselves, and pray and seek My face, and turn from their wicked ways, then I will hear from heaven, and will forgive their sin and heal their land."*[614]

---

[612] 1 Peter 4:17
[613] Luke 7:47
[614] 2 Chronicles 7:14

It Is Up to His Church

The final chapter of the pro-life movement is yet to be written, and it will not be until we can say we no longer need one. This happens when the hearts of the people turn back to God and He is Lord once again over our nation. This restoration starts with the people of God, as too many have been silent, refusing to be a voice for the voiceless. The violence and hatred that consumes our nation is a direct result of the slaughter of millions of innocent people denied their unalienable right to life, liberty, and the pursuit of happiness. "These rights have been given to all human beings by their Creator and which governments are created to protect." [615] As Thomas Jefferson so rightly put it:

> *"The care of human life and happiness, and not their destruction, is the first and only object of good government."*[616]

In Closing

Had abortion been illegal, had I seen an ultrasound or heard my baby's heartbeat, abortion would have never been an option for me. I suspect this is true for many women. My son, Jonathan, would be 44 years old this year. My choice brought a permanent consequence that we must fight to prevent. We need to step up. We need to be united as one, to reach out with love and compassion to women in need, while refusing to compromise on the notion that it is acceptable to take the life of even

---

[615] Declaration of Independence. (1776). An Act of the 2nd Continental Congress. (July 4, 1776).

[616] Jefferson, T. (1809, March 31). Letter to the Republican Citizens of Washington County, Maryland. Retrieved from http://voicesoffreedom.us/voices/thomasjefferson/thomasjefferson6.htm

one. It is time to possess the land. The only way America will be great again is for her people to embrace life!

In Loving Memory of Jonathan

Jonathan, dear Jonathan, my precious baby boy
Your life was one of sorrow instead of joy
I did not know your beauty; I could not see your eyes
No one would hear the sound of your silent cries
You were placed to nurture and protect within my womb
Little did you know it would become your tomb
There is but one thing comforting, there is one saving grace
To know you are in Jesus' arms and see Him face to face
And though your life is perfect now, it never was the plan
He placed you on this earth to become a godly man
Created in His image, the heavens sound one voice
But, alas, you would become just another choice
I know I stand forgiven and covered by His blood
But woe unto this land there comes a mighty flood
Of God's fierce wrath and judgment we will surely see
Unless we turn from our wicked ways and to Him bow our knee
Jonathan, dear Jonathan, my precious baby boy
One day I'll hold you in my arms and then there'll be such joy!

[Kitti Hataway is the Development Director for Personhood Florida, a state affiliate of Personhood Alliance. Kitti has been involved in pro-life ministry for more than 30 years. She is a licensed realtor in the Florida panhandle and an Auburn University alumnus. She considers being a mother and grandmother her greatest accomplishment, and her motivation is to see them grow up in a culture of life.]

CHAPTER 23

What Will You Do?

By Bill Kee, Executive Director, Defend Life Nebraska

Forty-four years and millions upon millions of legalized abortions have somehow numbed our sensibilities and disconnected us from the reality that God calls us to love our preborn brothers and sisters as we love ourselves.[617] This commandment implies that we need to protect them with as much vigor as we would protect our own families. To do so, we need to reawaken our sensibilities and reconnect with the reality of abortion. With this in mind, I present to you the following scenario.

What Will You Do?

It is 2030. Heated population control rhetoric has created a widespread panic surrounding an imaginary food shortage. In response to this manufactured crisis, the federal government passes a law that all children under 10 years of age are to be killed. You are a parent with

[617] Mark 12:31

three children, ages 7, 3, and 1. Soon, government agents will be coming to the door to take your children. How will you protect them?

Will you jump into action to help pass a bill that requires anesthesia prior to tearing children apart who are over 6 years old (a pain-capable law)? Will you lobby desperately for a bill that prevents the government from killing children by violently severing their spinal cords and removing their brains with a suction catheter (a partial-birth abortion ban)? Neither law will protect any of your three children.

Maybe you work to amend the law so that children over 4 years old are not killed (a ban based on gestational age). This way, you could at least save your oldest child, leaving your youngest two to be killed. Or perhaps the amendment could focus on saving children that have reached a particular stage of development, like physical coordination or more reasoned thinking, as long as these milestones were somehow measured and recorded (a heartbeat bill). Maybe you could champion a bill that tries to save children that can at least take care of themselves (restrictions based on viability).[618] Of course, these laws may seem too aggressive to pass in such a short amount of time. To make some progress, you could build exceptions into the laws to allow those who were conceived in rape or incest or born with genetic defects to be killed. After all, your children do not fall into these categories. But even so, these laws still would not save them.

Perhaps you could fight to pass a law to require government agents to obtain written consent from their superiors before killing your children

---

[618] Viability is a movable target. It is a measure of current medical technology capabilities and hospital intensive-care protocol, not life.

(an informed consent law) or watch your children's actions for a while first (an ultrasound law). What if you could make them wait two weeks after picking up your children before killing them (a waiting period mandate)? Would you risk the lives of your children on any of these laws?

Maybe you could instead go after the facilities in which the agents plan to kill your children or even the agents themselves. How often are the facilities inspected, what are the licensing criteria and inspection protocols, and are the hallways the same width as medical facilities that provide health care (safety and inspection requirements)? How much training does an agent need before being certified to kill your child (provider licensure standards)? Does he or she have the respect of a hospital board of directors within 20 miles of the killing facility (admitting privilege requirements)? Are these the laws you would work on to save your children from death?

If all of these laws seem inadequate, it is because they are. So why do we spend our time, money, and efforts passing and defending these laws in our quest to end abortion? Is this what we would do for our own family members? If not, why do we allow this for our preborn brothers and sisters? Is it because we do not love them as we love our own children? The Good Shepherd left the 99 in order to save the one.[619] As Christians, why do we do otherwise? When we as individuals and as His Church do not stand up to protect all children equally, it speaks volumes about what we really think of abortion.

---

[619] Matthew 18:12-14

Outside, you can hear the car doors slam and the shuffling of the agents' boots as they approach your front door. Will you give up some of your children, or will you fight with all of your strength to protect every one of them, regardless of the cost?

What Does the Personhood Movement Do?

Personhood advocates fight to protect the lives of every preborn human being. We will not promote any law that discriminates against any human being, whether that discrimination is based on method of conception, gestational age, the presence of a disability, or any other reason. Advocates work to educate and activate the pro-life grassroots, as well as legislators and policymakers, on the value and dignity of every preborn child. Our goal is to restore the right to life for all preborn human beings, through Personhood amendments at the state and federal level.

It is not enough in a time of war, in the midst of a holocaust in America, to simply raise our families and lead a "good" life. Our efforts to stop the killing of preborn children, in whatever way God calls us to do so, must be based on God's command to love our neighbors—our preborn brothers and sisters—as we love ourselves.

[Bill Kee is the Executive Director of Defend Life Nebraska and a board member of Personhood Alliance. He and his wife Jeanne have been active in pro-life work since 1993, as sidewalk counselors, pregnancy resource center workers, and street and campus evangelists. In 2008, Bill left his career to become a full-time pro-life missionary. Bill, Jeanne, and their two youngest children, Erin and Will, have participated in Personhood campaigns in Colorado, Mississippi, Montana, Missouri, and Alabama. Bill and Jeanne are blessed with 5 children, 6 grandchildren, and 1 great grandchild and currently reside in Lincoln, Nebraska.]

CHAPTER 24

STANDING ALONE IN THE PUBLIC SQUARE

By Daniel Becker, President, Personhood Alliance

"The prayer of a righteous person has great power as it is working. Elijah was a man with a nature like ours, and he prayed fervently that it might not rain, and for three years and six months it did not rain on the earth."[620]

I was alone and I was paralyzed. I struggled to breathe. My legs were rubbery and threatened collapse. I had never known the intensity of fear that engulfed me that July day in 1992. I stood on the square of our county courthouse hidden among a crowd of thousands—feeling abandoned, alone, and wholly inadequate to do what I believed God had called me to do—to be a voice for the voiceless. I was a new political candidate trying to honor God while seemingly standing alone against the tide of evil sweeping our land. I knew that the evil had to be confronted, but all I could do was cower on the sidewalk.

[620] James 5:16-17

The calculated, intentional, legal taking of innocent human life is arguably one of the most heinous evils of our day. It denies the basic right to life granted by God to each human person; a right without which all other rights are moot. As followers of Jesus, what are we to do against this injustice? One of the many duties of a follower is to do what Jesus did—to walk in His footsteps. This means we are to emulate His actions. Our behavior, directed by the Holy Spirit, should include the range of emotions, motives, and understanding of God that Jesus clearly lived out. The first prayer that He taught His disciples was, "Thy will be done on Earth as it is in heaven."[621] And Jesus said to the religious leaders, "The world cannot hate you, but it hates me because I testify about it that its works are evil."[622] To be like Jesus, I knew I must expose "the fruitless deeds of darkness."[623]

VICTORY: THE SPIRIT AND POWER OF ELIJAH

To confront evil in any form requires the courage to overcome one of life's greatest fears: The fear of standing alone. Let us be honest, this fear is one of the most debilitating forces to afflict our souls. Apart from God's grace, confronting evil by oneself can crush the will, poison the mind, and reduce one's emotions to abject fear.

We see this sequence playing out in the biblical story of the prophet Elijah. Elijah's courage in the public square turned to paralysis when he was threatened by Jezebel, the idolatrous queen of Israel. Even having been God's agent in a very public victory over pagan gods, he succumbed

---

[621] Matthew 6:10
[622] John 7:7
[623] Ephesians 5:11

to an all-consuming desire to flee from the constant onslaught of spiritual oppression and the threat of physical harm.[624] That is how I felt as I stood by the courthouse in July of 1992.

Looking back on the emotions of that day, I can say with certainty, that other than the death of my dear wife, it is the hardest thing I have ever faced. To this day, I remember the exact moment the power and Spirit of God enabled me to overcome fear, discouragement, and a deadly sense of aloneness in order to do what I did not think was possible. I took the first step toward a miracle. Little did I know that this one "step of faith" would be the hallmark of my pro-life efforts for the next 25 years.

It was Independence Day, a hot and muggy day in the Deep South. I was among a crowd of thousands who had come to enjoy our county's annual parade. From the front of the courthouse, a steady procession of antique steam engines fitted with rubber tires raucously tooted their way around the one-mile parade circuit. Interspersed with these steam-belching behemoths were floats from local civic groups and businesses. And, because it was an election year, there were several flat-bed trucks carrying Dixieland bands trumpeting their support for politicians promising entitlements to the masses.

I was a newly minted politician. Six weeks before, I had coordinated a statewide gathering of pastors at the Georgia capitol to pray for our beleaguered state. It was there that the Holy Spirit prompted me to run for federal office. Up until that point, I had never aspired to public office. Truth be told, the thought terrified me. In fact, I despised politics. After

---

[624] 1 Kings 19

seeking counsel from my pastors, parents, close friends, and most importantly, my wife, I was convinced that God was indeed asking me to run as a Republican for U.S. House. To compound the decision, Georgia's 9th Congressional District had not elected a Republican representative in over 120 years. It was obvious that the Lord was doing something very unusual in my life. For a brief time, I struggled with direction and focus for my political message.

Shortly after my surprise announcement, a friend came up to me at church and handed me an article about another Christian man that God was using in his run for Congress.[625] God was using his status as a federal candidate to boldly confront the main evil of the time, the "sacrifice" of innocent children through abortion. It was as if the spirit of Elijah had infused his political messaging. I recognized immediately that I was to do the same.

My chances of winning the seat were slim. There were four of us in the Republican primary to face a popular Democrat State Senator in the general election. I had aired my first pro-life campaign ad the week before the parade. It featured pictures of aborted children. According to the political pundits, my chances of winning the Republican primary[626] dropped from slim to nil.

Due to its unusual subject matter, the national media picked up the ad. All the major networks rebroadcasted my 30-second anti-abortion ad during the primetime evening news hour—for free. Millions of Americans saw it just before CNN began to air it to an international audience.

---

[625] Michael Bailey, Indiana's 9th Congressional District

[626] I faced three Republican opponents in Georgia's 9th Congressional District.

This airing was possible because there is a little-known federal law establishing that a federal candidate has the right to show and say whatever they desire in a television ad and the station must sell the time-slot for the ad at the lowest possible rate and without censorship. Like the godly congressional candidate, Michael Baily from Indiana, I used my 1st Amendment right[627] to broadcast graphic footage of a first and second trimester abortion. Over 6 million viewers saw the 30-second spot as it became news all over the world. My photo, campaign, or name appeared on the front page of the local Atlanta paper for an unprecedented six days in a row. America had been graphically confronted with the gruesome reality of modern child sacrifice.

I admit I relish the role of proclaiming truth and confronting evil. It is part of the spiritual DNA the Lord infused in me in the preceding years of my walk with Him. Elijah was a childhood hero of mine, and now became my biblical role model. I felt empowered by God in the same way that God had supported him during his very public challenge to the pagan gods who were appeased by child sacrifice. The Holy Spirit was filling me with courage to denounce the prophets of Baal in our own times. I knew that if I were to obey God it would require me, at times, to stand alone for His sake. I must confess I did not consider the impact this stand would

---

[627] My right to air the ad was challenged in federal court. See *Gillett Communications v. Becker*. (1992). 807 F. Supp. 757 (N.D. Ga. 1992). Retrieved from http://law.justia.com/cases/federal/districtcourts/FSupp/807/757/1968090/. I initially lost the right to air additional ads, thus becoming the first federal candidate in U.S. history to have my free speech censored by a federal court order. I won the case upon appeal 3 years later, and it is now taught to law students as a landmark ruling for free speech. See Walter, L.A. (1996). Case summary: *Becker v. Federal Communications Commission*: 95 F.3d 75 (D.C. Cir. 1996). *DePaul University Journal of Art and Entertainment Law*. (1996, Fall). Retrieved from http://j.tinyurl.com/zfrrbot

have on my family and friends and how it would expose my own character flaws.

Just a few days earlier, minutes after the first ad was aired, I received a call from a man I did not know. He told me his name and stated that he was a former Navy Seal. He claimed that the ads had traumatized his wife and small children and that he was coming to my home to kill me and rape my three teenage daughters.

ABC news anchor Bryant Gumbel interviewed me on *Good Morning America* and then muted my mic while he denounced me to the nation. Gumbel vilified me for showing the grisly details of aborted children, while he justified his network's graphic images of dead Bosnian children to change public opinion about the war. Ironically, he suggested that perhaps some attorneys in the audience should consider suing me for the "harm that I had done to children."

The press continually lampooned me. Politicians of both parties condemned me. Even some of my friends alienated me. Because of the unprecedented news coverage, I could no longer appear in public without being recognized as a troublemaker who had offended the nation's sensibilities by exposing the horror of abortion.

Fearing abuse and ridicule or perhaps something worse, I had asked my family not to accompany me to the parade that July day. It was against this backdrop that I approached the square and stood alone in the throng of thousands. I held a single prop—a yard sign hidden against my body that simply proclaimed "Becker for Congress!" At that moment, standing on the sidewalk, I was incognito. But I knew that as soon as I stepped off the curb and joined my fellow politicians in the parade, I would be stripped of the anonymity that cloaked and comforted me.

People talk glibly about "shaking in your boots." I was shaking and paralyzed. My overwhelming thought was "Lord, what have You gotten me into?" or more honestly, "What have I done?" I stood on the street corner until all of my fellow political opponents drove by with their professional-looking floats. I was the only political candidate without representation in this very important public event.

My prayer became, "Lord Jesus, you promised to be with me always. Give me the strength to take the first step." I have prayed many prayers in my life, some more earnestly than this, but none have been answered so dramatically. At that moment, one of the big steam engines entering the parade route paused while it built up the head of steam necessary to propel it further. This unexpected delay created an uncomfortable break in the steady stream of parade participants.

The Bible says, "Without faith it is impossible to please God."[628] I had walked most of my life with a desire to please God. But for me, in that moment, my leap of faith was 24 inches long and 4 inches down—off the curb and into the roadway. The next thing I had to do was to raise my yard sign over my head, take a breath, and walk that first step. By faith in God's promise to never leave me or forsake me,[629] I stepped out.

Before I had gone a few paces, a voice from the crowd said, "God bless you, Dan Becker." I looked up into the face of a friend from church in the company of his small children. My heart leapt as I received his blessing. It was if I had seen the face of an angel. He said, "Can we join you?"

---

[628] Hebrews 11:6
[629] Hebrews 13:5

And so it began. Every few steps, friends, neighbors, and perfect strangers joined the procession as we marched around the mile-long course. By the time we had reached the finish line in front of the courthouse, we had a crowd of over 300, a literal Gideon's army. The entire gap that had been created by the disabled steam engine had been filled to capacity with families and friends eager to identify with my pro-life message and to publicly declare their support to their neighbors and the culture at large. Later, it was hailed in political circles as one of the strongest displays of spontaneous grassroots support ever seen in Georgia politics. And in politics, grassroots support is everything. It became the hallmark of my campaign.

Whenever there was a parade that summer, my opponents would hire entertainers to carry their message. My message was carried by thousands of north Georgians who walked with an unlikely messenger with a decidedly unwelcome message. It was in the strength of this strong support that I defeated the three challengers in my Republican primary. My primary win defied all conventional political wisdom, confounded the pundits, and taught me that people admire politicians who stand on principle. And they will vote for them.

Later that fall, in the general election, I, like my Republican predecessors of the last 120 years, lost the race. But by God's grace, I believe we won something more precious. My message promoting the sanctity of life was heard throughout the district, the state, and the nation. Providentially, my Democrat pro-abortion opponent, Nathan Deal, got the message. In 1995, he switched parties and became a right-to-life convert. For over 14 years, he used his vote in Congress to defend the rights of the preborn, elderly infirm, and physically disabled. For the last eight years, he has been the Governor of Georgia and has signed every pro-life bill that crossed his desk. The Atlanta paper credited Georgia Right to Life PAC with providing the margin of victory in his narrow primary win in the 2010 gubernatorial race. His two terms as governor coincided with my two terms as President of Georgia Right to Life—former opponents, together for life.

If you had told me 25 years ago that this would be the outcome of my stepping off the sidewalk during my literal leap of faith, it would have made the decision much easier. However, it would have negated the faith. The author of Hebrews defines faith as "the assurance of things hoped for, the conviction of things not seen."[630] We do right, not by sight, but because it is right! Mother Teresa said that we are not called to be successful; we are called to be faithful.[631]

In Conclusion

I believe this type of faith is the need of the day. In Luke 1:17, an angel speaks prophetically of Zechariah's yet-preborn son, John the Baptist, who would prepare the people for Jesus:

> *"...He will go before him[632] in the spirit and power of Elijah,[633] to turn the hearts of the fathers to the children, and the disobedient to the wisdom of the just, to make ready for the Lord a people prepared."*

---

[630] Hebrews 11:1
[631] Arnold, C. (2013). A lesson from Mother Teresa. Retrieved from http://thepapist.org/a-lesson-from-mother-teresa/
[632] See Matthew 11:14
[633] See Malachi 4:6

May we demonstrate the "spirit and power of Elijah" in our time in history. Our culture needs ordinary individuals and groups that do not act merely on what is prudent or pragmatic—what the Bible calls "walking by sight."[634] Rather, we need those who are filled with the Holy Spirit, who will stand faithfully against the forces of evil in our day.[635]

My prayer is that you will find the courage to stand and be infused with the same Spirit that filled Elijah. Then, we will see those who oppose the living God either be converted as miraculous examples of God's grace or be exposed and removed like Jezebel and the prophets of Baal.

[Daniel Becker is the Founder and President of Personhood Alliance. He is also the former President and PAC Director of Georgia Right to Life and a former board member of National Right to Life. He studied at L'Abri Fellowship under the mentorship of Dr. Francis Schaeffer in 1973. A widower, Daniel enjoys investing in the lives of his 26 "grand-blessings."]

---

[634] 2 Corinthians 5:7

[635] The book, *Personhood: A Pragmatic Guide to Pro-life Victory and the Return to First Principles in Politics,* tells the story of one such group of people. The book is available at www.tkspublications.com

APPENDIX 1

Georgia Right to Life Personhood Affirmation

WHEREAS, the 14th Amendment to the U.S. Constitution states, "...nor shall any state deprive any person of life, liberty or property, without due process of law, nor deny to any person within its jurisdiction the equal protection of the law," Georgia Right to Life PAC affirms the principle that the right to life is the bedrock upon which all other constitutional rights are derived,

IN ADDITION, we believe in the face of compelling biological evidence that a continuum of human life and personhood begins at the moment of fertilization and ends at natural death, the ethical treatment of human embryos must include their "best interests,"

THEREFORE, as a candidate for public office, I affirm my support for a Human Life Amendment to the Georgia Constitution and other actions that would support these principles. This would assure that regardless of race, age, degree of disability, manner of conception or circumstances surrounding a terminal illness, the civil rights of the preborn at an embryonic or fetal level, and the elderly and those with mental or physical infirmities are protected by law; and are violated when we allow destructive embryonic stem cell research, therapeutic or reproductive cloning, animal human hybrids, abortion (in the rare case that the mother's life is indeed endangered by a continuation of the pregnancy, sound medical practice would dictate that every effort be made to save both lives), infanticide, euthanasia or assisted suicide.

The GRTL PAC will regard a vote for legislation containing language in violation to that described above as a vote in direct opposition to the Affirmation you signed. This action will result in immediate removal of your GRTL PAC endorsement and will be reported in subsequent communications from Georgia Right to Life to the grassroots activists in our state.

As a candidate for public office, I agree to uphold these principles and positions.[636]

---

[636] Georgia Right to Life PAC. (2017). Candidate endorsement procedure. Retrieved from http://grtlpac.org/endorsement-procedure/

APPENDIX 2

How to Join Personhood Alliance

Step 1

Contact the person who represents your state, listed in the table below. If there is no contact person for your state, proceed to Step 2.

State	First Name	Last Name	Email Address
AL	Bill	Fortenberry	life@personhoodinitiative.com
AK	Christopher	Kurka	christopher@alaskarighttolife.org
FL	Kitti	Hataway	khataway@personhoodfl.com
GA	Charlie	Powell	chuckpow49@aol.com
IA	Tim	Overlin	personhoodiowa@outlook.com
IL	Jim	Sable	permagraphics@sbcglobal.net
LA	Mary	Langlois	mlanglois4@yahoo.com
MI	Brad	Smith	bradjesi@gmail.com
MN	Mark	Vogel	mt_vogel@yahoo.com
MS	Les	Riley	rileydad10@gmail.com
NE	Bill	Kee	williamhkee@hotmail.com
NH	Darlene	Pawlik	gracefiles@comcast.net
NY	Dawn	Eskew	dawneskew@aol.com
OH	Dr. Patrick	Johnston	docjohnston@yahoo.com
SC	Richard	Cash	richardcashsc@gmail.com
VA	Gualberto	Garcia Jones	policy@personhood.org
WI	Matt	Sande	matt.s@prolifewi.org

STEP 2

Follow these steps to apply to form a Personhood Alliance state affiliate:

1. Go to https://www.personhood.org/index.php/press/who-is-national-personhood-alliance
2. Click the yellow link midway through the article to open the membership application form.
3. Print, complete, and submit the application as instructed on the form. Please understand that we only accept groups that fully agree with the Personhood Alliance Charter,[637] which defines us as a Christian, faith-based organization.
4. Once you are notified that your application is accepted, organize a founder's meeting in your state and notify the pro-life base that you are establishing a Personhood Alliance state affiliate.
5. At the founder's meeting, elect officers for the group and choose a delegate to represent the group.
6. Inform Personhood Alliance of your delegate's contact information, as he or she will participate in monthly conference calls as part of the Personhood Alliance national board.

If you have any questions about this process, please email us at webmaster@personhood.org.

---

[637] See Appendix 3

APPENDIX 3

PERSONHOOD ALLIANCE CHARTER

FAITH-BASED

WHEREAS, Personhood Alliance (PA) is a Christ-centered, biblically informed organization dedicated to the non-violent advancement of the recognition and protection of the God-given, inalienable right to life of all innocent human beings as legal persons at every stage of their biological development, and;

WHEREAS, without faith it is impossible to please God (Hebrews 11:6),

THEREFORE, PA recognizes that Jesus Christ is both Lord and God, and;

BIBLICAL PERSONHOOD

WHEREAS, the Bible affirms the personhood, sanctity, dignity, and value of every human being from the moment of our individual creation, as evidenced by the doctrine of Imago Dei and through the marital union of a man and woman (Gen 1:26-28), our being known by God even before being formed in the womb (Jer 1:5), the incarnation of Christ

(Luke 1-2), and the sacrifice of Christ to atone for the sins of humanity and restore fellowship between God and man (Rom. 5:12-21);

THEREFORE, PA affirms that we will uphold the biblical doctrine of the sanctity of human life as the primary objective of our organization, and thereby declare our essential unity; in areas of difference we declare liberty of conscience before God; and in all things—grace, and;

Education and Conscience

WHEREAS, two thousand years of Church history testify to the positive impact of this doctrine on the various cultures and nation-states where it has been recognized and embraced, and;

WHEREAS, the Church must, by example, be the primary means to form the consciences of nations regarding the moral demands of God, and;

WHEREAS, We will fully and ungrudgingly render to Caesar what is Caesar's. But under no circumstances will we render to Caesar what is God's, and;

WHEREAS, we honor justice and the common good, we will, by reason of conscience, advocate for non-compliance with any edict that purports to compel our institutions to participate in abortions, embryo--destructive research, assisted suicide and euthanasia, or any other anti--life act, and;

THEREFORE, PA will work to assist the Church as it seeks to affirm the personhood of every human being; and;

Legislation

WHEREAS, our nation's charter, the Declaration of Independence, states, "We hold these truths to be self-evident, that all men are created equal, that they are endowed by their Creator with certain unalienable Rights, that among these are life, liberty and the pursuit of happiness," and that governments are instituted in order to secure these rights, and;

WHEREAS, the 14th Amendment of the U.S. Constitution states, "nor shall any state deprive any person of life, liberty or property, without due process of law, nor deny to any person within its jurisdiction the equal protection of the law";

THEREFORE, the legislative objective of Personhood Alliance shall be the protection of every innocent human being and shall not be deemed completed until the personhood of all human beings, born and pre-born, is recognized and defended under the law; beginning at the local and state level and ending as ultimately expressed at a federal level, Personhood Alliance, Inc. shall not endorse any incremental legislation that excludes any innocent human beings from protection. No affiliate may endorse any legislative effort which explicitly identifies a class of human life that can be expressly exempted from the equal protection of the law;

Political Action

WHEREAS, all human beings, at any and every stage of life, in any and every state of consciousness or self-awareness, of any and every race, color, ethnicity, level of intelligence, religion, language, gender, character, behavior, physical ability/disability, potential, class, social status and regardless of manner of conception or creation are persons of equal and immeasurable worth and of inviolable dignity, and;

WHEREAS, they must be recognized and treated in a manner commensurate with this moral status;

THEREFORE, no political endorsement will be made which may explicitly identify a class of human life that can be expressly exempted from the equal protection of the law.

Unifying Principle

WHEREAS, the absolute sanctity of innocent human life will be the unifying principle of our Alliance, and;

WHEREAS, this is a confederation of independent groups who agree to link arms as equals,

THEREFORE, strength of unity can only be fully realized if we substantively agree on one consistent political endorsement criteria and a unified set of legislative measures that will allow local groups to achieve a national voice and footprint.

Statement of Faith

Personhood Alliance is a Christian organization and, as such, subscribes to the Apostles' Creed as expressed in our members' individual faith traditions.

INDEX

D

E

F

G

H

I

J

K

L

M

N

O

P

Q

R

S

T

U

V

W

Y

Z

PERSONHOOD

A Pragmatic Guide to Prolife
Victory in the 21st Century
and the Return to First
Principles in Politics

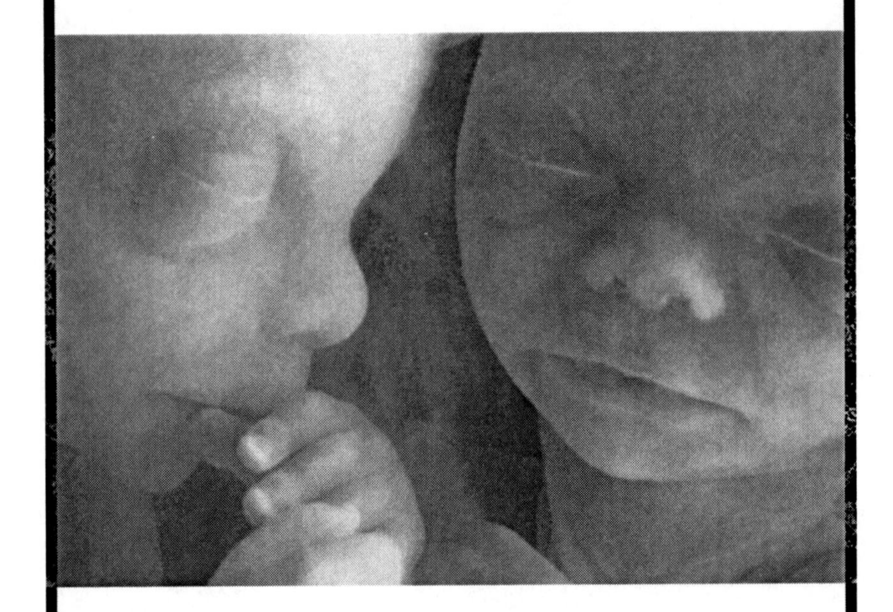

DANIEL BECKER

For additional reading on Personhood you can order this book at www.tkspublications.com. Get a copy for your pastor and lawmaker.

For comprehensive up-to-date coverage or to join the Personhood movement be sure and visit www.personhood.org.

"Dan Becker's book is a great blend of prudence, pragmatism and principled politics; it is certain to cause us to rethink pro-life strategy in the 21st century."

Dr. Donald Wildmon Founder and Chairman Emeritus
of American Family Association and American Family Radio

"History will one day look upon the movement to affirm the personhood of unborn children in the same way we now look upon the abolition of slavery and the end of the Holocaust. Dan Becker has been a reliable and principled voice for the unborn. His book advancing personhood for the most vulnerable among us is like a sound of the trumpet that will reverberate throughout time. The Holocaust of the unborn is the darkest chapter in American history and Dan Becker's book is a call to turn the page and restore a culture of life. It is a must read."

Mathew D. Staver Dean and Professor of Law
Liberty University School of Law

"All believers in God should insist, without compromise, that the human law must always treat every innocent human being as a person entitled to the right to life. Dan Becker courageously affirms this truth."

Professor Charles Rice, Emeritus Professor of Law
University of Notre Dame

"'Personhood' is at the very heart of the 21st Century Civil Rights Movement. My Uncle Martin once said that to deny a person is " to say that he has no right to existence." Whether it is Dred Scott, Sojourner Truth, 1968 Sanitation Workers, or a baby viewed in a 3D Ultrasound, from conception until natural birth, a person is a human being, entitled to life, liberty and the pursuit of happiness. This right to personhood is a civil right. So, this book is an essential tool for these times."

Dr. Alveda C. King (Niece of Dr. Martin Luther King, Jr.)
King for America, Priests for Life

CPSIA information can be obtained
at www.ICGtesting.com
Printed in the USA
FFOW02n2351230218
45183804-45720FF

9 780983 190370